THE AFTERLIFE OF S
A CRITICAL REVIEW
BY SAMUEL HEILMAN AND M

RABBI CHAIM RAPOPORT

OPORTO PRESS

ב"ה

The Afterlife of Scholarship:
A Critical Review of 'The Rebbe' by Samuel Heilman and Menachem
Friedman

By Rabbi Chaim Rapoport

For interviews with the author, or to purchase this book in volume, email:
therebbebook@gmail.com.

ISBN-13: 978-0615538976 (Oporto Press)
ISBN-10: 0615538975

•

ACCEPT THE TRUTH FROM WHATEVER SOURCE IT COMES.

MAIMONIDES, SHEMONAH PERAKIM

•

In Afterlife of Scholarship, Chaim Rapoport offers a meticulous critique of Samuel Heilman and Menachem Friedman, The Rebbe: The Life and Afterlife of Menachem Mendel Schneerson, published by Princeton University Press, 2010. Rapoport challenges many of the assumptions made by Heilman and Friedman, and argues, through close textual reading, that these assumptions are based on interpretive flaws and/or lack of knowledge of Hasidism in general and of Habad in particular. Despite the overtly polemical tone, Rapoport's criticisms are never offered ad hominem. On the contrary, he painstakingly documents every point of contention, and has thereby provided ample evidence to allow other readers to assess his arguments against the portrait of the Rebbe presented by Heilman and Friedman. Whatever one might decide on the merits of his analyses, Rapoport's volume provides an invaluable treasure-trove of sources for future generations of scholarship on the seventh Rebbe of Habad-Lubavitch.

Elliot R. Wolfson
Abraham Lieberman Professor of Hebrew and Judaic Studies
New York University

TABLE OF CONTENTS

A NOTE TO THE READER

After reading 'The Rebbe: The Life and Afterlife of Menachem Mendel Schneerson' (Princeton University Press, 2010, 382 pages) a recent book by Samuel Heilman and Menachem Friedman, I felt it was incumbent that somebody else share their viewpoint on the topic.

In this essay, I propose to appraise the methodology of the authors of the above-mentioned book, their use of sources and their particular pre-suppositions. I also attempt to judge this biography in terms of its quality as a work of scholarly research and analysis. Although the biography of the Rebbe and the history of his movement are presented by the authors as intrinsically intertwined, I intend to focus primarily on the biographical section of the book.

This essay is not intended as an alternative biography of the Rebbe. Instead it is an elaborate review essay on Heilman and Friedman's efforts. It is my hope that future scholars can build upon the sources I have collected here, thereby avoiding many of the errors of fact and judgment that these authors have made. While this work is written in a polemic style geared toward the layman, I have heavily footnoted the text in order to facilitate the research of future scholarly biographers of the Rebbe.

This particular version of my comments actually represents a second draft. The first was posted on the Internet (on the Seforim blog located at http://seforim.blogspot.com), and evidently made an impression on the authors themselves. After my initial comments went online on June 14th, 2010, Heilman and Friedman chose to respond to my comments in their own essay, which was also published on the Seforim Blog. Over the next few weeks a fascinating public dialogue emerged between myself and the authors of the book: six essays and rebuttals were eventually published, three by myself and three by Heilman and Friedman.

It is my contention that the errors in Heilman's and Friedman's work are so fundamental and pervasive that they actually serve to disqualify this work as a serious historical or biographical document.

In the months following our internet exchanges, I have come to realize that it would be beneficial for readers to read the 'The Rebbe: The Life and Afterlife of Menachem Mendel Schneerson' in conjunction with this essay in order to be aware of the numerous flaws in the original work. I have synthesized my three essays, revised them and added significant material based on subsequent investigation, the sum product of which has yielded this work. Where I have seen fit, I have also incorporated relevant critique from Heilman and Friedman's essays into the footnotes.

It must be noted that my original review essays on the Seforim Blog – as well as the current edition – are a critical review of the first edition of Heilman and Friedman's book which was published in the Spring of 2010. After having exposed some of their serious factual errors in my original essays, the authors hinted that future editions may ultimately be amended. Future editions published by the authors, therefore, may not exactly match the original pagination or text upon which this essay was based.

A note about myself and biases:

There are those who would have it that only non-Israelis (and Arabs) can pass judgment on the Arab-Israeli conflict, only atheists can write impartially about religion and only non-citizens can take stock of a particular country's governance.

I disagree.

I am an orthodox Jew. I also consider myself to be a disciple of the late Lubavitcher Rebbe. Although I studied in other Yeshivot (Manchester and Gateshead) and therefore am familiar with a broad array of Orthodox theologies, my main training was in Lubavitch. While I acknowledge that I may not be able to achieve the maximum degree of objectivity with regard to Jewish Orthodoxy or Lubavitch, on the other hand, I do believe that my first-hand experience of Orthodox and Chasidic life actually affords me certain advantages that outside scholars often lack.

Moreover, the viewpoint of the outsider is itself not always free from bias. Not all external expertise is objective, nor are all insiders blind. In this context it is appropriate to direct the reader to Professor Heilman's own published comments on this theme, since they relate both to his work and, to a certain extent, my own:

> I am not so naïve as to believe that my account is a neutral, "tropeless discourse that would render my realities 'exactly as they are,' not filtered through [my] own values and interpretive schema." Nor do I believe that I can remain invisible in this account. [...] If I seem to insert myself, my impressions, or my person into the account of the other people's lives, it is because I admit that 'all ethnography,' as Clifford Geertz argues, 'is part philosophy, and a good deal of the rest is confession' (from the prologue to Heilman's 'Defenders of the Faith,' Schocken Books, 1992).

I therefore appeal to the reader to avoid pre-judging my essay by resorting to the knee-jerk rejoinder: 'Well, he is a Lubavitcher; what value can he add to this discussion?!' Rather I implore the reader to review my contribution and judge my analysis with the utmost objectivity that he or she is able to achieve.

Before I conclude these words of preface, it is my duty and privilege to express my gratitude to all those who have helped me in the preparation of this book. I particularly acknowledge, with deep appreciation, the sterling work of Eliezer Leib Rubin.

I offer special thanks to Menachem Butler of the Seforim Blog, whose enthusiasm for, and commitment to, the dissemination of Jewish scholarship has broadened the horizons of so many people. His commitment to public dialogue and his quest for the truth allowed the initial exchanges between myself and Heilman and Friedman to take place in a dignified and fair manner.

Last, but by no means least, I thank my wife Rachel Clara and our wonderful children for their tremendous encouragement, support and assistance throughout this project. Without them, it would have been impossible to complete this work.

Chaim Rapoport
London, England
Nissan, 5771 / Spring 2011

Section I

1. Two Books in One

This book 'The Rebbe: The Life and Afterlife of Menachem Mendel Schneerson' is comprised of two studies.

Firstly, there is a sociological study of the Lubavitch 'mission establishment' (shlichus); a layman's guide to the now global phenomenon of Shluchim[1], shluchos and their Chabad Houses, as they have become organized over the last two or three decades. The authors describe the dedication of these emissaries; their ambitions, achievements and the ethos that (they believe) spurs them to work tirelessly and passionately on behalf of the Jewish people.

In this section they speak, often quite fondly, of the sterling work performed by the Shluchim and their families who go and live in small towns, far-flung cities and secular university campuses in order to re-ignite religious life; providing Jewish amenities for both residents and

---

[1] In their first endnote on the book, Heilman and Friedman express surprise that Lubavitch emissaries are referred to as shluchim: "The precise Hebrew or Yiddish word for emissaries would be "shlichim," but for whatever reason, Lubavitchers have chosen to use the term "shluchim," perhaps to distinguish themselves from all other types of emissaries, religious or otherwise" (chapter 1 note 1).

This comment bespeaks a lack of familiarity with classical Hebrew. Whilst it is true that in Modern Hebrew (the Ivrit of Ben Yehudah) the plural shlichim is used, in rabbinic Hebrew (and therefore Yiddish) it is virtually **unused**. On the other hand, the term shluchim and its derivatives are found in hundreds of places in rabbinic writings. For a couple of **random** examples, see: (a) the mishnaic phrases: "*sholchim shluchim be-chol ha-mekomot*" (*Sanhedrin* 11:4), "*shluchei mitzvah peturin min ha-sukkah* (*Sukkah* 2:4), and "*shluchei bet din*" (*Yoma* 1:5; *Menachot* 10:3); (b) the Talmudic phrases: "*shluchei mitzvah eynan nizokin*" (*Pesachim* 8b); "*shluchei Nissan*" (*Rosh Hashanah* 21a); "*mitzvah bo yoter mi-bishlucho*" (*Kiddushin* 41b); (c) the midrashic phrases: "*nitnah reshut li-shluchim le-chabel*" (*Mechilta deRashbi* on Exodus 19:21); "*shluchim sheshalach Moshe* (*Bemidbar Rabbah* 16:1). The famous maxim "*harbeh shluchim la-makom*" will resonate with those who are conversant in rabbinic literature. The Talmudic-Aramaic term often employed by rabbinic delegates and emissaries, "*shluchei de-rabanan*" (שד"ר = שלוחי דרבנן) will also be familiar to many.

Whilst on the topic, I am not sure what to make of the odd transliterations and spellings scattered throughout the book, such as "*Yatir mibehayekhon*" for "יתיר מבחיוהי", (Heilman and Friedman page 60) *bey-shakhayim* for "בית החיים" (page 12 in footnote). Perhaps these are mere typographical errors.

itinerants, observant or otherwise, across the globe. They emphasize the novelty of this phenomenon, in contradistinction to other chasidic and haredi groups who tend to retreat into their insular communities, shunning exposure to the outside world and its religiously threatening elements. They depict the 'equal rights' and privileges of women on shlichus, describing the uniqueness of this somewhat 'egalitarian' phenomenon within an otherwise ultra-orthodox group. They explore the motives that they believe drive so many young, talented and charismatic couples to choose such a challenging life-long career, and describe how they maintain the high level of inspiration, stamina and perseverance that are essential for success in this vocation. Finally, they demonstrate how such families see themselves, as astonishing as this may seem, to be acting as emissaries of Rabbi Menachem Mendel Schneerson (born in 1902), the seventh Rebbe of the Chabad Lubavitch Hasidic dynasty [henceforth: 'the Rebbe']; who passed away in 1994.

Secondly, and more importantly for this essay, the authors present us with an attempt to record the life-story of the Rebbe. Heilman and Friedman do not merely endeavour to reconstruct the factual data of his life, much of which, they claim, is shrouded in mystery, but they also venture to penetrate the deepest recesses of his psyche. They attempt to reveal his unspoken thoughts, feelings, incentives, and at times, they second-guess his actions or reactions at various times of his life, often portraying them as though they are given facts. As one reviewer of this book has put it, the authors "take a psycho-bio approach to Schneerson's life, trying to get inside the man's head to uncover his motivation" – a tall order indeed!

2. Credentials and Expertise

While Professors Heilman and Friedman have many qualifications as erudite scholars, it appears that the study of Hasidism in general, Chabad-Lubavitch in particular, and most specifically the intellectual output of the late Lubavitcher Rebbe lies beyond their particular fields of academic expertise.

The authors' lack of awareness of Chabad practices becomes readily apparent early in the book. There are numerous blatant errors in the first chapter alone. For example: Describing the customs of chasidim

when visiting the gravesite of the Rebbe, the author's state categorical-
ly:

> Even *Kohens* – Jews who are considered the descendants of the
> ancient priestly tribe and who normally cannot visit the
> cemeteries because of death's capacity to defile their special
> purity – are allowed by Lubavitcher custom to visit the Rebbe's
> tomb, based on the principle accepted by Chabad that while
> presence near a dead body is defiling, even a Kohen cannot be
> defiled by the corpse of a *Zaddik.*

This statement is not sourced and was probably made on the assumption, supported possibly by hearsay, that Chabad accepts this
principle. In fact, although some other (non-Chabad) chasidim have
adopted this permissive ruling, and there may well be Kohanim belonging to other Orthodox sects who do not refrain from contact with
the graves of the righteous, Chabad chasidim do refrain from such contact. Chabad practice on this matter follows the Rebbe's authoritative
ruling (that has been published in numerous places[2]), according to
which a Kohen must keep the requisite distance from the grave of a
Rebbe[3]. It is for this reason, the Rebbe writes, that a special wall was

---

[2] See the Rebbe's ruling published in his *Igrot Kodesh* (Kehot Publication Society:
Brooklyn, 1987-2009), vol. 6, page 349 and his *Likuttei Sichot* (Kehot Publication
Society: Brooklyn, 1962-2001), vol. 22, page 316:

"רובם ככולם מחמירים בזה, וכן משמע ג"כ פס"ד עדת חב"ד וכדמוכח מתשובת מהרי"ל מיאנאוויטש (אחי
אדמו"ה"ז) שנדפס באחת מחוברות התמים (חוברת ו' ע' לח) בעניני המחיצה שעשו בהאדיטש מסביב
להקבר, וכבר הובא ג"כ בהספרים שהביא השדי חמד אשר נעפ"כ הרבה מקילים בזה, ובפרט החסידים
בנוגע לנשיאיהם. ואעפ"כ אין דעתי נוחה מזה מפני תשובת מהרי"ל הנ"ל, וכן אמרו לי אשר בליובאוויטש
בהאהל היו סימנים בתור מחיצה שעד כאן נגשים כהנים ותו לא ... בנוגע לאהל כ"ק מו"ח אדמו"ר הנה
נסדר שסביב הקבר נמצאת מחיצה גבוה עשרה טפחים והכהנים עומדים במרחק ד' טפחים מהקבר וגם
המחיצה בכלל. וכיון שהאהל נמצא בתוך בית החיים, הנה הכהנים באים לשם באותא סגור, היינו שיש לו
דין אהל, ואהל זרוק בכגון דא - אהל הוא כיון שענין הריחוק דד' אמות מביה"ק אינו אלא מדרבנן לכל
הדיעות".

See also *Igrot Kodesh* vol. 11, page 220 and *Sha'arei Halachah uMinhag* (Heichal
Menachem: Jerusalem 1993), vol. 3, chapter 150 (pages 394-395).

[Please note: There are several series of *Igrot Kodesh* that are referred to in this
booklet. For the sake of brevity, unless stated otherwise, references to *Igrot Kodesh*
always refer to those of Rabbi Menachem Mendel Schneerson (the Rebbe).]

[3] For details of the variant halachic opinions in this regard, see Rabbi Mordechai
Spielman, *Tziyon L'Nefesh Chayah* ['a treatise concerning the presence of kohanim at
the graves of tzadikim'] (Brooklyn 1976).

erected around the grave of his father-in-law, the sixth Lubavitcher Rebbe, Rabbi Yosef Yitzchak Schneersohn (Rayatz: 1880-1950) (this wall now encompasses the Rebbe's grave as well).

In a similar vein, they seem to be unaware of the traditional Chabad practice to avoid eulogies at a funeral[4]; that each mourner leads a separate prayer service (to facilitate multiple recitations of the Kaddish[5]) and that one does not sit down when visiting the *Ohel* [=gravesite of a Rebbe][6].

The above items, while not on the scale of some of the larger flaws I will identify shortly, are indicative of poor sociological research. For these are matters of common practice among thousands of chasidim,

---

[4] See Heilman and Friedman page 37, who cite the novelty that no tributes were offered at the funeral of Rayatz and suggest that this calls for explanation. See, however, Rabbi Yechiel Michel Tukachinsky, *Gesher haChayim* (Jerusalem 1960), vol. 1, chapter 13, page 121 (subsection 4) who offers several reasons for this custom amongst Chabad and other "holy communities". See also *Likuttei Sichot* vol 2, page 504.

[5] See Heilman and Friedman page 38. See, however, *Igrot Kodesh* vol. 3, page 459.

[6] See Heilman and Friedman page 236.

The following Hebrew text is a segment of a memoir the Rebbe wrote in which he documented his father-in-law's practices and the customs he adhered to at the wedding of his youngest daughter and son-in-law Mendel Horenstein (*Reshimat HaYoman*, Kehot Publication Society: Brooklyn, 2006, pages 239-240):

"[הקידושין] בטבעת של זהב דוקא. [כ"ק מו"ח אדמו"ר שליט"א] צוה שיגררו מקודם הפראבע. החתן - ציווהו שיפשוט שעונו, זאפאנקעס (cufflinks), ואם יש יש אצלו עוד איזה שוה כסף (ארנקי וכו') [- שלא יהיו אצלו בעת הקידושין]. גם התיר קשר עניבתו".

Heilman and Friedman (page 112) rephrase the Rebbe's words in the following paragraph: "A brief recollection is provided by Mendel Schneerson, and it subtly underscores his new brother-in-law's modernity. . . At the wedding, the groom, who gave his bride a gold ring, was wearing a fashionable tie (an unusual accoutrement for a Hasidic groom, as his new brother-in-law noted, which was nevertheless permitted), a gold watch, and cufflinks (the latter were to be removed under the wedding canopy)".

In addition to the characteristic inaccuracy and exaggeration in the authors' paraphrase of the Hebrew, it appears that due to lack of familiarity with traditional customs they misconstrued the significance of the removal of the watch and cufflinks and the difference between these items and the tie. See *Sefer HaMinhagim–Chabad* (Kehot Publication Society: Brooklyn, 1967), page 76; *Igrot Kodesh* vol. 5, page 87; *Likuttei Sichot* vol. 29, page 454 and the sources cited in Rabbi Gavriel Zinner, *Nitei Gavriel-Hilchot Nisuin* (Jerusalem, 1998), vol. 1, pages 117-118 notes 13 and 14.

not obscure citations in hard-to-find-works in a language foreign to the authors.

The authors are also apparently unfamiliar with many aspects of the Chabad vernacular. Thus when explaining the term *"pnimi"* that was used to describe the Rebbe, they write: "one of us, an insider"[7]. This may be the colloquial meaning of the term in ultra or modern Orthodox Israeli circles, but it has no connection with the term as used in the Chabad lingua franca[8].

In Chabad vernacular the title *"pnimi"* refers exclusively to an individual who acts upon pure inner conviction, shying away from recognition and fanfare[9].

On one occasion, the authors implicitly attribute to Chabad followers an arguably idolatrous practice. In their description of the "cottage" at 226-20 Francis Lewis Blvd., Cambria Heights, N.Y. which is located in close proximity to the Rebbe's gravesite they write: "The largest room inside the cottage has a library and chapel where people may pray (facing east toward the tomb and Jerusalem) and study the enor-

---

[7] Heilman and Friedman page 57.

[8] There exists a substantial literature on the meaning of the term *"pnimi"* (related to *penimiyut*). See, for example, Rashab, *Torat Shalom* (Kehot Publication Society: Brooklyn, 1957), pages 42, 118, 168, and 218 and Rayatz, *Likuttei Dibburim* vol. 4 (Kehot Publication Society: Brooklyn, 1958), page 1429. See also *HaYom Yom* (Kehot Publication Society: Brooklyn, 1943), entry for 24th Tammuz; *Chanoch LeNa'ar* (Kehot Publication Society: Israel, 1991), page 53 and Rayatz, *Igrot Kodesh* (Kehot Publication Society: Brooklyn, 1982-2011), vol. 4 (letter dated 18th Tammuz 5699), page 542 (end). Suffice to say, Heilman and Friedman are way off the mark with their definition of the term.

[9] Another example of ignorance of Chabad vernacular is displayed by the authors on page 22 where they write: "the temimim, the unblemished and pure of heart, as they were called, and because they went to the yeshiva of that name." Although the Hebrew word *'tamim'* can mean 'unblemished and pure,' the name of the Chabad yeshivah system, *Tomchei Temimim*, was chosen by its founder, Rashab, because its students were to be *'tamim* – **complete'** in their study of Torah, by virtue of studying both its revealed and esoteric dimensions. See, for example, Rayatz, *Igrot Kodesh* vol. 10, page 368.

mous body of literature, published talks, and letters the Rebbe produced in his lifetime and that are now part of his legacy'"[10].

This paragraph clearly suggests that the daily prayers (at least those that according to Jewish Law must be recited facing Jerusalem, namely the *Amidah* prayer) that are held in this "chapel" are directed towards the tomb. Any visitor to the Rebbe's tomb can easily see that this is not the case.

I have personally prayed (and led services) in the house near the *Ohel*; I have likewise participated in the services that are held in the miniature sanctuary that is immediately adjacent to the *Ohel*, and I have never seen anyone direct themselves towards the Rebbe's grave. The ark in all of these 'chapels' faces Jerusalem ('*mizrach*'), as do virtually all synagogues in the USA and the world over. The Chazan and the congregants pray towards Jerusalem – not the *Tziyon*[11].

In some cases, eagerness to find corroboration for their thesis led the authors to jump to conclusions based on careless reading and evident inadequacy in understanding a primary source.

---

[10] Heilman and Friedman Page 17.

[11] Rather than acknowledge this obvious inaccuracy Heilman and Friedman in their response on the Seforim blog dug in their heels: "Much is made of the fact that we mention that prayers at the Ohel face the Rebbes' tomb. Does Rabbi Rapoport deny that the worshippers face in the direction of the Tomb? An examination will demonstrate this to be the case. Indeed, a look at people inside the ohel will note that wherever they stand, all face toward the tombs while they recite prayers".

To which I responded: To be sure people **inside the Ohel** ... face toward the tombs while they recite prayers" (those included in the traditional *Ma'aneh Lashon* etc.); this is of course nothing unique to the Rebbe's gravesite. I have never seen anyone pray at any gravesite facing in any direction other than the tomb. Indeed both at the Rebbe's gravesite and other gravesites these prayers are often recited in positions that do **not** face Jerusalem.

[See also Samuel C. Heilman, *When a Jew Dies: The Ethnography of a Bereaved Son* (London: University of California Press, 2001), **front cover design.**]

Yet this in no way justifies Heilman and Friedman's published claim that the daily prayers that are held **in the chapel** and that must be recited towards Jerusalem are actually directed towards the tomb. The facts are readily observable to the degree that they need no further subtstantiation. See Figure 1 (satellite image) at the end of this book.

For example, one of the central theses of the book is that the Rebbe's original 'life-dream' was to become an engineer enjoying the secular life of the European capitals rather than leading the life of a devout chasid and disciple of his father-in-law, the sixth Lubavitch Rebbe, Rabbi Yosef Yitzchak Schneersohn. Whilst it is true that the Rebbe studied engineering, and, apparently, he had initially hoped to earn a livelihood through this science, Heilman and Friedman suggest that engineering was not merely a means to an end for the Rebbe, it was the end itself. In their narrative, becoming and living as an engineer would have been the fulfilment of the Rebbe's existential "dream"[12].

In this context, the authors breathlessly describe the Rebbe's excitement upon receipt of his degree in engineering:

> At last, on March 25 1938, Mendel Schneerson, who was now thirty-six years old, received his diploma. He was finally an engineer with a degree. His pride in his new status could be seen in the fact that on the letters he sent to his parents he

---

[12] Heilman and Friedman page 152, even assert that he never really 'relinquished' this dream. Even when he became Rebbe it was because he "could not help but realize that in the end, he was here in 'Lubavitch', and all his other plans would have to be set aside, not because he wanted to give them up (whenever he found a visitor able and willing to talk about technology or engineering or mathematics and science, he still hungered for conversation about it)". In a footnote the authors add: "When, for example, in the early 1960s he met with a couple before their impending marriage and learned [that] the groom was working for IBM, he spent almost the entire visit, which he extended, asking for the young man's opinion about the merits of FORTRAN and other computer languages, even as the line outside his office grew longer and his assistants tried to urge him to conclude."

This story would have been illuminating if this type of behavior on the Rebbe's part had been out of the ordinary. In reality, however, literally hundreds of people who sat with the Rebbe in private audience reported the same behavior. The Rebbe would **routinely** extend his audiences past the usual three to five minute limit, and he would **routinely** ignore his secretaries' messages reminding him of the growing line outside his door. The Rebbe did this not only for discussions relating to science or **whichever career his visitor was engaged in**, but also – and much more so – for discussions relating to Jewish belief, education and communal affairs. The sources that report such behavior are too numerous to list, but they can be found in numerous interviews published in the *Kfar Chabad* magazine, and in dozens of video testimonies recorded by JEM.

marked his return address on the envelope as "Eng. M. Schneerson"[13].

The authors found this discovery so illuminating that they have reproduced a copy of the envelope inscription as "figure 14" in their book[14].

This argument appears convincing.

There is one problem. The Rebbe never wrote "Eng." on the envelope.

As a mere glance at the photograph of the envelope will reveal what he actually wrote is "Exp. M. Schneerson"[15]. Exp. is an abbreviation for Expéditeur, which means simply "sender", and, until this day, is often prefaced to the address of the one sending the letter; just as in English, the one dispatching the letter will typically preface his return address with the word: "Sender" or "From". Indeed, had the Rebbe, who at this point had never been to an English speaking country, wanted to document the title of his profession on the back of the envelope, he would have used the Russian инженер or the French Ingénieur, but surely not (an abbreviated form of) the English "Engineer"[16].

---

[13] Heilman and Friedman pages 121-122.

[14] See Heilman and Friedman on the pages that follow page 162. They describe the illustration as: "Envelope from 'Eng[ineer] M. Schneerson', from Paris".

[15] In chapter 4 endnote 90 Heilman and Friedman indicate to the photograph published in *Kovetz Chof Menachem-Av* (Kehot Publication Society: Brooklyn, 2004), pages 53-56 [see Figure 2 at the end of this book]. They add that "Eng." (standing for "Engineer") was underscored.

[16] **In their response on the Seforim blog** Heilman and Friedman have no choice but to acknowledge this obvious mistake, but they continue to cling to their unsupported thesis. They offer alternative evidence for R. Schneerson's pride and excitement in "M. Schneerson's listing in the Paris directory, where he made sure to be listed as "Ing. Electr. Mecan" as an engineer" (See also Heilman and Friedman chapter 4, note 93).

To which I responded: The telephone directory demonstrates, **at the very most**, R. Schneerson's concern with finding employment. R. Schneerson had initially wanted to reach a stage that would make him financially independent from the court and able to earn his own living from a respectable professional vocation. It would therefore follow that when he received his degree he would seek to advertise his qualifications in a manner that may lead to employment, namely in the telephone directory.

Another serious error occurs in the same context. In a letter that the Rebbe penned to his parents soon after he received his degree in engineering, he told them:

בא אונז קיין נייעס פאר דער צייט איז ניט צוגעקומען. עס איז דא אלערליי חלומות,
ועגען א שטעלע, אדער שותפות אין מיין ספעציעלנאס. א טייל פון זיי איז שוין נפתר
געווארען, אז עס איז נאר א חלום.

In English, this segment of the letter may be paraphrased as: 'We have no special news to share. There are all sorts of remote possibilities (in Yiddish the Hebrew word for dreams is used: "*Chaloimes*") for employment involving either a 'position' (a *shtele*) or a partnership in my area of expertise. However, some of these possibilities have already proven to be mere dreams (in Yiddish the Hebrew word for dream is used: "*a Cholem*")'[17].

Moreover, even though one may safely assume that the Rebbe was pleased when he thought he would be able to become financially self-sufficient, it is unlikely that he would have chosen the Parisian telephone directory as the venue for his expression of joy or pride. Therefore, it is likely that such a phone-listing would have been intended purely to facilitate employment.

Finally and **most importantly**, a perusal of the page in the telephone directory on which the Rebbe's listing is found illustrates that it was the norm for all persons to list their names together with their qualifications or occupations. Thus the vast majority of names on this page (as on all the pages of the directory) are accompanied with a brief job-description or qualification of the individual listed.

Thus, for example, on the page that lists "Schneerson M." as an engineer virtually everyone is listed with their professional credentials. For example: a tailor, a postal officer, a dentist, a banker, an actor, a printer, a decorator, a professor, a builder, an accountant, an architect, a doctor, a pharmacist, a music teacher, a joiner and a funeral director. There are also other engineers on the same page. See Figure 3 at the end of this book.

The guidelines for registration in the telephone directory also indicate that it was the norm to be registered together with the title of one's vocation. See Figure 4 at the end of this book.

Consequently, it is clear that the contents of the 1939 telephone directory do not illustrate any pride or joy on behalf of the Rebbe, nor do they reveal what the Rebbe's dreams may have been. At the most, the telephone inscription demonstrates his pragmatism, and minimally it teaches us about his ability to register his contact details in accordance with accepted societal norms.

[17] This letter was published in *Kovetz Chof Menachem-Av Shishim Shanah 5704-5764* (Kehot Publication Society: Brooklyn, 2004) page 54.

Whilst there are ambiguities as to the exact connotations of these sentences, one thing however is clear: that the use of the term *Cholem* in the vernacular refers to a remote and far-fetched possibility of finding employment. (Even though the term *Cholem/Chaloimes* may also have the connotation of 'hope', the subject of the hope in the context of this letter would clearly be employment, not the nature of the career).

The authors however interpreted the term *Cholem* in the above-mentioned letter to mean an existential dream or a deep-set aspiration (as in, 'a dream of becoming president'). They therefore understood the Rebbe to discussing the (aborted) realization of his vision and goal of becoming an engineer, and therefore misleadingly refer to this letter on multiple occasions as if it supports their claim that R. Schneerson's life-dream was to become an engineer.

Whilst neither Yiddish nor French are the authors' native tongues, the inordinate occurrence of mistakes such as these illustrates an unwarranted haste on the part of the authors, and, more importantly, demonstrates the existence of a preconceived conclusion that evidently made the occurrence of such errors an almost inevitable phenomenon.

3. The Rebbe's Scholarly Output

It appears that the authors are unfamiliar with some of the ideas, primary texts, practices, and cultural norms that are relevant to their subject of research[18].

Indeed, in their entire book (including the endnotes) negligible reference is made to the thirty nine volumes of the Rebbe's magnum opus, his *Likuttei Sichot*, which contain, not only a significant share of his in-

---

[18] There is even the odd confusion with names, typical of researchers engaging in a field with which they lack familiarity. Heilman and Friedman refer to the second Rebbe of the Chabad dynasty as "Baruch" rather than "Dovber" (page 41, in footnote).

On page 115 they refer to Edmea Schneerson who was "like Moussia a granddaughter of the fifth rebbe, Rabbi Shalom Dovber". As a matter of fact, the fifth rebbe, Rabbi Shalom Dovber had no granddaughters other than Moussia and her sisters Chanah and Sheina – the only children of his only son. Again, this may be a typographic error.

tellectual output, but also information that is of biographical interest[19]. And when they do choose to reference the *Likuttei Sichot*, the references are often inaccurate or wrong[20]. With the exception of one solitary discourse[21], none of the Rebbe's approximately 1500 *ma'amarim*[22] are referred to or discussed. Nor do his *sichot* (talks) figure prominently as a

---

[19] See the reference to *Likuttei Sichot* below, footnote 164, for one example.

[20] In one endnote (chapter 8 note 17) they refer to "*Likutei Sichos*, 35:113-19 and sources cited there". They refer to this volume as a source for the Rebbe's discussion of the concept that "the *shliach's* actions and accomplishments are attributed to the one who empowered him to act in his stead". There is nothing in that section of *Likuttei Sichot* that relates to this issue.

In chapter 5 note 80 they refer to "*Likutei Sichos*, 23:274, for a talk given in the summer of 1986". No such talk can be found on that page (or any other page of this volume), nor could it have been found in this volume, since *Likuttei Sichot* vol. 23 was published (for the first time) in 1984.

The only arguably significant references that I have found to the scholarly writings in *Likuttei Sichot* are to vol. 5 pages 223 and 382 (Heilman and Friedman chapter 5 endnote 99 and chapter 6 endnote 51).

[In general their references are often misleading and should be checked out. See, for example: (a) Heilman and Friedman page 33 where they make the spurious claim that: "Barry [Gourary] had been his assistant for years, watching the Rebbe's every move and coming whenever his grandfather rang the bell for him". In chapter 2 endnote 13 they refer to Uri Kaploun, *A Prince in Prison* (Sichos in English: Brooklyn, 1997) as the source for this information. However that monograph records nothing of the sort; (b) in chapter 4 (page 107ff) they write that Rayatz wanted the future rebbe to accompany him on his trip to the Land of Israel in 1929, but "his younger son-in-law refused, first because his passport did not allow him to travel to Palestine and (*sic*) second because he was involved in his studies". In endnote 48 they refer to Rabbi Yehoshua Mondshine's *Derech haMelech* (Brooklyn, 2000) page 14 as a source for this. However there is nothing in Mondshine's publication that indicates this. Similarly the next reference to Mondshine's *Derech haMelech* (chapter four endnote 48) also leads us to a non-existent source.

[21] The first Chasidic discourse the Rebbe delivered in 1951, an **English translation** of which they refer to several times.

[22] The Rebbe presented a total of 1558 *ma'amarim* (of which all are extant and transcribed except 49) many of which he edited over the years. Six volumes of the Rebbe's *ma'amarim* were edited and published by the Rebbe himself (*Sefer ha-Ma'amarim Melukat*, Kehot Publication Society: Brooklyn, 1986-1992).

significant source[23]. His scholarly *Reshimot*, or notations, which were written in his younger years (the period in his life on which our authors focus vigorously), receive but passing mention[24]. [These *Reshimot* began to appear in print in instalments after the Rebbe's passing in 1994. Subsequently, one hundred and eighty-seven *Reshimot* were reprinted and produced in five bound volumes by Kehot Publication Society in 2003].

Whilst the authors do refer to some of the Rebbe's letters, their lack of familiarity with the Rebbe's published correspondence in both Hebrew and English is readily apparent.

Thus when they refer to the Rebbe's view on college education, they source it in a book by author and journalist, Sue Fishkoff, rather than the Rebbe's own Hebrew and English letters and his *Likuttei Sichot*[25]; when they discuss the Rebbe's views on the controversial issue of the non-denominational prayers in American public schools they refer only to newspaper articles and seem to be unaware of the Rebbe's handwritten letters on the subject[26], and when they discuss the Rebbe's

[23] It is estimated that he spoke publicly for approximately 11,000 hours. Some of these talks are recorded on audio or video. The vast majority of these have been transcribed in the original Yiddish and more than half have been translated into Hebrew. The 39 volumes of his *Likuttei Sichot* (above note 2) and twelve volumes of his *Sefer HaSichot* covering the years 5747–5752 (Kehot Publication Society: Brooklyn, 1989-1998), were edited for publication by the Rebbe's own hand.

[24] See Heilman and Friedman pages 57 and 109.

At one point, the authors seem to forget entirely about the existence of the relevant *Reshimot*. Hence, on page 119, the authors note the lack of new entries in the Rebbe's "**diary**" from 1938 to 1941, whilst, in reality, during this period the Rebbe penned over a dozen scholarly essays in his *Reshimot* – including the longest one to be found in all of his journals, *Reshimat HaMenorah* (Kehot Publication Society: Brooklyn, 1998). The essays of this 'forgotten' period include many which were composed by the Rebbe while he and his wife were on the move through southern France and Portugal fleeing from the Nazis – at least one of which was even delivered publicly in a synagogue – a fascinating fact one would have expected the authors to enthusiastically report in their quest to build a thoroughly "complex" image of the Rebbe's inner life.

[25] See references cited below, notes 140 and 142.

[26] See, for example, the Rebbe's letters dated 15th Tammuz 5723, (*Igrot Kodesh* vol. 22, page 475) and 2nd Ellul 5723 (*Igrot Kodesh* ibid., page 496).

advocacy of a Menorah with diagonal branches they offer their own fanciful reasons for his choice of the Maimonidean model and do not tell us what the Rebbe himself had to say on the matter[27].

In fact, many of their presentations of the Rebbe's statements or opinions are based on hearsay[28] and at best on secondary sources, English articles posted on various websites, Hebrew newspapers and popular circulars and sound-bites gleaned from educational videos – specifically those videos that are designed for popular consumption[29].

---

[27] See *Likuttei Sichot* vol. 21, page 168ff. Needless to say the Rebbe does not even allude to the idea that Heilman and Friedman suggest.

[28] For example, on page 55 Heilman and Friedman write: "The Rebbe often compared himself to Joseph, separated from his family for so many years only to be reunited with them as a leader". [They then proceed to explain one of the Rebbe's talks in light of this analogy]. The authors do not provide any source for this statement. The reason for this is because it must have been based on hearsay, if not imagination. The Rebbe sometimes did compare his father-in-law (Rayatz) – whose first name was Joseph and who was not separated from his family – to the biblical Joseph (see, for example, his talk on 10th Shevat 5734, *Sichot Kodesh* 5734 vol. 1, page 345), but there does not appear to be any evidence that he did so of himself.

There exists anecdotal evidence that in 1947 upon his reunion with his mother, who had remained trapped behind the Iron Curtain for 20 years after the Rebbe had left with his soon-to-be wife's family, the Rebbe referred in a public talk – in the presence of his mother – to the Biblical precedent of Jacob who was separated from his parents for twenty two years while living at the house of his uncle, Laban. The Sages tell us that as "punishment" for not fulfilling the obligation to honor his father and mother for twenty-two years, G-d took Jacob's own son, Joseph, away from him for an equal number of years (JEM interview with Rabbi Nochum Yakobovitch, 2006). The authors appear to be referring to this talk in Paris 1947 on page 140 of their book, but they again claim that the Rebbe was comparing himself to Joseph, not Jacob.

[29] Their degree of expertise in the Rebbe's letters can be judged from the fact that it was only with the help of an academic and a chasid (Dr. Maya Katz and Rabbi Eliezer Shemtov) that they were able to locate (evidently in the eleventh hour) a letter in which the Rebbe explains the reason for his preference for married women covering their hair with wigs rather than with kerchiefs (see Heilman and Friedman page 5 in footnote). There are numerous letters and talks, scattered throughout the 30 volumes of the Rebbe's *Igrot Kodesh* and the 39 volumes of *Likuttei Sichot* and other collections, in which the Rebbe states the reason for his preference. See, for example, *Igrot Kodesh* vol. 10, page 92 (letter dated 28th Marcheshvan 5715); ibid, page 186 (letter dated 1st Tevet 5715); vol. 15, page 199 (letter dated 14th Sivan 5717); vol. 19, page 488 (letter dated 10th Ellul 5720); *Likuttei Sichot* vol. 13, pages 187 and

Thus, when discussing the central Chabad doctrine of '*dirah be-tachtonim*' (that is, G-d's desire for man to make a 'dwelling place for Him in the physical world'), they are again out of their depths. The authors write, apparently based on an erroneous understanding of secondary sources, that the Rebbe had transformed or replaced the original meaning of the idea to suit his own purposes. Whereas in the past this philosophy meant that G-d wanted man to overcome his "animal nature, and material being and thus make space for the Divine Presence to enter into him, into this lower form of existence", the Rebbe, the authors suggest, "turned that idea around. It was G-d who wanted to descend to man's level, to transform that mundane reality into his dwelling place"[30]. Even a neophyte in the study of the Rebbe's theology ought to recognize how inaccurate this presentation is. Sadly, the authors' self-acknowledged lack of familiarity, or interest, with the sources does not deter them from making broad-sweeping statements about the Rebbe's theology[31].

---

189. See also *Likuttei Sichot* vol. 28, page 317; *Sha'arei Halachah uMinhag* (above note 2), vol. 4, page 143ff.

[30] See Heilman and Friedman page 157.

[31] See next footnote, for a quote of the authors themselves saying that they did not consider it their responsibility to study the Rebbe's teachings in depth before attempting to write a "psycho-biography" about his life.

On the Seforim Blog the authors even made the claim that the Rebbe's texts have become corrupted by editors.

To which I responded: "Firstly, this is clearly an *ex-post-facto* 'justification.' This is not an assertion that you made in your book and, even now, you do not point to even one *sichah* or *ma'amar* that you have reason to suspect or that corroborates your claim in any way.

Secondly, if you seriously had qualms about the authenticity of the texts, you would not have relied on many of the **secondary** sources and **websites** (that you quote so often), for these sources have gleaned their information from these very texts that you now suggest you could not use because they are 'suspect.'

Thirdly, even if you believed this to be the case, you could have listened to the hundreds of hours of recordings that are available on Chabad.org, (a website which you refer to repeatedly) for all and sundry to listen to, free of charge! [Were you to have done so, you would have become convinced that the unedited versions of the Rebbe's talks, the so-called *hanachot bilti mugahot*, are indeed reliable transcripts!]

The authors' lack of appreciation of the Rebbe's essential works, calls into question their ability to construct the narrative of his life, es-

---

Fourthly, the edited *sichot* and *ma'amarim*, those that were included in the thirty-nine volumes of *Likuttei Sichot* and the six volumes of *Sefer haMa'amarim Melukat* were **finally** edited, often with pain-staking meticulousness, by the Rebbe himself. These volumes (45 in total) were all published with the Rebbe's verbal and written approval during his lifetime and his good health. To dismiss the *Likuttei Sichot* that were by the Rebbe's own testimony, his finished product, in favor of sound-bites gleaned from all sorts of websites, fliers and magazines (*sichat ha-shavua, sichat ha-geulah* etc. etc. – which are neither *mugah* nor *bilti mugah*) constitutes a horrendous indictment of the Rebbe's honesty and a callous, audacious in the extreme, dismissal of his scholarly output."

To this the authors countered back in a follow-up response: Rapoport suggests that our assertion that texts of the Rebbe were subject to emendations and changes is made ex-post-facto. In fact, beginning on p.65, we write about the difficulty of using Chabad sources. Anyone reading Rapoport's explanations can see how even now a hasid's reading and description of what his Rebbe said requires looking at texts through a very narrow view."

I, in turn, responded: On page 65 of your book you write: 'The life of a Hasidic Rebbe is often shrouded in Hagiography . . . myth, mystery and reconstructed memory. Obviously such an attitude often makes it difficult to sift through internal accounts by those who look upon the Rebbe as their spiritual leader and guide.'

To be sure, I had not failed to notice your preoccupation with the recurring theme of hagiography in your book. Yet in the section of my rejoinder that you refer to, I was not talking about chasidic narratives or story books; I was addressing the fact that you rely on secondary rather than primary sources, and more generally your failure to engage in the Rebbe's *sichot, ma'amarim and Igrot* etc. – one of the most shocking facets of your 'biography'.

I never thought for a moment that (on page 65 or anywhere else for that matter) you were actually suggesting that the Rebbe's formal publications (for example his *Likuttei Sichot*) were the stuff of myth "and reconstructed memory"!

Even if, for arguments sake, you actually believe that the published sources of the Rebbe's Torah are not worthy of trust, is it not more likely that the secondary sources (and the circulars or websites that draw from them) which you do refer to, are even less accurate and even more suspect?

Finally, are you suggesting that the audio and video recordings of the Rebbe's public addresses are also shrouded in Hagiography? If you believe they are, how could you have used the clippings from JEM? And if you do acknowledge that the documents edited by the Rebbe's own hand are reliable, why did you ignore these addresses? Surely they would have helped you in your quest to read the Rebbe's mind!

pecially one that attempts to read the mind as well as the body, to record not only the dry facts, but the internal psycho-dynamics that governed his choices and decisions throughout his life.

To be sure, there is more to a man than the books he writes[32], but familiarity with the relevant literature is arguably a pre-requisite to conclusions and publications on the subject of one's biography. One who writes an authoritative biography of Maimonides, for example, ought to first acquire, at the very least, a basic familiarity with his *Mishneh Torah*, Letters and *Guide for the Perplexed*.

I therefore consider it pretentious for professors Heilman and Friedman to undertake the production of what is purportedly a serious biography of the Rebbe, while apparently lacking the requisite qualifications to do so.

---

[32] **In their response to this paragraph in my original review essay on the Seforim blog, authors Heilman and Friedman write:** "The argument p. 5 that only the books that a person writes are the basis of a biography (using the example of Maimonides – we leave aside the hubris of suggesting MMS and Maimonides are parallel [indeed not only is the Rebbe compared to Maimonides but also to Moses and David p. 6] as Rabbi Rapoport suggests is an opinion we do not share, particularly if those books and publications leave out a whole section of a person's life and are subject to emendation by Hasidim. As we write at the outset of our work, our goal was not to plumb these writings."

To which I responded: "It is clear that you did not read what I wrote in this regard. What I wrote was that you are 'insufficiently familiar with the primary texts, practices and cultural norms that are relevant' to your subject of research. I then wrote: 'To be sure, there is more to a man than the books he writes, but familiarity with the relevant literature is arguably a pre-requisite to conclusions and publications on the subject of one's biography, especially if the biographers (like yourselves) attempt to read the mind of their subject'. I stand by this assertion and believe that it is entirely reasonable."

Section II

1. Point of Departure

Several decades ago an early biographer of the Rebbe[33] suggested that the Rebbe initially engaged in scientific studies (such as engineering[34]) in order that he should be able to earn a livelihood (and be able to observe the Sabbath) in the circumstances that prevailed in communist Russia[35]. Clearly, a young man in the 1920s could hardly have expected to earn a stable livelihood from the rabbinate under the anti-religious communist regime[36] [37].

It is likewise axiomatic to students of Lubavitch history, that the Rebbe did not initially envisage himself as the successor of his father-in-law. As we know, even after the passing of his predecessor he was

---

[33] A journalist by the name of Nissan Gordon: 1918-1990. I should note that Mr. Gordon was born to a Chabad family, though his primary work was for Yiddish newspapers.

[34] Later he was to use his knowledge in these areas in his capacity as a Jewish leader. See, e.g., Nissan Mindel, *The Letter and the Spirit* (Kehot Publication Society: Brooklyn, 1998), page 245 (letter dated 1966): "... in view of the Rebbe's academic training in engineering, several years ago the Rebbe considered it his duty to make public two *responsa* wherein he clearly and in detail set forth the facts about the inevitable and repeated *Chilul Shabbat* involved in the operation of the said ships on *Shabbat*".

For the Rebbe's lengthy Hebrew letters in this regard, see *Igrot Kodesh* vol. 13, pages 285–293 (letters dated 23rd Tammuz 5716); pages 315-319 (letter dated Rosh Chodesh Menachem Av 5716); pages 321-323 (letter dated 2nd Menachem Av 5716); pages 333-335 (letter dated 4th Menachem Av 5716).

See also letters of the Rebbe dated 29th Iyar 5713; 21st Shevat 5718 published in *Letters from the Lubavitcher Rebbe* vol. 4 (Brooklyn, 1998), pages 6-7; 13-17.

[35] See Nissan Gordon (using the pen-name of N. ben Yochanan) in *Di Yiddishe Heim*, vol. 5, no. 4 (Adar 5724), page 5.

[36] Additionally, his general shunning of the limelight may have contributed to his reluctance to enter the rabbinate.

[37] Later ('University Education for a Chasid') I will suggest additional reasons for the Rebbe's study of the sciences.

reluctant, in the extreme, to assume the mantle of leadership[38]. Rather it was fate and destiny (what chasidim call Divine Providence) that led him, arguably against his will, to assume this role. It is therefore reasonable to assume that in his earlier years – certainly before he became engaged to the daughter of Rayatz – he did not seriously entertain this idea, although it is possible that others may have done so.

The authors clearly worked with similar premises and presuppositions, yet, as we shall see, they depart into more radical and unsubstantiated claims.

In order to facilitate structure, I shall break down their narrative into segments, in accordance with the different stages of and milestones in the Rebbe's life, and examine their findings in light of the above criteria.

2. Reb Levik: The Rebbe's Father and Teacher

They begin their biographical narrative with much of the same information that may be found in the writings of Lubavitch chroniclers, although they (do not always appear to give sufficient credit to the initial researchers and) sometimes curiously omit some significant details or cast undue doubt on established facts[39].

---

[38] See for example *Igrot Kodesh* vol. 3, pages 260; 308; 485. See also *Igrot Kodesh* vol. 4, page 70. The topic of the Rebbe's reluctance to assume leadership after Rayatz's passing is treated more fully in 'Appendix Two: The Ten Lost Years'.

[39] One example typical of many: In their discussion of the arrest of Rayatz by the Soviet authorities in 1927 they write: "[I]n **one version** (emphasis added) of the story, as they took Yosef Yitzchak away to prison, one of the two former Lubavitchers, perhaps with irony, offered to carry the Rebbe's bag of *talis* and *tefillin* (prayer articles), saying, 'as my grandfather your Hasid once carried your packages for your grandfather, so will I now carry them for you.' The Rebbe **reportedly** (emphasis added) held on to these articles in defiance." The authors then continue: "Rabbi Yosef Yitzchak was imprisoned and, according to **Lubavitcher versions** of the events, sentenced to death." (Heilman and Friedman page 80).

There is only one account of the arrest, and that is the one that Rayatz himself penned (and subsequently published) in his own personal diary. See *Likuttei Dibburim* vol. 4, page 1218ff. There are no other 'versions' of this story. On what basis do the authors cast doubt on the authenticity of Rayatz's own narrative of his arrest?

They tell the story of a bright boy, born and bred in the home of a rabbi of a "small Hasidic community"[40], Yekaterinoslav (later Dnepropetrovsk) in the Ukraine[41]. Mendel (as they call him) who was born to Rabbi Levi Yitzchak and Chanah Schneerson[42] was given a comprehensive Jewish education in the local Cheder and, subsequently, by his learned father – a follower and supporter of the fifth Rebbe of Lubavitch, Rabbi Shalom Dovber Schneersohn (Rashab: 1860-1920). Although Mendel never attended the local gymnasium, he was taught languages and science in an extra-curricular capacity – his parents evidently wanted him to have a broad education.

In this context, the authors contend that not only Rabbi Levi Yitzchak, but also Rashab, valued secular knowledge, at least as a useful political tool in communal affairs. Whence do they know this?

The authors explain:

In a letter of recommendation written by the fifth Lubavitcher Rebbe in support of his rabbinical selection in Yekaterinoslav, Levi Yitzchak was described as superior 'in Torah and the fear of God,' but also as someone who *'knows and understands worldly matters'*[43]. The Lubavitcher Rebbe of the time understood that this last point would carry weight - this in spite of the fact that ChaBaD rebbes had generally been prominent opponents of the idea of Jews receiving a general or university education.

In a footnote they add:

He [Rashab] tried hard, and even went so far as to suggest that his cousin, Levi Yitzchak, try to acquire an additional

---

[40] Heilman and Friedman page 67. They fail to mention that in 1920 Rabbi Levi Yitzchak became the Rabbi of the entire Jewish community of Dnepropetrovsk. See Zvi Harkavy in *Shanah beShanah* (Heichal Shlomo: Jerusalem) 5729, page 288.

[41] They write that Rabbi Levi Yitzchak came to Yekaterinoslav in 1907. As a matter of fact, it was in 1909 (see Rashab, *Igrot Kodesh* vol. 4, Kehot Publication Society: Brooklyn, 1986, page 327).

[42] For some biographical details see Rabbi Naftali Tzvi Gotleib, *Toldot Levi Yitzchak*, 3 volumes (Kfar Chabad 1995).

[43] Heilman and Friedman page 69 (the emphasis in the italics is theirs).

ordination or at least a letter of recommendation from the non-Hasidic yeshiva head, Rabbi Haym (*sic*) Soloveitchik of Brisk[44] (Brest-Litovsk) in Lithuania (*sic*), indicating that the broader the education, both in Torah studies **and in other matters**, one had, the greater the likelihood of getting hired by the Jews of the increasingly cosmopolitan region of Russia"[45].

Whether, and to what degree, Rabbi Levi Yitzchak or Rabbi Shalom Dovber appreciated the importance of secular education is beyond the scope of this essay. What is clear, however, is that Rashab's letters from which the authors infer this, have absolutely no bearing on the issue at hand.

Firstly, the Hebrew words that Rashab uses in describing Rabbi Levi Yitzchak's knowledge are "וגם יודע ומבין דבר במילי דעלמא", a phrase that has nothing to do with secular knowledge or education. [Secular knowledge is typically referred to as '*madda*', '*chochmot chitzoniyot*' or simply '*limudei chol*'] The term "*mili de-alma*", which Rashab employs in a letter written to an Orthodox rabbi, is a generic term and refers, in both classical rabbinic writings[46] and later works, to domestic or communal matters that are not intrinsic to Torah. A person who "knows and understands worldly matters" simply means a person who is not just book-wise, but also has an astuteness that enables him to deal with the entire spectrum of issues that a communal rabbi has to contend with. Whether or not one appreciates the value of secular education, no one would deny the need for a rabbi to have the necessary acumen and insight to deal with matters that extend beyond 'the four cubits of halachah'.

The fact that Rabbi Shalom Dovber "went so far as to suggest that his cousin, Levi Yitzchak, try to acquire an additional [rabbinic] ordination" from Rabbi Chaim Soloveitchik of Brisk (1853-1918) has nothing to do with the premise that "the broader the education, both in Torah

---

[44] It is noteworthy that Rabbi Levi Yitzchak did indeed receive this ordination. For some details of the examination leading to the ordination see *Likuttei Sichot* vol. 9, page 91.

[45] Heilman and Friedman page 69.

[46] See, for example, *Pesachim* 113a; *Bava Metzia* 9a.

studies and in other matters" the more chances there were to succeed in the rabbinate.

The reason for the suggestion is explained by Rabbi Shalom Dovber himself in the very letter they refer to (but in the section of it that they do not cite): כאשר דורשים סמיכה מבריסק צריך לנסוע לשם. ('If they insist on an ordination from Brisk, you must travel there'). Clearly, the community stipulated his appointment on his receiving ordination from Rabbi Soloveitchik of Brisk.

Whilst the above-mentioned issue has no bearing on the central thesis of Heilman's and Friedman's biography, I have nevertheless included this section in my review, because their 'reading' of Rashab's letters regarding Rabbi Levi Yitzchak is illustrative of their method of selective quotation and inaccurate translation.

3. The Rebbe's Date of Birth

The authors assert:

Like so much else in his story, even the date of his birth is ambiguous. While the accepted birthday, according to his own word, was Sabbath eve, April 18, 1902 (11 Nissan 5662, according to the Jewish calendar), his soviet passport indicates an earlier date, March 2, 1895, a discrepancy having to do with the constant need of the Jews born under the rule of the czars to find ways of avoiding the army draft, which many understood meant the inevitable loss of young Jewish boys to secularity and unbelief. Mendel Schneerson claimed he had received a student deferment from the Russian army in 1915. Perhaps when he applied for his passport in 1927 he gave the earlier date so that he could exit Russia at an 'older' age, when he would no longer be as likely to be called to serve as a soldier"[47]. In an endnote they conclude: "Given that we find a letter to Mendel from his father in 1937 greeting him on his

---

[47] Heilman and Friedman page 66.

thirty-fifth birthday[48], we **tend to believe** (emphasis added) the
1902 date to be the true one[49].

However, even if one is not prepared to take the Rebbe's word for
it, there is no reason to doubt the authenticity of this date, since the
Rebbe's birth was registered (in 1902) by his parents in the Nikolaev
Jewish communal records and these have been preserved in the government's archives. These documents have been published[50]; even cursory research would have enabled the authors to access them.

If further evidence is required, the Rebbe's grandfather's diary has
been published, and in his entries for the year 1915 we find reference to
his grandson's forthcoming bar mitzvah[51].

Their ambivalence regarding the date of the Rebbe's birth has far-
reaching ramifications. For later in the same chapter they refer to an affidavit that records that the Rebbe had "served in the Russian military
from March to August 1915, before being released to become a student;
what he did during those six months of army service remains unknown"[52].

In light of the fact that the Rebbe was only born in 1902, any suggestion that the Rebbe had served in the Russian military in the year

---

[48] To be precise, Rabbi Levi Yitzchak's blessings to the Rebbe on occasion of his 30th,
33rd, 34th, 35th and 36th birthdays have all been preserved and published in *Likuttei
Levi Yitzchak–Igrot* (Kehot Publication Society: Brooklyn, 1973). It is unclear what
Heilman and Friedman found unique in the blessing for the 35th birthday.

[49] Heilman and Friedman, chapter 3 note 1.

[50] See *The Early Years*. vol. 1 (Jewish Education Media: Brooklyn, 2005). See also
Figure 5 at the end of this book.

[51] See the diary notes of the Rebbe's paternal grandfather, Rabbi Baruch Schneur
Zalman Schneerson (1853-c.1927), *Reshimot HaRabash* (Kehot Publication Society:
Brooklyn, 2001). On page 141 (entry for 20th Adar **5675**) he records how he
requested a blessing from Rashab on the occasion of his grandson's (the Rebbe's)
forthcoming bar mitzvah. See also *ibid.* page 130 (entry for 7th Adar **5675**):

"בליל ראשון פרשת תצוה הי' הסיפור אודות בני לויק שי', ואודות בנו מענדל שי', שצריך להניח תפלין
ביום חמישי הבעל"ט אי"ה, י"א אדר, כי **ל"א ניסן הבעל"ט אי"ה יהי' בר-מצוה** ... **והוא נער טוב בלימוד
על-דרך הפלגה** בעזה"י. ושבכלל הם נערים טובים הם השלושה בנים שלו יחיו. ולויק שי' מדריכם בדרך
התורה ועבודה, והולכים בדרך הישר והטוב".

[52] Heilman and Friedman page 73.

1915 is highly unlikely, for what military role could he have played at the tender age of thirteen[53]?

4. The Rebbe's Youth and Education

In Heilman and Friedman's work, they tell us that a childhood acquaintance of the Rebbe, Zvi Harkavy[54] recalled that the Rebbe and his brothers were tutored in languages and mathematics by a certain Israel Eidelsohn, "a confirmed socialist and Zionist", and Yeshaya Sher[55] recalled that the Rebbe was exceptionally "gifted in translation and in mathematics"[56]. Heilman and Friedman speculate that Eidelsohn may have served as a "role model" for the Rebbe (and his brothers) and are confident that "he had a profound intellectual and moral impact upon them". This because the "tradition of respecting one's teacher was deeply ingrained in the Jewish ethos ... and that held true even if the teacher taught them matters beyond the boundaries of tradition"[57]. Aside for these speculative remarks, Heilman and Friedman have precious little to tell us about the Rebbe's life in his father's home.

They seem to have ignored the Rebbe's classmates' accounts and eschewed any of the Rebbe's and the Rebbe's mother's recollections of his youth-time.

According to the Rebbe's own testimony, Rabbi Levi Yitzchak had employed a Torah scholar, a great *lamdan*, to live in their home so that the children would always have a teacher on hand[58].

Rebbetzen Chanah Schneerson and many other people who lived in the Rebbe's vicinity in the years of his youth have been interviewed, and spoken of his diligence, studiousness and specific accomplish-

---

[53] See 'Appendix One: The French Affidavit'.

[54] Heilman and Friedman page 71.

[55] Heilman and Friedman page 72.

[56] They do not mention his interest and prowess in astronomy, something which Sher discusses in detail, and is ostensibly reflected in several of the Rebbe's later writings.

[57] Heilman and Friedman page 72.

[58] See the Rebbe's conversation in *Sichot Kodesh* 5733 vol. 1, page 456.

ments[59]. His mother had described, for example, two fascinating and revealing episodes of the Rebbe's life during the turbulent times of his youth in the Ukraine[60]. Even when the authors attempt to quote her, they do not manage to get it right[61].

The Rebbe himself remarked that as the first born of the family, who was also fluent in the Russian vernacular, he was summoned every so often to the offices of the powers that be – in connection with his parent's communal work, and he was witness to the stereotypical communist anti-religious oppression and brutality[62].

These biographical sources are inexplicably ignored, as are numerous others[63].

5. The Rebbe's Rabbinic Credentials and Ordination

The Rebbe received *semichah* (rabbinic ordination) in 1924 from his uncle, Rabbi Shmuel Schneerson, chief rabbi of Nikolaev. A facsimile of

---

[59] See Nissan Gordon in *Di Yiddishe Heim,* vol. 5, no. 3 (Kislev 5724), page 3ff; idem. no. 4 (Adar 5724), page 4ff; idem.

[60] See Nissan Gordon (based on interview with the Rebbe's mother) in *Di Yiddishe Heim,* Adar–Iyar 5722, pages 4-5.

[61] This is true even with regard to matters that are inconsequential to their thesis. Thus, for example, the Rebbe's mother had recalled how he came back home to Yekaterinoslav for the festival of Sukkot 1927, an experience that she described in detail and was reported by Nissan Gordon in *Di Yiddishe Heim* vol. 6, no 3 (Kislev 5725), page 20ff.

Heilman and Friedman cite this visit from a secondary source (which they refer to as a "Lubavitcher hagiography"): "One Lubavitcher version of the events has him travelling back ... to his parents to spend the Sukkot holidays with them ... he then purportedly journeyed on with his mother" (page 84).

[62] *Sichot Kodesh* 5732 vol. 1, page 593; *Sichot Kodesh* 5739 vol. 3, pages 565-566.

[63] Another typical example of the biographical information ignored by the authors is the following testimony broadcast on Israeli television by an Israeli politician, Yona Kesse, who in his youth frequented the Rebbe's parents'home: "I witnessed his intense diligence in Torah study, I always found him learning in a standing position, never sitting down ... I remember him as an extremely private person, an introvert; his entire being, as I recall it, was Torah." (Morashah program, broadcast on Israeli Television 16th Kislev 5733). Kesse (1907-1985) was an irreligious Israeli politician who served as a member of the Israeli parliament between 1949 and 1965, most of the time as a member of the left-wing Mapai party.

this *semichah* is available[64]. Heilman and Friedman were evidently not aware of this and therefore cast aspersions on his credentials as a 'rabbi'.

Although, they write, a Lubavitch biographer "claims Mendel received *semicha* from the ... so-called '*Rogatchover Gaon*'"[65] and "Menachem Mendel would claim this as well in his booklet *HaYom Yom*... we have found no documents of ordination to support this claim[66]". To be sure, the claim that the Rebbe received rabbinic ordination from Rabbi Yechiel Yaakov Weinberg[67] is cavalierly dismissed[68].

Concerning the Rebbe's "claim" that he received rabbinic ordination from the '*Rogatchover Gaon*', Heilman and Friedman toil in vain to knock down a straw man. Why? Because the Rebbe never made such a claim![69].

---

[64] See Figure 6 at the end of this book.

[65] The Rogatchover Gaon, Rabbi Yosef Rosen (1858–1936) was one of the most prominent Talmudic scholars of the early 20th century.

[66] Heilman and Friedman page 87 in the second footnote.

[67] Rabbi Yechiel Yaakov Weinberg (1884-1966) was a noted European Orthodox rabbi who headed the Hildesheimer Rabbinical Seminary in Berlin.

[68] "A story repeated among Lubavitchers that Menachem Mendel Schneerson received rabbinic ordination *(semikhah)* while in Berlin from Rabbi J. J. Weinberg, who taught and also served for a time as a rector at the seminary, has no apparent evidentiary basis" (Heilman and Friedman page 87).

[69] The authors refer to "Ha-Yom Yom (Brooklyn: kehot/otsar Hasidim 1943"21) on October 1944 (Tishrei 5685)". Once again they err. Firstly, the original edition of *HaYom Yom* (published in 1943) did not include any biographical data about the Rebbe himself, since the biographical section in the preface of the book was meant to offer timelines of the lives of the **Rebbes** of Chabad (not the sons-in-law of the Rebbes). In 1944, when the first edition was published, "Mendel Schneerson" was still years away from becoming the seventh rebbe of the Chabad movement. Secondly, the entry about the Rebbe having received rabbinical ordination from the Rogatchover Gaon was added only in the 1982 edition, in which the publishers added an expanded biographical sketch of the Rebbe's life. It has been confirmed by this author with the printers of that edition that the Rebbe never personally edited the biographical information added about him in that edition.

With regard to the Rebbe's *semichah* from Rabbi Weinberg, I refer to the expert opinion of historian Professor Marc Shapiro[70], a specialist on Weinberg, who has concluded that the weight of evidence suggests that the Rebbe did indeed receive rabbinic ordination from Weinberg[71].

At any rate, the issue that Heilman and Friedman really wish to raise here, albeit under the thin veil of the ordination saga, is whether the Rebbe was really a Torah scholar of the calibre that would impress the likes of Rabbi Weinberg and the *'Rogatchover Gaon'*.

To this end, they would have done well to explore the substantial remnants of what appears to have been part of an on-going correspondence between the Rebbe and the Rogatchover[72]. In one such letter (available in manuscript facsimile and published[73]) which the Rebbe sent from his home at twenty-three years of age, he responds to the Gaon and, remarkably, frames his response in a fashion that resembles the Gaon's own idiosyncratic style; terse phrases replete with numerous references to voluminous Talmudic literature.

Even a cursory perusal of these letters (as well as the one item of correspondence that has survived from his written communication with Rabbi Weinberg[74]), in addition to the correspondence, in diverse and multi-faceted areas of Jewish Law, Homiletics and Chasidism, which he would later engage in with other prominent rabbis of his day[75] – adequately demonstrate, that whether or not the Rebbe received

---

[70] Shapiro is the author of *Between the Yeshiva World and Modern Orthodoxy: The Life and Works of Rabbi Jehiel Jacob Weinberg, 1884-1966* (London; Portland, Or.: Littman Library 1999).

[71]   See   http://seforim.blogspot.com/2009/09/marc-b-shapiro-responses-to-comments.html

Professor Shapiro concludes: "From now on, whenever I am asked if the Rebbe received *semikhah* from Weinberg, I will reply yes".

[72] See *Igrot Kodesh* vol. 1, pages 1-2 (a facsimile of the Rebbe's letter is published at the beginning of the volume, page 22); ibid. page 14; *Reshimot* no. 33, pages 4-16; no. 159, pages 8-15; no. 104, pages 3-8 and 10-11.

[73] See *Igrot Kodesh* vol. 21, pages 1-6. A facsimile of the Rebbe's letter is provided in Figure 7 at the end of this book.

[74] See *Reshimot* nos. 127 and 128.

[75] See *Reshimot* no. 3, pages 3-9; no. 34; no. 58; no. 96, pages 13-14; no. 124; no. 139; no. 147, pages 6-10; no. 151, pages 15-20; no. 161; no. 174, pages 7-14.

ordination from the *Rogatchover Gaon*, he certainly would have been a worthy candidate.

The authors conclude their discussion of the Rebbe's *semichah* with this suggestive remark:

Why Yosef Yitzchak [=Rayatz] did not ordain him is not clear.

This speculative comment illustrates the authors' unawareness of Chasidic norms. It is common knowledge that Rayatz never ordained anyone, even relatives. (Neither did his father, Rashab, and neither did his son-in-law, the Rebbe). Apparently, they saw such rabbinic ordination as the function of a halachic authority (who, in contrast to a Rebbe[76], their primary occupation would be with legal matters) and outside of the purview of their roles as 'Rebbes'[77].

6. A Flawed Psycho-Biographical Hypothesis

According to Heilman and Friedman, the Rebbe dreamt from an early age of becoming an engineer[78], a career choice that took him from his hometown to Leningrad, and ultimately to Berlin and Paris where he finally received his degree. As the authors have it, it was in France that his dreams were shattered with the rise of European anti-Semitism

---

[76] See, for example, *Igrot Kodesh* vol. 9, page 123; vol. 23, page 393.

[77] Many Chasidic courts had in-house 'rabbis' who would serve as the authority on legal issues that arose in the Rebbe's home or amongst their Chasidim.

When the Rebbe was consulted on strictly halachic matters he would usually refer his interlocutors to halachic authorities. For a few random examples see *Igrot Kodesh* vol. 26, page 412 and page 497; vol. 27, page 123; vol. 28, page 141; *Nitzutzei Ohr* (Kehot Publication Society: Brooklyn, 1999) Hebrew section, page 91.

See also *Igrot Kodesh* vol. 29, page 269 where the Rebbe refers to Rabbi Moshe Feinstein (1895-1986):

"ע"פ מכתבה השני – **צורך** בחוו"ד רב מורה הוראה - שיספרו לו אופן הנישואין (שלפני הנישואין למר [...] שי') ויאמר ההי' צורך בגט ומה לעשות וכו'. והרב פיינשטיין שי' עונה לכל השואלים – גם כשאינו מכירם (ולפעמים גם ע"י טליפון) ונשאר בסוד, כמובן".

See also the biography of Rabbi Feinstein published in his *Igrot Moshe* vol. 8 (Jerusalem, 1996):

"אדמו"ר רמ"ם מליובאוויטש זצ"ל הי' מקורב במיוחד לרבנו והי' מפנה אליו שאלות רבות בהלכה".

[78] See above regarding their play on the word *chalom* in which they interpret it to refer to a **life-long aspiration** of becoming an engineer.

and the outbreak of the second-world-war. The Holocaust and its consequences did not allow him to realize his professional aspirations.

Another journey unfolded in the Rebbe's life during this time. In
the early 1920s he met his distant cousin and future father-in-law, Rabbi Yosef Yitzchak Schneersohn. Mendel became attached to the court of
Rayatz and was involved in its activities. After a lengthy courtship
Mendel married Rayatz's middle daughter, Moussia, a marriage that
would, in the length of time, lead him to become his father-in-law's
successor as the seventh Rebbe of the Chabad dynasty.

The authors claim that Mendel had not been particularly interested
in Chasidism in general and Chabad Orthodoxy in particular. Although he begrudgingly 'ran a few errands' for Rayatz[79], his real interest was to lead a primarily secular life, first as a student in the scientific
academies of his choice, and then as a worldly engineer living in cosmopolitan Paris.

The authors posit that whilst the Rebbe was always "observant" of
Jewish Law - indeed when academic courses clashed with the observance of the Sabbath, he "simply left early on Fridays, without explanation"[80] and later "successfully petitioned the administration for
permission to leave early on Fridays"[81] - "Sabbath was not to be denied"[82] - he had decided, when moving to Berlin, to abandon the Chasidic way of life. In the course of time, the authors posit, familial ties
and his own childlessness drove him towards a greater Chasidic orientation.

Although there was a small East European Chasidic community in
Berlin, Heilman and Friedman contend that Berlin was not a place for a
chasid to be, it was rather "a magnet to those who sought to leaven
their religious attachments with the supplement of Western Civiliza-

---

[79] In one passage of the book, at the top of page 152, the authors state in remarkably
poor taste: "He had escaped from pogroms, communists, many of the missions of
his father-in-law, and now the Nazis."

[80] Heilman and Friedman page 118.

[81] Heilman and Friedman page 121.

[82] Heilman and Friedman page 120.

tion"[83]. The Rebbe was no exception. He went there to escape from the world of ultra-Orthodoxy and Chasidism, although at one odd juncture they assert, somewhat paradoxically:

> There is no evidence of Mendel's presence in Berlin's Synagogues during this time. We do know he was pious and perhaps as well a bit ascetic[84].

The authors hypothesize that the Rebbe was immersed in Parisian culture, and was a source of embarrassment to his father-in-law. He lived, they state "in the cultural capitals of Western Europe in ways that seemed to border on the cosmopolitan and secular" [85]. The correspondence between the Rebbe and his father-in-law, Rayatz, was limited to the mundane and the trivial[86].

While there are many reports that when the Rebbe was in Berlin and Paris, he remained a steadfast chasid[87] – moreover that his personal life was an exemplary combination of Chasidic piety and modesty and his pursuit of scientific knowledge was a mere adjunct to his engagement with Torah and Mitzvot – these reports are dismissed as mere 'hagiography'.

When confronted with the Rebbe's diary[88], hundreds of pages filled with Torah ideas, Chasidic vignettes, ethical aphorisms and detailed transcriptions of his father-in-law's talks recorded over a lengthy time in terse language and precise handwriting, Heilman and Friedman remain perplexed. Is it really possible that a man whose scholarly interests were invested primarily in the hard sciences and whose social intercourse was amongst the un-godly residents of bourgeois Paris should simultaneously be engaged in Chasidic lore and pietistic ruminations?

---

[83] Heilman and Friedman page 85.

[84] Heilman and Friedman pages 88-89.

[85] Heilman and Friedman page 39.

[86] See Heilman and Friedman page 105.

[87] See, for example, below, 'On Synagogues and Distances', and footnote 125.

[88] The manuscript of this diary was found in the Rebbe's study after his passing and was published, first in installments and ultimately as *Torat Menachem-Reshimat HaYoman* (Kehot Publication Society: Brooklyn, 2006).

The authors provide us with one of their central psycho-biographical hypotheses:

The Rebbe led a "double life as both a Hasid and as a student at the university"[89]; He lived the Chasidic life when he was in the court of Rayatz and reverted to the secular when he was back in Berlin or Paris[90]... "Mendel managed to switch easily from one mind-set to the other, from his secular to his Hasidic interests and religious concerns"[91].

This hypothesis leads the authors to a number of flawed conclusions which I will discuss shortly.

7. Correspondence: Omissions and Fabrications

Heilman and Friedman claim that both the Rebbe's father (who was trapped in the Soviet Union) and his father-in-law who had established his court in Riga (Latvia) were concerned about the state of his religious observance. To this end they sent him, we are told, letters of encouragement and guidance in addition to books of Jewish learning, to ensure that he remained observant in the manner that they preferred[92].

Yet what does the correspondence **itself** actually indicate?

The Rebbe and his father engaged in an on-going correspondence for almost the entire duration of time that the Rebbe lived in the European capitals. A perusal of the available letters demonstrates that they reciprocally sent each other their original Torah insights – sometimes mini-tracts on Talmudic and Kabbalistic intricacies, and often added supportive or critical remarks to each other's output[93].

---

[89] Heilman and Friedman page 95.

[90] See Heilman and Friedman page 95. See also page 104: "They lived a kind of bifocal life: in one they were young newlyweds in Berlin, students tasting the cosmopolitan life of the German capital - a life in which they would go out together, usually on Monday nights to enjoy the city, establishing their own home together . . . On the other hand, they were still firmly connected to the family and court from which they came, and would return to it for holidays and family events".

[91] Heilman and Friedman page 106.

[92] Heilman and Friedman page 104.

[93] The following snippets from Rabbi Levi Yitzchak's letters, all published in *Likuttei Levi Yitzchak–Igrot* (above note 48) are illustrative:

In one such letter father writes to son:

With regard to your written *chiddushei Torah* that G-d has
graced you with ... you asked that I should inform you of my
opinion without any reservation whatsoever. Let it be known
to you that the discourse (*ma'amar*), in general, is very good; it
combines sharp thinking with vast knowledge in both *nigleh*
and *nistar*; correct and penetrative insights in the
understanding of both the revealed and the hidden dimensions
of the Torah. Thank G-d for the understanding, knowledge and
wisdom He has gracefully endowed you with ... indeed, your
ma'amar is excellent ... However, my cherished son, my faithful
advice to you is that you should see, in all such matters, to add
'salt and pepper', namely to ensure that what you write should
be anchored much more in the 'True Wisdom', the *kabbalah*"[94].

On another occasion (in an unpublished letter dated in 1936) the father praises his son's erudition:

With regard to your *chiddushei Torah*, I disagree with you. You
belittle yourself and write that they contain nothing novel. This
is not so, my son. 'Though you may be little in your own eyes,
etc. [are you not the head of the tribes of Israel?" (1 Samuel
15:17)]. Your *chiddushim* are very good ... My heart rejoices on
account of my son's wisdom. (See Figure 8 at the end of this book
for a facsimile of this handwritten letter.)

"וע"ד הערותיך על מכתבי נהנתי מהם מאד, ואם חכם בני ישמח לבי גם אני כו', ומי יתן והי' שתעשו
הערות גם על שארי העניינים האמורים בו .. הערתך הא' שרצית לומר .. הערתך הב' שרצית לומר ..
הערתך הג' .. הערתך הד' .. ע"ד קושייתך בביאורי הזהר פ' וישלח כו'"; "טוב הדבר שאמרת .. ואעירך על
הד' חלוקות שבגמרא שם .. והי' לי לעונג מה שהיית במסיבה בשמחה ואמרת דברים טובים ונכונים,
וטהור ידים יוסיף אומץ גם על להבא .. בסיימי המכתב נזכרתי שבמכתבך הקשת על המבואר בלקו"ת
כו'"; "וע"ד קושייתך עוד הפעם על האמור בלקו"ת .. וע"ד קושייתך בהמבואר בתו"ר בדרושי פורים";
"נהניתי מביאורך שאמרת על המארז"ל ברבה ור' זירא שאכלי סעודת פורים בהדדי .. וזכורני שדברתי
קרוב לזה עוד בהיותך אצלנו"; "מכתבך בני .. קיבלתי .. וע"ד הערותיך תדע, כי גם ממני לא נעלם מ"ש
בערוך וברית יוסף, אפס לפסק הלכה פסקינן .. ע"ד ההערה שהקטניות הוא לא בתור שכר כו'"; "ע"ד
הערותיך בחדושי תורה. א) בפסקי דינים ליור"ד .. ב) בתרגום יונתן פ' מטות .. ג) בלקו"ת בביאור דחקת ..
ואשאלך אני, מה דאמור בעירובין .. גם למה לא הובא המימרא דסבי דפומבדיתא כו'"; "ואעירך בראשי
פרקים, בדבר המאמר דרבב"ח .. שדברת אודותיו .. ובאתי עתך רק לאעירך בעניניך".

[94] *Likuttei Levi Yitzchak-Igrot* pages 307-308.

Rabbi Levi Yitzchak then again goes on to tell his son that he should seek to find support in and anchor his ideas on the wisdom of the *kabbalah* and then responds to his son, in detail, regarding his *chiddushim*.

In the Hebrew:

בדבר החידושי תורה שלך, אין דעתי כדעתך, מה שאתה מקטין את עצמך וכותב שאין בהם שום חידוש, לא כן בני, אם קטן אתה בעיניך הלא ראש כו', המה טובים מאד, ומכוונים אל האמת בכלל, אם חכם בני ושמח לבי גם אני, ורק יותר תבלין צריך בהם, הוא מה שכתבתי לך מכבד, שנצרך יותר יסודות מקבלה בהם, והרגל את עצמך לתמוך ולסמוך את החידושים על יסודות הקבלה, ואז יעלו ויתכוונו הדברים לאמתתן. ואעירך בראשי פרקים ...

Heilman and Friedman must surely have been aware of the nature of Reb Levi Yitzchak's numerous letters to his son, many of which have been published, but they choose to ignore and even misrepresent their nature. Which letter do they select?

A letter on the eve of Yom Kippur in late 1938 is typical. It begins with a review of the laws and practices of this holiest day of the Jewish year, complete with references to Talmud and other sacred literature, as well as the expressed hope that these lessons 'will not be lost from you and your progeny forever'[95].

They project an image of a father who must remind his son about the "the laws and practices" of the Day of Atonement and pray that he and his offspring will remain committed to their observance. This suggestion speaks volumes about the son's religious standard and is clearly intended to influence the reader's impression of who and what the "son" was.

There is only one problem. Not only is such a letter not "typical", it simply does not exist!

A letter was in fact written on that date by Rabbi Levi Yitzchak to the Rebbe. That is about the only 'grain of truth' in the authors' narrative. The letter focuses on the Kabbalistic dynamics of Erev Yom Kippur and Yom Kippur, and concludes with abundant blessings including a fervent prayer for the birth of a male grandson ("progeny")

---

[95] Heilman and Friedman page 128.

and for the arrival of the Messiah. But there is no "review" of the "laws and practices" of Yom Kippur in this letter (or in any other letter written by father to son). Nor does it include a blessing or an exhortation that the "laws and practices" of Yom Kippur should not be forgotten from the son and his potential offspring[96]. Indeed, how could a letter mailed on Erev Yom Kippur, and which would inevitably arrive days, if not weeks, after Yom Kippur, have possibly been intended as a review of the laws of Yom Kippur?!

In fact, the vast majority of letters between father and son deal exclusively with intensely deep Torah matters. The letters which are written in terse style, and that cover over 200 pages of small print, have been available for all to explore for almost four decades. They address intricate Talmudic matters; they introduce us to a 'to-and-fro' on, for example, the commentaries on the Jerusalem Talmud; and, primarily, they deal with deep and subtle Kabbalistic esoterica. Many of the letters are likely to exceed the grasp of many a seasoned Torah scholar who is unfamiliar with abstract Kabbalistic ideas.

Were Heilman and Friedman to have revealed to their readership the true nature of the correspondence between father and son rather than fabricating a 'sample' letter that, were it to exist, would have been atypical in the extreme, they would have come closer towards an accurate biographical account.

In another attempt to 'illustrate' the nature of the father's letters to his son, Heilman and Friedman write as follows: "About a week before his wedding, Mendel received a letter from his father filled with a whole series of directions" including a request that the Rebbe wear a

---

[96] The letter is published in *Likuttei Levi Yitzchak–Igrot*, pages 421-422. [The authors assert that this is the letter they refer to (see chapter 4, endnote 112)]. Over the course of our back and forth discussions on the Seforim blog, the authors had ample opportunity to simply admit their error and thereby demonstrate their objectivity and honesty. Instead, they insisted that their 'interpretation' was valid.

To settle this matter once and for all, I have included the full original Hebrew text of the letter (as published in *Likuttei Levi Yitzchak*), which consists of two paragraphs, in Figure 9 at the end of this book.

silk garment (*sirtuk*) for the duration of the chupah[97]. A "close reading" of the letter, they say, reveals "a concern on the father's part for the son's proper religious behavior".

"After explaining why this confession, normally recited on Yom Kippur (Day of Atonement), was also part of the wedding preparations, Levi Yitzchak suggested to his son that excessive weeping during these prayers and the fasting that precedes marriage 'is to be praised'"[98]. The authors continue: "Finally he urged his son to 'meditate with fear of G-d' under the wedding canopy, and after the wedding to pray wearing the special 'belt' (gartl) that Hasidim use and forever after don an extra pair of Tefillin according to the specifications of Rabbenu Tam".

Then comes their argument:

> Are these the directions of a father to a son who knows what is expected of a Hasidic groom, who himself is preparing to lead a life of piety and devotion, who is on the verge of entering the court of a Hasidic Rebbe ... Or are these the words of guidance given by a father who is very much a rabbi and is addressing a son who he knows has embarked on a life's journey that has taken him to the heart of secular culture, the university, and the capitals of Western culture and who, the father believes, needs to be reminded of the religious nature of marriage and of the holiness of this day[99].

Again, Heilman and Friedman are 'grasping at straws', seeking support for their thesis where none exists. In the process, they completely distort the tone and message of this touching letter from a loving father who is unable to be present at his eldest child's wedding, and must offer his parental guidance from afar.

---

[97] Note that the Rebbe Rashab had likewise asked the Rebbe's grandfather, who was on all accounts a man of exceedingly great Chasidic devotion, that he should wear a silk garment under the *chupah*. See *Reshimot HaRabash* (above note 51), entry for 17th Marcheshvan 5673 (pages 52-53): "אמר לי שצריך לילך להחופה בבגד של משי".

[98] Heilman and Friedman page 99.

[99] Heilman and Friedman pages 99-100.

At the outset let it be stated, that it is in perfect keeping with traditional practice for a father to remind his son, and for a mentor to remind his student, about the auspicious nature of his forthcoming *Yom ha-Chupah*.

The truth, however, is that a mere glance at the letter will demonstrate that it was never intended to remind the son about the "religious nature of marriage", rather the letter serves as an instruction manual (typical of those found in ethical wills and similar documents) in which the father (writing from a distance) advises his son, who has never experienced such a moment before, exactly which customs were part of his family's traditions and the finer nuances of these customs that he wishes him to adopt[100].

What about the "explanation why this confession, normally recited on Yom Kippur, was also part of the wedding preparations"; did a pious groom need an explanation for this?

The answer is, once again, that no such explanation is found in the letter. Heilman and Friedman evidently did not understand the meaning of the Hebrew. The father does not explain this, for, as Heilman and Friedman themselves explain, this knowledge is axiomatic to anyone who leads "a life of piety and devotion". The father merely mentions, in passing, that in Mishnaic teaching (*Ta'anit* 4:8) the day of Yom Kippur (on which the penitential confession is also recited) is actually related to the phenomenon of marriage, wherein after the conclusion of Yom Kippur Jewish bachelors would choose their brides.

Yet, what about the warning to meditate on the fear of G-d beneath the wedding canopy; would this not be a superfluous reminder for a devout groom?

A look at the entire text will help us. The father writes:

When beneath the wedding canopy, meditate the entire time on the Fear of Heaven, (this is what my Rebbe of blessed memory[101] told me before my own marriage) [102].

---

[100] For the full text of the letter (as published in *Likuttei Levi Yitzchak-Igrot*), see Figure 10 at the end of this book.

[101] "אדמו"ר ז"ל נבג"מ זי"ע", namely Rashab.

In other words, the father was merely employing the traditional vocabulary of his own mentor, linking the words of encouragement to his son with those that his own Rebbe gave to him. Moreover, his instruction to the groom is more than a reminder regarding the fear of G-d; it directs him to meditate on that "the entire time" that he is beneath the *chupah* (wedding canopy), focusing fully without permitting himself to be distracted. Instead of presenting the full context, Heilman and Friedman conveniently selected odd snippets that, when read in isolation, would support their thesis[103].

A similar flaw is found in Heilman and Friedman's approach to the correspondence between father-in-law and son-in-law. The authors ignore the published documents that record how Rayatz found no one better to refer his queries in the intricate laws of *Mikvaot*, than his son-in-law in Berlin[104]. They may not have been aware that Rayatz sent the bulk of his talks and discourses to be edited by the Rebbe prior to their publication[105]. Rayatz even turned to his son-in-law for an assessment of the illustrious Gaon and Rosh Yeshivah of his flagship Yeshivah in Otwock[106], Rabbi Yehuda Eber[107].

---

[102] *Likuttei Levi Yitzchak–Igrot* page 207.

[103] See the testimony of Rabbi Althaus cited in 'Appendix Two' to this essay ('Personal Encounters').

[104] See *Reshimot* no. 142.

[105] See *Rayatz, Igrot Kodesh* vol. 15 and the editor's preface to the book. This volume contains the letters of Rayatz to his son-in-law Rabbi Menachem Mendel and to his daughter Rebbetzen Chaya Mushka Schneerson. Significantly, the volume also includes relevant extracts from Rabbi Menachem Mendel's letters to his father-in-law. The vast majority of these letters were written between 1927 and 1941, during which the Rebbe and his wife lived for several years in Berlin and then in Paris. Many details of his whereabouts and activities come to light, and many tasks of a private or communal nature are detailed, in which Rabbi Menachem Mendel was engaged on his father-in-law's behalf.

Heilman and Friedman cannot be faulted for glossing over this particular volume for it was released after their book was complete. It nevertheless points to the weakness of their thesis.

[106] See *Sefer HaTemimim* (Kehot Publication Society: Brooklyn, 1991), page 267. [Heilman and Friedman (page 112) err in this regard when they assert that "there was a Temimim yeshiva in the town" of Otwock even prior to 1926].

In typical fashion, Heilman and Friedman refer to a couple of seemingly trivial exchanges between Rayatz and his son-in-law, as if these were indicative of the nature of their relationship and the extent of their correspondence, and ignore the large body of material that contradicts their pre-conceived conclusions about their relationship.

All the above is in addition to the evidence from the scholarly Reshimot – and I do not refer to the *Reshimat haYoman* (the 'diary' with Chasidic vignettes) – which portray a person deeply engaged in Chabad and other Torah scholarship. It is only because they choose not to pay any attention to the above that Heilman and Friedman could suggest that the reader dismiss the reports that the Rebbe "had been involved with ChaBaD and other Torah scholarship throughout his years outside the court" as ex-post-facto claims, "emerging later, after his star had risen in the Lubavitch leadership"[108].

The authors begrudgingly concede that

> [t]here is some evidence (or at least ex post facto Lubavitcher claims) that he [the Rebbe] was involved with the editing of a new Lubavitcher publication called *HaTamim*[109]; however, his name does not appear in it among the three mentioned as editors[110].

---

[107] See *Rayatz*, letter dated 13th Nissan 5690, published in *Teshurah LeHaMishtatfim Be-hitva'adut Chasidim* (Agudas Chasidei Chabad: Brooklyn, 1997), page 13:

"בטח דברת עם ידידנו הרב ר' יהודא שי' עבער, בדברי תורה, ובבקשה לכתוב לי דעתך אודותו".

In the Rebbe's response (published in conjunction with Rayatz's letter in his *Igrot Kodesh* vol. 15, pages 86-87) he writes:

"על דבר י. עבר נ"י, קשה לי להחליט דבר מה ברור על יסוד שיחות קצרות ושטחיות. אבל דבר טוב ניכר בו גם בהשקפה ראשונה, שדרכו בלמוד הוא על אתר גופא – אויף אַן אָרט – בלא ורמינהו וראיות ממרחק, כ"א בסברא במקומו. ועוד אחת, שלא הכרתי בו, במשך עת דברנו, מציאות הגאות והרגשת עצמו. והרי הב' אי-מצוי במאד מאד. ועכ"פ אין זה אלא רושמיים שטחיים. בקשתיו לתת לי חדושיו מהרשום אצלו בכתב לעיין בהם".

For some of Eber's biographical details, see the preface of his disciples to his *Sha'arei Yehudah, Chidushim al Masechtot Ketubot, Gittin, Kiddushin* (Kehot Publication Society: Brooklyn, 1958), pages 5-8.

[108] Heilman and Friedman page 40.

[109] A scholarly rabbinic journal that was published periodically from about 1935 until the outbreak of World War II.

[110] Heilman and Friedman page 119.

What they did not state is that there is a published facsimile of a hand-written letter of Rayatz to his daughter, Chaya Mushka (the Rebbe's wife), in which he states that although other names will appear in print, "the entire work" in the production of this journal is that of "my dear and beloved son-in-law, the Rabbi"[111]. There are several published letters that give additional testimony to the Rebbe's involvement in HaTamim [112]. Indeed, as in many other issues of Torah scholarship, the Rebbe assumes the role of in-house advisor to his father-in-law[113].

Finally, recently published correspondence will shed some additional light on the nature of the Rebbe's religious orientation during his university years in Berlin. The following letter was written by the Rebbe to Rayatz in Weimar Berlin in the summer of 1929 in anticipation of the forthcoming High holidays:

> I am reminded that the month of Ellul is imminent, it being a month of preparation [for Rosh Hashanah] and return [to closer communion with G-d]... But how can I find a way and a solution to ensure that I internalize this message?

In a personal and extremely candid display of introspection, the Rebbe continues to bare the inner recesses of his heart, as only a true chasid can before his Rebbe:

> Looking deeply into my heart, perhaps all this is only externality on my part [i.e. the preoccupation with preparation

---

[111] See the letter of Rayatz (dated 22nd Sivan 5695) published in Teshurah LeHaMishtatfim Be-hitva'adut Chasidim (Agudas Chasidei Chabad: Brooklyn, 1997), page 13 and Rayatz, Igrot Kodesh vol. 15, pages 207-208:

בעזה"י דורך דער ארבעט און אינטערעס מאישך הנכבד חתני יקירי וחביבי הרב שי', ועהט אין[ן] געכין גידרוקט ווערין זייער א ויכטיקער שזורנאַל מיט דעם נאמען "**התמים**". רעדאקטאָרין אויף פאפיר ועהלין זאַיין אנדערע, אבער די גאַנצע ארבעט איז זיינע. אָן עין הרע גאָר גאר א ויכטיקער יונגערמאַן, השי"ת זאהל אייך בעגליקן בגו"ר.

[112] See, for example, Rayatz, Igrot Kodesh vol. 3, page 400. Teshurah LeHaMishtatfim Be-Kinus HaShluchim Ha-Olami 5761 (Merkos L'Inyonei Chinuch: Brooklyn, 2000), pages 12-13. See also Rayatz, Igrot Kodesh vol. 15 and the preface thereto.

[113] See, for example, Rayatz, Teshurah (previous note) pages 14-15:

"וסמכתי כי בודאי תבין כוונתי לסדר את המאמר ולתקנו הן בהחשבונות והן בסגנונו וביטוייו הכל כאשר לכל בחזקת חבר גמור, כי עלה בדעתי ליתן מאמר זה בהתמים חוברת ג' ... ובודאי צריכה בקורת בקורת חדה".

and return is merely subconscious pretence] and maybe the truth is that it does not truly matter to me.[114]

In reply Rabbi Yosef Yitzchak reassures him that he was in fact being true to himself in expressing his aspiration that the Divine service of Ellul should affect him, for "when one learns Chasidut, especially matters of [Divine] service, in a way that affects one through one's service of the heart, which is prayer, through contemplation and communion – one begins to speak in a different language, one understands and grasps things differently and automatically one's aspirations are very different..."

In another letter dated 4th Shevat 5691 (22nd January 1931) the Rebbe implores his father-in-law to evoke Heavenly mercy upon him that he may succeed in understanding and internalising the teachings of Chasidut. In this letter he expresses his faith that his father-in-law has the ability to help him "either through a blessing or through (intercessory) prayer"[115].

Are these the ruminations of a student who has embraced secular culture and become detached from his Chasidic roots, who "needs to be reminded of the religious nature of marriage and of the holiness of this day", or are these the words of a pious and introspective young man whose deepest desire is for religious growth and genuine, intense connection with G-d?

---

[114] The Hebrew text of the Rebbe's letter is published in Rayatz, *Igrot Kodesh* vol. 15, pages 63-64:

"והנני נזכר שחדש אלול ממשמש ובא, וה"ז חדש להכנה ותשובה וכו', ואי' איפוא הדרך, ומהי העצה, שיפעול עלי, וסו"ס יהי' עכ"פ יר"ש נגע בלבי, וגם פה למטה בפו"מ, שגם "אני" ארגיש את הַשִּׁינוּי?

ובעיון בלבבי, שאולי כ"ז מצדי אינו אלא מן השפה ולחוץ, ואינו נוגע לי באמת. אבל בין שנוגע בין שא"נ, הרי עכ"פ הדבר אמתי, שהוא ללא תורה וללא יר"ש וכו'. ומהו תכלית זה, ועד מתי?"

[115] The Hebrew text of the Rebbe's letter is published in *Igrot Kodesh* (previous note), page 101:

"מה שבקשתי ברכה בהשגת תורת הדא"ח, התעצמות אתה וכו', הוא רק מפני שמשתוקק אני לזה. וכתבתי לכ"ק בקשת ברכה זו, כי מאמין אנכי שאם יחפוץ בזה באמת מקול"ע, הרי, בתור ברכה או בתור תפלה, וועט ער קאנען פועל זיין למע' שיקוייימו כל דברים אלו בי בפו"מ למטה"."

8. On Synagogues and Distances

As mentioned above, Heilman and Friedman claim: "There is no evidence of Mendel's presence in Berlin's Synagogues during this time" on Sabbath and at "the services each day that a Jew is required to attend"[116]. The same is true, they claim, with regard to the Rebbe's time in Paris. Heilman and Friedman imply that the Rebbe rarely if ever went to services whilst in Paris. Why? Because in Paris "the Jewish quarter, dominated by the so-called Pletzel, the square at its centre, was ... about two and a half miles away" from where the Rebbe lived. "We find little evidence that either of the Schneersons was commonly seen in this district"[117]. When the Rebbe moved in 1938 to a new residence, at 7 Villa Robert Lindet, it was not, they write with no small measure of cynicism, "based on its closeness to the Jewish ghetto". On the contrary, "[f]rom a distance of about three miles to the Pletzel, they were now more than eight and one-half miles away, and from having been four miles distant from rue Dieu, they were now more than five miles away"[118] – how could the Rebbe get to the synagogue on the Sabbath?

Let us respond to these arguments:

The 'evidence' – or more accurately, lack of evidence – presented about the Rebbe's synagogue attendance in Berlin is based on the testimony of one person[119]. In Paris, no particular person at all is credited with 'not having seen' the Rebbe attend prayer services.

---

[116] Heilman and Friedman pages 88-89.

[117] Heilman and Friedman page 115.

[118] Heilman and Friedman page 122.

[119] Heilman and Friedman pages 88-89.

At the end of page 88, they write that "**visitors** (emphasis added) to the few Hasidic congregations in Berlin report never having seen him there at the time." In the endnotes (chapter 3 note 66) we learn that the basis for this statement is the fact that Menachem Friedman was allegedly once told by Yosef Burg who was "a student at the Hildesheimer Seminary and often visited Hasidic congregations" that he "never encountered Mendel Schneerson or heard about his activities".

[In a similar vein the authors state that "as late as 1947, while he was in France, they [the Chasidim in Paris] and he [the Rebbe] displayed an unfamiliarity with one another". They refer to Mordechai Menashe Laufer's *Yemei Melech* (Kehot Publication Society: Kfar Chabad, 1989-1991), vol. (2) [3], page 948 as the source. Maximally this source illustrates that he was unfamiliar with one Russian

Whilst it may be true that one person did not recall seeing the Rebbe in the synagogues that that person himself attended in Berlin, other people certainly did see the Rebbe in synagogue, and not just in Berlin, but in Paris as well. Jewish Educational Media (JEM) has published video-recorded testimonies that illustrate this fact adequately[120]. In addition, there are several published testimonies of the Rebbe himself about customs he observed and ideas he learned in the synagogues of Berlin and Paris[121]. Finally, Heilman and Friedman seem to be unaware

---

immigrant who had arrived in Paris at the beginning of the month of Nissan that year].

[120] Regarding the synagogue the Rebbe frequented in Berlin, see for example the testimony of Rabbi Naftali Rubin, son of Rabbi Yissachar Ber Rubin, the Dombrover Rebbe of Berlin, in *Early Years* vol. 2 (Jewish Educational Media: Brooklyn, 2006): "Every Shabbos for two years straight, he came to pray...it took him to walk it could be 40 minutes or 45 minutes. . . Germany was like America . . . when he passed the Jewish section . . . it was like Williamsburg or Crown Heights or Boro Park on every block there was a study hall, a small synagogue, a large synagogue, a Mikva . . . He must have passed between 20 to 25 synagogues until he came to the Dombrover Synagogue".

Regarding the Rebbe's prayer habits in Paris, JEM conducted a video interview with Mr. Bernard Lax, who grew up in pre-war Paris. His father, Reb Yankel Lax, who was not a Lubavitcher Chasid, was not only a close acquaintance of the Rebbe in Paris (in fact, it was he who later gave the Rebbe the money he needed to leave France for America before the Nazis invasion) he also used to host Rayatz at his home on Shabbos on many of Rayatz's visits to France. Bernard, who was in his early twenties at the time, had this to say about the Rebbe's prayer habits: "Every day he went to the Pletzel – the Jewish district – which had Rue Des Rosier [and] two *shteiblach*... Number 17 was Chabad and 25 was everything what you want [all kinds of Jews prayed there]. The Rebbe hardly ever went to [the synagogue at] 17, and my opinion is because he didn't want the *kavod* [honour] among Chabad Chasidim [which] they would have given him ... he shunned every *kavod*".

Lax's fascinating testimony, which also mentions the Rebbe's research of ancient Jewish manuscripts at the St. Geneviève in Paris, one of the great libraries of Europe, was published by JEM in *The Early Years* vols. 3 and 4 (Brooklyn, 2007, 2008).

[121] See, for example, *Sichot Kodesh* 5736 vol. 2, page 174; the remarks of the Rebbe on 22nd Sivan 5727 (*Sichot Kodesh* 5727 vol. 2, page 408).

of the published transcripts of public discourses that the Rebbe delivered in synagogues in Paris[122].

Moreover, on page 86, the authors write: There is a report from one
seminary student who recalled seeing him standing at the back of a
room [when Rabbi Yechiel Yaakov Weinberg lectured] and listening
intently to some lectures." In a footnote on the following page they relate:

> One report of a sighting in class comes from Pini Dunner, who
> writes that his grandfather, Rabbi Yosef Tzvi Dunner . . . was
> asked if he recalled seeing Mendel Schneerson from his time in
> Berlin. He replied that 'he remembered him well – he was the
> rather modern-dressed young man . . . who stood at the back of
> the shiur [class] room'.

Curiously, the authors do not quote Rabbi Dunner's sentence in its
entirety, as reported by his grandson on the website referenced by the
authors themselves:

> I asked him if he remembered the Rebbe from his time in
> Berlin. He smiled and said he remembered him well – he was
> the rather modern-dressed young man . . . who stood at the
> back of the shiur room and who would talk in learning after
> **almost every shiur** with Rav Yechiel Yaakov Weinberg z"l."
> (emphasis added).

Were the authors not to have truncated R. Dunner's sentence they
would have provided the reader with ample evidence that the Rebbe
was deeply enagaged in Jewish life when he lived in Berlin.

Finally, concerning the Rebbe's religious standards in Berlin, there
is the published testimony of several of his contemporaries, including
the testimony of Rabbi Joseph B. Soloveitchik[123] (a colleague of the

---

[122] See *Reshimot* nos. 66 and 125. It is unlikely that the Rebbe would have been
invited to address the congregants of a shul if he rarely attended synagogue
services!

[123] Rabbi Joseph Ber Soloveitchik (1903–1993) was a leading Orthodox rabbi,
Talmudist and modern Jewish philosopher who served as Rosh Yeshivah of Rabbi
Isaac Elchanan Theological Seminary at Yeshiva University in New York City. He

Rebbe in Berlin[124]) – as recorded by several of his prominent students and published by JEM, that the Rebbe immersed himself, daily, in a

---

attended classes at the University of Berlin at the same time as the Rebbe, ultimately earning a PhD in philosophy from the school.

[124] It is noteworthy that the friendship between the Rebbe and Rabbi Soloveitchik continued throughout their lives.

Rabbi Soloveitchik visited the Rebbe when he was sitting *shivah* for his mother in 1964 (on the 8th Tishrei 5725). Snippets of their conversation have been preserved in *Torat Menachem Menachem Tziyon* (Kehot Publication Society: Brooklyn, 1994) vol. 1, page 98ff. Rabbi Soloveitchik also attended the Rebbe's *farbrengen* on the 10th Shevat 5740 (marking thirty years since the Rebbe had assumed leadership of Lubavitch). See also Rabbi Hershel Shachter, *MiPeninei HaRav* (Flatbush Beth Hamedrosh: Brooklyn, 2001), page 187.

There are a number of items of correspondence between the two rabbis that have been published. See *Igrot Kodesh* vol. 23, pages 273-274; vol. 24, pages 276-277.

The immense respect that Rabbi Soloveitchik had for the Rebbe finds expression in a letter that he sent to the Rebbe on the occasion of the latter's seventieth birthday (published in his *Igrot Kodesh* vol. 27, page 386):

כבוד אדמו"ר, הגאון הגדול, עטרת ישראל, הודו ותפארתו, צדיק יסוד עולם, מרן מנחם מ. שניאורסון, שליט"א,

שלום וברכה רבה ונאמנה! אני מגיש בזה את ברכתי הדלה, ברכת הדיוט, למעכ"ג, שליט"א. יחד עם אלפי מעריציו בכל קצוי ארץ אני מתפלל ומתחנן לא' מרום, כי יפרוש את סוכת שלומו עליו וכי יאריך את ימיו ושנותיו בטוב ובנעימים, ללמד תועים בינה וצמאים יראה, חכמה ודעת, עד כי יבא שילה.

יפוצו מעיינותיו חוצה, ילכו רבים לאורו ותמלא הארץ דעה. אך טוב וחסד ירדפוהו תמיד כל הימים.

בהערצה ובחיבה גדולה, יוסף דוב הלוי סולוביצ'יק, ברכת מועדים לששון ולשמחה, חג כשר ושמח! יום ב' י"ב ניסן תשל"ב

See also Rabbi Soloveitchik's letter to the Rebbe's brother-in-law Rabbi Shmaryahu Gourary (Rashag) dated 11th Tishrei 5739 in which he writes:

ואני תפלה כי ד' יאריך ימיו ושנותיו של אדמו"ר עטרת ישראל ותפארתו שליט"א, ויזכהו להשקות את הצמאים במעיינות הנגלה והנסתר ולהאיר עיני רבים עד כי יבא שילה. כולנו צריכים לו וכולנו מתפללים עבורו.

A facsimile of this handwritten letter is available on http://theantitzemach.blogspot.com/2011/02/blog-post_23.html

In 1983, two of Rabbi Soloveitchik's students, Rabbis Moshe Sherman and Yosef Wolf, sent a letter to the Rebbe asking if he would submit a Torah essay to be included in an album honoring Rabbi Soloveitchik on his 40th anniversary as Rosh Yeshivah. In response, the Rebbe strongly encouraged the project, but apologetically explained that the custom of his predecessors precluded his participation.

In paragraph three, Rabbi Soloveitchik's students write:

"יודעים אנו כמה אדוקים הם קשרי הידידות, ההוקרה, וההערצה בין כבוד קדושתו שליט"א לבין מורינו ורבינו שליט"א"

Mikveh, a ritual not required by Jewish Law and not practiced by non-chasidic Jews.

In the words of a disciple of Rabbi Soloveitchik:

The Rav told me that he was a great admirer of the Rebbe. He said that their relationship began when they met in Berlin where they were both studying at the University of Berlin. During that period, they would often meet at the home of the *Gaon* Rabbi Chaim Heller. It was in the course of these meetings that a strong friendship developed between the two men, both of whom were destined to become outstanding spiritual leaders of the century. The Rav recalled that the Rebbe always carried the key to the *mikvah* (ritual pool) with him when he attended lectures at the university. 'At about two or three o'clock every afternoon when he left the university he would go straight to the *mikvah*. No one was aware of this *minhag* [custom] and I only learnt about it by chance,' the Rav said. On another occasion, I offered the Rebbe a drink. The

---

The Rebbe circled their words יודעים אנו, and added in the margin: "הרבה יותר מאשר יודעים"

(See *Krinsky Teshurah*, 16th Ellul 5770, page 20 – reproduced in Figure 11 at the end of this book).

Further testimony regarding the relationship between the Rebbe and Rabbi Soloveitchik can be found in David Holzer, *The Rav Thinking Aloud – Transcripts of Personal Conversations with Rabbi Joseph B. Soloveitchik* (published privately, Florida, 2009) page 42.

This volume also records Rabbi Soloveitchik's support for the Rebbe's position with regard to the propriety of making 'aliyah' to Israel: "In this regard I subscribe to the opinion of the Lubavitcher Rebbe. He said it and he's right" (Holzer, page 241). See also Holzer, ibid., page 169ff. The testimonies included in *The Rav Thinking Aloud* are taken from tape recordings of Rabbi Soloveitchik.

See also Rabbi Soloveitchik's letter (dated 15th June 1962) published in *Community, Covenant and Commitment: Selected Letters and Communications* (KTAV New Jersey, 2005) page 251 where he quotes (approvingly) the Rebbe's view on one of the issues of the day: "Rabbi [Menachem Mendel] Schneersohn of Lubavitch has commented that Ecumenical Council is a strictly Catholic wedding and it would be undignified if we were to crash the party. Unfortunately, Jewish political leaders in America possess neither a sense of dignity nor an awareness of Jewish historical continuity".

See also http://www.yutorah.org/lectures/lecture.cfm/719953.

Rebbe refused, but when I pressured him I understood that he was fasting that day. It was Monday and the Rebbe was fasting.' 'Imagine that,' Rabbi Soloveitchik said to me, 'a Berlin University student immersed in secular studies maintains this custom of *mikvah* and fasting. These things made a huge impression upon me. Additionally, the Rebbe had an amazing memory.' The Rav described the Rebbe's memory as *'gevaldig'* (astounding). 'In all my life, I never encountered someone with such a memory.' Then the Rav proceeded to describe his understanding of the Rebbe's Torah. 'Those of us who emanate from Brisk don't adhere to the pilpul system perpetuated in Poland,' the Rav said, "but the Rebbe has a *gevaldiger* [astounding] comprehension of the Torah. There were other Jewish students from other communities in the university, studying together with us at the time. Some of them are considered today to be famous *gedolei* Torah [Torah giants]. In the university they behaved the same way as other university students, but this Jew (the Rebbe) behaved like a Jew from Warsaw or from Russia. Berlin made absolutely no impression upon him at all'.[125].

Could it really be that the Rebbe who, even according to Heilman and Friedman, had become extremely 'pious' and went beyond the strict letter of the law in matters of ritual observance[126], would have failed to observe "the services each day that a Jew is required to"? Is it plausible that this 'pious ascetic' was simultaneously an individual so irreligious as not to attend the synagogue? Yet, what are we to make of the marathon distance between the Rebbe's home in Paris and the synagogue?

The answer is: It is simply inaccurate to suggest that if the Rebbe wanted to pray in a synagogue on the Sabbath in Paris, the only way he

---

[125] This is the testimony of Rabbi Sholem B. Kowalsky ((b. 1920. d. 2007. Kowalsky was a leading Young Israel rabbi during the second half of the twentieth century) in his *From My Zaidy's House* (American Friends of Keren Dorsehi Zion: Brooklyn, 2000) pages 274-275:

[126] Heilman and Friedman pages 128-129.

could do that would be to walk the distance to the Pletzel neighbour-hood.

In their intense preoccupation with the plausibility of the Rebbe's synagogue attendance, Heilman and Friedman fail to mention the fact that there was a synagogue in much closer proximity to his house than the Pletzel.

One of the most prestigious Synagogues in Paris was located not far from where the Rebbe lived, in the 15th arrondissement of Paris it-self. I refer to the Synagogue built on Rue Chasseloup-Laubat, which was established in 1913 to accommodate, in part, the influx of immi-grant Jews in the area[127]. This synagogue was located at a distance of 1.6 miles from the Rebbe's first residence in Paris (9 Rue Boulard), 0.6 miles from his second residence (78 Rue Blomet) and 1.4 miles from his last residence (7 Rue Robert Lindet) and this would have provided an alternative place of worship for the Rebbe if he was, for some reason, unable or unwilling to walk all the way to the Pletzel[128].

---

[127] In an interview (11th July 2010) with Mrs. Jacqueline Lebrecht (currently in London, England) she related to this writer that her late (ultra-Orthodox) father Mr. Neftali Theodore Klein (who, incidentally, knew the Rebbe in Paris before the war), often used to attend the synagogue on Rue Chasseloup-Laubat when their family lived in the 15th arrondissement of Paris (on Boulevard Lefebvre) in her childhood years.

Lebrecht also confirmed that which I have verified with numerous Parisian Jews and scholars who specialize in the history of the Jews of Paris during that era, namely that Orthodox Jews were widely dispersed throughout the multiple districts of Paris and often used to walk long distances on Shabbat to attend synagogues of their choice.

She also stated that there were various *shteiblach* and even ad hoc 'cottage *minyanim*' that were held by small pockets of orthodox Jews dotted across the many districts of Paris.

[128] The authors take issue with the fact that I only revealed the existence of this local synagogue in my second response to them, rather than in my first.

In their "final word" on the Seforim blog they write: "The discussion of the 'local' synagogue nearer to MMS's residence is a new wrinkle in Rapoport's argument. Readers will recall he told us how much the man liked to walk and assured us it was no problem for him to walk to the synagogues in the Pletzel. Now suddenly he talks about this large nearby synagogue (which he wonders that we did not mention nor did he, why?) but conveniently fails to mention that MMS was not seen

Secondly, contrary to what Heilman and Friedman write, the Rebbe never lived more than 3.8 miles away from the synagogue he evidently frequented. In those days this was not at all unusual; Orthodox Jews, especially those (who, like the Rebbe) lived on a modest income and had to struggle to make ends meet, sought accommodation wherever the rent was most reasonable or the conditions were most convenient, even if it entailed a longer walk to the synagogue on the Sabbath[129]. For a man in his thirties it would not be an athletic feat to walk this distance on the Sabbath, especially for someone who, like the Rebbe, was a brisk walker. How Heilman and Friedman measured eight and a half miles from the Rebbe's second address to the synagogue in the Pletzel is beyond me. A simple check on googlemaps reveals that this 'distance' has no basis in reality[130]. Geography is clearly not their area of strength[131] [132].

---

there, nor did he take any active role as teacher in this synagogue. Where is the evidence he went there?"

To which I now respond: In my first response I was merely working with the information that the authors provided their readers which clearly portrayed that the closest synagogue in town was located at the pletzel. It was only over the course of my later investigation that I learned of the existence of the synagogue at Rue Chasseloup-Laubat.

As for their ex-post-facto justification, namely that since they found no evidence that the Rebbe attended that synagogue, this means that "he was not seen there", I respond: (a) the fact that after 70 years they did not encounter witnesses who could testify about the Rebbe's presence in the synagogue does not prove that he did not attend it; (b) moreover, their failure to mention the existence of this synagogue (or the lack of available testimony regarding his possible attendance there) in their book, implies that they did not investigate this possibility; (c) regardless of whether or not any 'evidence' that the Rebbe attended this synagogue can be found **seven decades later**, and after the decimation of European Jewry, the very existence of the synagogue demonstrates the fallacy of their claim that if the Rebbe wanted to attend prayer services his only option was miles away.

[129] It is also possible that living in closer proximity to the university would have minimised his need to miss lectures on short Fridays.

[130] **In response to this point in my original review essay on the Seforim blog, the authors responded:** "The distance between 7 Villa Lindet and the Pletzel (Rue Ferdinand Duval) is 4.25 miles, and a round trip of eight and a half miles. The word roundtrip was dropped by accident from our text, and will be added in the next edition."

To which I responded:

"(a) Granted that the word "roundtrip" was accidentally dropped from your text as you now suggest, it is still misleading. To be precise: the distance between 7 Villa Lindet and **25 Rue Des Rosier (the synagogue)** is 3.8 miles.

Look here: http://is.gd/d43bP for one possible route.

The round trip would be 7.6 miles, not "more than eight and one-half miles."

(b) Even if for some mysterious reason you felt compelled to measure the distance between the Rebbe's home and **Rue Ferdinand Duval** (a tiny road that is less central to the 'Pletzel' than Rue Des Rosiers and on which there are no synagogues), you could not have arrived at the sought-after "more than eight and one-half miles away" roundtrip, because in actual fact the distance between 7 Villa Robert Lindet and Rue Ferdinand Duval is, to be precise, 3.85 miles, namely 7.7 miles roundtrip. You would therefore still have to account for the additional distance of close to a mile that you added.

(c) It is highly unlikely that the word "roundtrip" was dropped by accident. For you wrote: "From a distance of about three miles to the Pletzel (actually it is exactly 2.5 miles, see http://is.gd/d436F), they were now more than eight and one-half miles away, and from having been four miles distant from rue Dieu, they were now more than five miles away."

Firstly, if the word "roundtrip" would have originally been in the document it would have read "they were now **more** (emphasis added) than eight and one-half miles roundtrip away" – a rather awkward phrase.

Secondly, the other distances which you refer to in the same clause (before and after) are given in terms of single – not round – trips.

Thirdly, the reference to a distance between home and synagogue is not usually described in roundtrip format, and in our context it is misleading, taking into consideration the fact that in between the '2 legs' of the round trip there is ample time for 'recuperation.'

It is therefore more likely that your description of the "accident" [namely your writing "more than eight and one-half miles away"] is more akin to hagiography than to history."

131 Another example of a simple – albeit harmless – geographic mistake the authors made is worthy of mention. On page 81 Heilman and Friedman write: "he [the Rayatz went to rest in the resort town of Malakhovka in the Zhitomir district of Ukraine". As it happens Malakhovka is located approximately 30 kilometers away from Moscow - nowhere near the Ukranian Zhitomir!

132 It should be noted, as Heilman and Friedman point out on page 114, that for the majority of their stay in Paris, the Rebbe and Rebbetzen lived in the 14th District at 9 rue Boulard, in the very same building as their sister and brother-in-law, Shaina and Mendel Horenstein. Heilman and Friedman assume (page 113) that the Horensteins **followed** the Rebbe and Rebbetzen to Paris. Yet in reality it was the reverse. The

9. University Education for a Chasid

The authors report that a few nights after the Rebbe's wedding, Rayatz gave a talk to a large assembly that had gathered in honor of Yud Tes Kislev (the 19th of Kislev, one of the most important days on the Chabad Chasidic calendar[133]), in conjunction with the Rebbe and Rebbetzen's fifth *Sheva Berachot*.

Heilman and Friedman suggest that this talk was prompted, at least in part, by Rayatz's consternation with the Rebbe's occupation with secular studies (and the size of his beard). Here is their account of the event:

> A few days after the wedding, however, Yosef Yitzchak would give a hint of what must have been on his mind, even in the midst of his joy at his daughter's wedding. On Saturday night, the day after the wedding party had returned from Warsaw, a *sheva berakhot* gathering, part of the seven days of festive meal that follow a traditional Jewish wedding, was held in Riga, a city where even the observant Jews had absorbed many of the views and institutional patterns of the neo-orthodoxy of

---

Rebbe and his wife arrived in Paris after the Horensteins were already settled there. See Rayatz, *Igrot Kodesh* vol. 15, page 131 and editor's footnote thereon.

If the Horensteins had moved to the 14th District first, and there was an adequate Jewish presence in the local area, it would only have been natural for the Rebbe and Rebbetzen to move in next to their own kin. On page 122, the authors themselves quote Moussia's letter to her in-laws in which she writes that it was "important" to her and the Rebbe to live close by to the Horensteins. Thus, even in 1938 when they moved to 7 Villa Robert Lindet in the 15th District, the Rebbetzen writes that two main concerns for her and her husband were to find an inexpensive apartment and for the Horensteins – who moved at the same time – to find a new place close by to them. It is not entirely unreasonable to assume, then, that these were also deciding factors in their original choice of dwelling in 1933.

See also Rayatz, *Igrot Kodesh* vol. 15, page 134, where Rayatz instructed the Rebbe that immediately upon arriving in Paris in 1933, he should develop a closer relationship with Mendel Horenstein and take him under his wing.

[133] The 19th of Kislev was called by Rayatz's father, the Rebbe Rashab, "The Rosh Hashanah of Chasidus". It commemorates the day of liberation of the founder of the Chabad movement, Rabbi Schneur Zalman of Liadi (the Alter Rebbe: 1745-1812) from Czarist prison in 1798.

German Jewry. With his new son-in-law sitting near him - the same son-in-law with the trim beard who was about to return to Berlin and the university, where he and his new wife, Moussia, would take courses - Rabbi Yosef Yitzchak spoke to the assembled Tseirey Agudas Yisroel, the youth of the fervently orthodox community. After two years in Riga, the Rebbe knew well the views of the young people, who had embraced higher education and secular culture as a part of their world view, who appeared in modern dress, many of them barefaced or with the short beards, and who probably looked at the new son-in-law sympathetically as one who shared their values and ethos. Before this audience Yosef Yitzchak gave an impassioned sermon against the mixing of the sacred and the profane, arguing that the neo-orthodox approach that combined religious and secular studies was only 'good for those who would otherwise, heaven forefend, be even worse,' but that for those who were truly pure, the temimim, this was not the way. Then he denounced those who trimmed their beards or who shaved them off altogether. All of this he said while his new university bound son-in-law with a beard that for all intents and purposes looked as if it were trimmed sat there, and his two young daughters (one of whom was the bride), who everyone in the room likely knew shared an outlook of modernity, were in a room nearby. Did he mean that this mixing of torah and secular learning was alright for the bride and groom because otherwise they 'would be even worse'? After all, he would help support them financially when they returned to pursue this way of life in Berlin. Or was he trying to warn them against the way of life they had apparently chosen? He was of course nominally speaking to the audience, but could his message to his own children be lost on them?[134]

---

[134] Heilman and Friedman page 102.

In other words, they would have us believe that Rayatz used this *Sheva Berachot* celebration as an opportunity to publicly admonish his new son-in-law for his engagement in secular studies!

The source for this episode is given in an endnote[135]. It is in the record of the event penned by Rayatz himself in a letter he wrote to Rabbi Menachem Zemba (1883-1943) on the 1st Shevat 5689 (12th January 1929) and published in his *Igrot Kodesh* vol. 2, pages 152-153.

Indeed their account of the words of Rayatz regarding the mingling of the secular and the profane is, relatively speaking, loyal to their source (although, on that occasion, Rayatz did not actually discuss beards – trimmed, shaven or fully grown – altogether), except that their entire hypothesis is built on a false premise. The address to the Orthodox youth of Riga, was actually given, as Rayatz himself wrote in the above-mentioned letter, not in the year 5689/1928 (the year of his daughter's marriage) but in the previous year (19th Kislev) 5688/(13th December) 1927. In the words of Rayatz:

בחג הגאולה י"ט כסלו **שנה העברה** כנהוג באו בלא ע"ה הרבה בע"ב וחסידים מקומיים ואורחים יחיו, ובסעודת מצוה אחרי אמירת חסידות מצאתי לנכון לדבר עניני התעוררות בדבר הרבצת תורה ותורה תמימה ומדי דברי על דבר תורה תמימה נגעתי בענין הנהגת צעירי אגודת ישראל יחיו ואופן הלימוד בבית הספר 'תורה ודרך ארץ' וכמובן אשר בקרתי בסכינא חריפא לאמר טוב טוב תורה ודרך ארץ מדרך ארץ ותורה כי בכל השילובים הראשון גובר אבל הטוב האמיתי הוא 'תורה תמימה' תורה ויראת שמים.

Indeed Rayatz's speech was reported in the Yiddish newspaper entitled *Der Ruf*, 29th Tevet 5688 (22nd January 1928)[136].

At the celebration on the 19th of Kislev that was held a year later in conjunction with the Rebbe and Rebbetzen's fifth *Sheva Berachot* (2nd December 1928), Rayatz did not address secular studies as he had done the previous year on that date[137]. The contents of his address on this oc-

---

[135] Heilman and Friedman chapter 4, endnote 31.

[136] See Figure 12 at the end of this book.

The editor of *Sefer HaSichot* (next note), page 58, footnote 19, also erred in this regard and suggested, albeit tentatively, that Rayatz' talk that he described in his letter to Rabbi Menachem Zemba was delivered at the 19th Kislev celebration of 5689. The editor has acknowledged his error in writing to this author.

[137] See Rayatz, *Sefer HaSichot* 5688-5691 (Kehot Publication Society: Brooklyn, 2002), page 55ff.

casion have been preserved, partly by his son-in-law, the Rebbe him-self[138].

All the above notwithstanding, we must address the authors' question: how could it be, that the Rebbe studied in a university when his father-in-law, Rayatz, had "denounced" the "pursuit of a university education"[139]. At face value, this is a good question. An even better question is how the Rebbe himself could oppose attending university[140], when he himself did just that! Why did he not practice that which he preached?

In order to answer this question, it is necessary to explain why Rayatz and the Rebbe, generally speaking, advised against university education[141].

An enquiry into the relevant sources, informs us that this advice was predicated upon several propositions.

---

[138] Rayatz's talk on that occasion characteristically dealt with many different subjects, and includes a vehement protest against some of the elders of the Chasidic community in Riga who had evidently deviated from the Chasidic practice and had cut their beards. See *Sefer HaSichot* (previous note) pages 57-58:

"א חסידישער איד דארף דעם באַרד ניט שערן, מאכן א שפּיץ בערדל, א פּראנצוסקי בערדל, פּע, דער זיידע זאגט אז עס איז א איסור דאורייתא, און ער איז דער מרא דאתרא ביי חסידים. איר אלטע וואָס איר זייט געוווען ביי דעם טאטן, ביי די פּעטערס, ביי די שוועסטער-קינדער, איר האט אלע געזען גילוי אור, ווי אזוי זייט איר מחלל את השם, איך וויל אייך גאָרניט זען אזוי, מילא די יונגע וואס האָבן נאָך קיין אור ניט געזען, זיי דארף מען מקרב זיין, אבער איר אלטע ווי ווערט דאס בא אייך רעכט תירוצים אבנק וכו', דער זיידע דער מרא דאתרא האט דאך אבער גע'אסר'ט, (ובכה הרבה באמרו הדברים האלה)".

[139] Heilman and Friedman page 97.

[140] See *Likuttei Sichot* vol. 15, pages 43-44. *Sha'arei Halachah uMinhag*, vol. 5, *Hosafot uMiluim* (Heichal Menachem: Jerusalem 2002), chapters 134 and 135, (pages 237-238). See also *Igrot Kodesh* vol. 27, pages 387, 520 and 525. See, however, *Igrot Kodesh* vol. 28, pages 339-340 for examples of circumstances in which the Rebbe encouraged those who had already invested time and energy in the pursuit of secular studies to complete their degrees. See also *Letters from the Lubavitcher Rebbe* vol. 5 (Brooklyn, 2001), pages 22-23 (letter dated 15th Av 5720) that one who is, for whatever reason, engaged in secular studies should endeavour to work in his field with efficiency and "attain the objective fully". In the course of time he will find the "opportunity to utilize these efforts in many ways" and his secular studies will give him a "good advantage".

[141] See for example Rayatz, *Igrot Kodesh* vol. 10, page 325 (3rd Tevet 5710):

"במענה על כתבך אודות ההרשמה בקאלעדזש, בשלילה גמורה".

Firstly, they believed that as a prerequisite to any other pursuits, one must be well immersed in Torah and imbued with the Fear of Heaven.

Secondly, they were concerned about the contaminating influences that secular studies can have on those who engage in them without a halachically recognized purpose and focus.

Finally, with regard to the study in college and university, the Rebbe was most apprehensive on account of the permissive ambience and heretical perspectives that usually dominate present-day campuses and study-halls. He believed that, for the rank and file student, it would be irresponsible to expose oneself to the university culture and the religious challenges it presents; for very few people have the requisite stamina and discretion to engage with the package deal of university life and emerge unscathed[142].

Yet both Rayatz and the Rebbe knew that there were exceptions to the rule. As the authors acknowledge themselves, Rayatz paid for all the Rebbe's tuition expenses and helped facilitate his studies throughout[143]. Moreover, although they do not acknowledge this, Rayatz ultimately recorded his pride in the Rebbe's academic achievements. A few months after the Rebbe obtained a degree in engineering, Rayatz described his talent and accomplishments in the field of *handasah* as something he shared with their illustrious ancestor (the third Rebbe of

---

[142] In addition to some of the sources cited in note 140 see the letter of the Rebbe dated 28th *Cheshvan* 5715 published in *Return to Roots* (Lubavitch Foundation of Great Britain: London, 1980) page 203. See also *Letters from the Lubavitcher Rebbe* vol. 1 (Brooklyn 1997), pages 111-116 (letter dated 23rd Sivan 5718); vol. 2 (Brooklyn, 2001), pages 8-11 for a lengthy English explanation. [In that letter the Rebbe writes: ["I can therefore state with the fullest measure of conviction and responsibility that he who sends his child to college during the formative years subjects him to shock and profound conflicts and trials and invites quite unforeseen consequences. In view of all the above, it is my definite and considered opinion that all Jewish children, upon completing their compulsory secular education, should devote at least several years to the exclusive study of the Torah, without the interference of the other studies, not even training for a trade, in order to obtain the maximum insurance against all risks and dangers that their future life may hold, when they attain adulthood and settle down to a family life"].

[143] See Heilman and Friedman page 94. See also ibid. page 106 and endnote 42.

the Chabad dynasty), Rabbi Menchem Mendel of Lubavitch, the saintly Tzemach Tzedek (1789-1866)[144]. [145]

Noteworthy in this context are the words of Rayatz:

Chochmot chitzoniyot ('exterior sciences') constitute an opposition to the Torah and attempt to soil it, but one whose

---

[144] In a letter dated 25th Tammuz 5698 (published in Riga in that same year and republished in Rayatz, *Igrot Kodesh* vol. 4, page 377ff) Rayatz wrote:

"דער עלטער-זיידע דער באוואַסטער רבי מיט דעם וועלט-נאמען 'צמח צדק' איז געווען א גרויסער גאון אין נגלה, אין קבלה וחסידות, און איז אויך **געווען זייער גרויס אין חכמת ההנדסה.** זיינע קינדער און אייניקלעך זיינען געווען גרויסע גאונים אין נגלה קבלה וחסידות, נאר קיינער פון זיי איז ניט געווען אזוי גרויס אין חכמת ההנדסה. נאר גראד **איינער פון זיינער אור-אייניקלעך** האָט געירשנט דעם גרויסן כשרון פון אונזער הייליק גרויסן רבין 'צמח צדק' אין חכמת ההנדסה".

[145] **In their response to this paragraph in my original review essay on the Seforim blog, the authors write:** "Whatever (p. 21) the Rayatz said about his son-in-law's accomplishments as an engineer, his grades and his inability to find employment as one speak for themselves. What the engineering abilities were of the 'saintly Tzemach Tzedek,' as Rabbi Rapoport refers to MMS's namesake, we cannot say. Rabbi Rapoport is obviously the expert on this."

To which I responded: "Once again you attempt to side-step the issue. Firstly, I never spoke about the Tzemach Tzedek's 'engineering abilities.' I referred (citing book and page number) to the fact that Rayatz described the Tzemach Tzedek as being great in the field of '*handasah*'. Whilst in modern Hebrew *handasah* means engineering, the term *handasah* as used in traditional (in contrast to modern) Hebrew (and Arabic), and employed by Maimonides, means studies associated with mathematics, in particular: geometry [or חכמת השיעור]. (See also Rabbi Yomtov Lipman Heller (1578-1654), *Tosafot Yomtov* on *Avot* 3:18). Thus there is nothing fantastic in the idea that the Tzemach Tzedek was accomplished in the field of *handasah*.

Consequently, it should come to you as no great surprise that Rayatz congratulated the Rebbe for his knowledge in *handasah*, because, as you write yourselves (page 117), the Rebbe took courses in Geometry (knowledge of which is required for Engineering) and "particularly excelled in mathematics."

Secondly, and most importantly, let me remind you of what I wrote: "Rayatz...knew that there were exceptions to the rule...Rayatz ultimately recorded his pride in the Rebbe's academic achievements...a few months after ... the saintly Tzemach Tzedek."

Clearly, the point here was not to highlight the Rebbe's or the Tzemach Tzedek's level of expertise in Engineering or Geometry, but rather to highlight Rayatz's pride in the Rebbe's academic achievements and the fact that he described these in terms of a 'continuum' that started with the "saintly Tzemach Tzedek" (Rayatz's epithet, not mine)."

fear of sin precedes his wisdom can deflect the uncleanliness with his Torah study and indeed becomes one of those whose merit helps the multitudes through the wisdom which was added to his Torah knowledge[146], as was the case with Rabbi Saadia Gaon and Maimonides and Nahamanides of eternal luminescence, each in his generation[147].

In light of all the above, there is no need to assume that the Rebbe's own preoccupation with the sciences in Berlin and Paris was a symptom of his 'selling out to the forces of modernity'. It is more likely that it was based on his own religious convictions, as reflected in his own writings[148] (which have clearly escaped the attention of Heilman and Friedman) which led him to believe that there can be both utilitarian and existential meaning in the study of the sciences, and that for the exceptional few there is religious sanction to pursue these studies even in a university environment.

It is also important to emphasize that neither Rashab, nor Rayatz nor the Rebbe were opposed to their chasidim earning a living from a trade or vocation. Some of their most esteemed followers were businessmen and professionals. It was rare, in pre-war Europe, for chasidim – even those who served as representatives and delegates of Rayatz – not to have some sort of vocation from which they earned a living. Indeed, Rayatz described his older son-in-law, Rabbi Shemaryahu Gourary (Rashag) as someone who was "engaged in commercial enterprise and had a good reputation amongst the well-known businessmen"[149].

---

[146] See also *Letters from the Lubavitcher Rebbe* vol. 4, page 156 (letter dated 2nd Adar 5739) wherein he underscores the special religious influence that Orthodox scientists can have on others.

[147] Rayatz, *Igrot Kodesh* vol. 5, page 284.

[148] See the Rebbe's discussions in his *Igrot Kodesh* vol. 3, pages 122-126; 169-171.

[149] See letter of Rayatz, written in 1921, (*Igrot Kodesh* vol. 13, page 88) where he describes Rashag as:

"עוסק במסחר ויש לו שם בין הסוחרים הידועים".

Moreover, many chasidim, and possibly the Rebbe himself, wanted to achieve financial independence and not be eternally reliant on charitable religious organizations for their livelihood.

In addition to all the above, in light of the Rebbe's own writings, it is possible that he believed that his engagement in the sciences would, in the course of time, enable him to reach out to more of his brethren to whom he would show that the sciences can actually help facilitate a deeper appreciation of the divine[150]. [In this context it is noteworthy that the Rebbe spoke about the scientific and technological discoveries that we have witnessed in recent generations as being precursors to messianic times – an era in which the world will be filled with knowledge of G-d[151]].

10. Why was the Rebbe Fasting?

The authors who paint a picture of the Rebbe as one who had travelled, both geographically and existentially, "to the heart of secular culture", who may have even neglected the "religious customs of Hasidism" on the day of his wedding[152], encounter a problem which threatens to undermine their thesis.

They write:

During these years Mendel's father, Levi Yitzchak, was also concerned about his son's religious life. In 1929, for example,

---

[150] See also Rayatz, *Igrot Kodesh* vol. 7, pages 389-290 (letter dated 15th Ellul 5703):

"מלימודך באוניברסיטה בלימוד חכמת החימי', אשר בכל מדע, ובפרט במדע זה **יכולים להבין גדולת ה' מענין הבריאה אשר הוא ית' הטביע בנבראים ובהרכבתם סגולות נפלאות,** אבל כותלי האוניברסיטה הם להיפך ... מכותלי בית הכנסת ובית המדרש אשר הסביבה גורמת זכות המוח וטהרת הלב ... וחלופיהן בכותלי האוניברסיטה וצריכים **שמירה מעולה וסיעתא דשמיא**".

[151] See *Likuttei Sichot* (cited above note 140) page 42ff.

[152] See Heilman and Friedman pages 99-100.

At one stage they describe the Rebbe's later 'return' to the Chasidic way of life as analogous to the path of a *ba'al teshuvah* (religious penitent). In their words: "He believed that this journey away from parochial Jewish identity, belonging, and practice was not irreversible or permanent. One could be made to abandon those aspirations, to counter acculturate and turn back to the most parochial of Jewish identities, to escape the seductions of contemporary culture and embrace the tradition and old practices even more powerfully. He knew all this because he had experienced it himself." (Heilman and Friedman pages 164-165).

he sent a letter[153] in which he reported that Moussia had complained to him that Mendel was fasting every day until the time of the afternoon prayers. 'Where,' Levi Yitzchak asks, did his son acquire this practice? Entreating him to desist, he adds, 'You are not a Samson in strength'. Such is not 'the way of Torah or repentance' ... Why was Mendel fasting? We do not know for certain (though we offer a hint of an answer at the end of this chapter)[154].

Clearly, a young man who has little interest in the requisite spiritual preparations for his wedding would hardly be a candidate for pietistic asceticism. How do the authors propose to reconcile this contradiction? We wait with bated breath to the end of the chapter. Here comes the promised "hint". The authors turn to discuss the fact that "Mendel and Moussia" had no children, a matter that was, judging by his letters, of great concern for R. Levi Yitzchak. In this context they write:

Perhaps that was why Mendel had begun his fasting, hoping to move heaven to 'remember' him and his wife by his actions of piety ... Mendel was becoming increasingly pious, the anxiety of their childlessness weighed heavily on the couple and their parents[155].

The problem with this thesis is that the above-mentioned letter in which R. Levi Yitzchak tells his son to stop fasting is dated 2nd Adar Rishon 5689 (4th March 1929)[156]. This was just two and a half months after the couple had married! Could it be that the young man's anxiety about his childlessness had kicked-in within the first couple of months of his marriage?[157] [158].

---

[153] *Michtavei HaChatunah* (Va'ad Agudat Chasidei Chabad HaOlami: Brooklyn, 1998) page 8.

[154] Heilman and Friedman pages 105-106.

[155] Heilman and Friedman page 128.

[156] See Figure 13 at the end of this book.

[157] Considering the fact that it would have taken some time for the correspondence to be initiated by Moussia and for the mail to travel from Europe to the Ukraine and

back, it is reasonable to assume that Moussia learned of her husband's pietistic practices quite shortly after her marriage, and having failed to dissuade her husband herself she appealed to her father-in-law for assistance.

[158] **In their response to this question in my original review essay on the Seforim blog, the authors write:** "Rabbi Rapoport intimates (p. 22) that anxiety about childlessness does not 'kick in' after a few months of marriage. Actually, the work of one of us on haredi sexuality (see *Defenders of the Faith* [Samuel C. Heilman, *Defenders of the Faith: Inside Ultra-Orthodox Jewry* (University of California Press: London, 1992)]) suggests that Rabbi Rapoport may not even be close to correct. Moreover at Moussia Schneerson's age of 28/9, the question of pregnancy may indeed have been a concern. The fact remains, the couple had no children."

To which I responded: "In my initial essay I had objected to your suggestion that the Rebbe: (a) could possibly have become anxious about his childlessness within just the first two months of marriage; and (b) had consequently embarked upon a daily penitential program involving ascetic-style deprivation from food. [In other words: the only reason you can find for the Rebbe's piety is his childlessness; otherwise why would someone who, you suggest, ran away from Chasidic life and absented the synagogues (and later may have visited the outrageously bohemian cafés of Montparnasse), indulge in religiously oriented fasting?]

You now respond to these objections by arguing that "the work of one of us... (see *Defenders of the Faith)* suggests that Rabbi Rapoport may not even be close to correct." Here you refer to your study of some sensational ignorance or obsessive anxiety that you discovered in your explorations of charedi society in Israel in recent times.

As if to support your ill-conceived notions that you have now reiterated, you conclude with the empty rhetoric: "The fact remains, the couple had no children."

To which I respond: "You have merely added insult to injury. Apparently, in order to defend the indefensible you are ready to stoop to the grotesque levels of sleazy tabloids and exploit a human tragedy to advance the goals of your 'objective' scholarship. You are, it appears, ready to compare the Rebbe to some retarded teenagers or neurotic clients that you have explored in your (Samuel's) book on ultra-orthodox Jews.

Since your objective here is clearly not history, it came as no surprise to me when I discovered another unfounded accusation and unwarranted slander that you (Menachem) have hurled against the Rebbe, once again with regard to his childlessness.

In the *Ha'aretz* newspaper, in the year 2007, you spread (without objection) the totally unfounded rumor which amounts to a scandalous accusation against the Rebbe, namely that the Rebbe deliberately avoided bringing children to the world. In other words, you make the libelous suggestion that the Rebbe committed the grave sin of abstention from pro-creation, without a shred of evidence to support it.

Moreover, is it really possible that he underwent a radical trans-
formation in such a short period, from being a religiously callous
groom (to whom a father must remind about "the religious nature of
marriage") to a deeply pious person engaged in daily penitential fasts?

If indeed he had indeed made such a leap already in 1929, just a
few months after arriving in Berlin, and evidently sustained it – this
can be seen from the fact that the father continues to periodically admonish his son on account of his excessive pietistic practices, including
his abstention from food and sleep[159] – does it make sense to suggest
that he was simultaneously 'living it up' as would a young secular-
minded student, removed from Chasidism and pietistic devotion?

I find it difficult to believe that a person who allegedly may have
preferred theaters to synagogues and prioritized the secular over the
sacred, would be concurrently engaged in intensive fasting and adopting time-consuming non-mandatory religious practices.

So in one place you give credence to a piece of baseless gossip that suggests that the
Rebbe avoided having children, and in another you suggest that his extra-ordinary
acts of religious piety (first in Berlin and then in Paris) were stimulated primarily by
his quest for children, even as he continued (you claim) to avoid synagogue and
religious quarters."

As far as Heilman's book *Defenders of the Faith* shedding light on our current
discussion, the reader can decide if Heilman's findings there indeed have any
relevance here.

The only section of that book the authors could possibly be referring to is the
discussion on pages 333-335 about a particular couple's failure to conceive. The gist
of the story is summed up in these few sentences (bottom of page 333): "Neither he
nor his wife knew exactly what to do... For over a month and a half they failed to
consummate their marriage. As time went by and Shimon's wife 'Ruth' failed to get
pregnant as expected, this caused the couple and their parents considerable
consternation. Maybe they were indeed cursed."

[159] In an (unpublished) letter dated 1935 father writes to son: "My beloved son, I
hereby warn you not to undertake additional stringencies in matters of eating and
drinking and the like in the forthcoming 'ten days of penitence' please G-d, see to it
and endeavor to look after your health. See Figure 14 at the end of this book for a
facsimile of this handwritten letter.

In another (unpublished) letter dated 1936: "Please guard your health and do not be
more stringent than necessary". See Figure 15 at the end of this book for a facsimile
of this handwritten letter.

Finally, it is noteworthy that in the mid-1930s a committee of ultra-Orthodox Jews in Paris had approached the Rebbe, and subsequently his father-in-law Rayatz, regarding their search for a rabbi. These Jews, who represented the ultra-Orthodox synagogues that were not affiliated with the communal *Consistoire de Paris*, sought to appoint a rabbi who would preside over what may be described as the Parisian *Austrittsgemeinde*. To this end they sought to interest the Rebbe in this position thereby hoping to secure his candidacy. The Rebbe was evidently not at all forthcoming, resulting in the aforementioned representatives approaching his father-in-law who himself actually tried to persuade the Rebbe to give serious consideration to this opportunity[160].

The very fact that the Rebbe would have been a viable candidate for this position clearly indicates the esteem in which he was held by those devout Jews who frequented ultra-Orthodox (or shteibel-style) synagogues in Paris. It also demonstrates that the Rebbe's reputation for religiosity and erudition was well established.

11. Four Pairs of *Tefillin*: Wherefore?

Heilman and Friedman became aware of another pietistic practice that the Rebbe had assumed whilst living in cosmopolitan Paris. He started wearing four pairs of *Tefillin*, a practice that was observed by

---

[160] See Rayatz, *Igrot Kodesh* vol. 15, pages 211-212, letter to the Rebbe and the Rebbetzen dated 14th Tammuz 5695:

"די טעג האב איך גיהאט א בריף מידידנו היקר והנעים מר ריינין שי', ועגין די רבנות אין פאריז בכלל, און ער שרייבט טאמער ואהלט הרב ר' מנחם מענדיל שי' גיוואהלט, מר מערקין שי' האט גיפרעגט צי קאן מען איבער דעם טראכטין.

אין פאריז האט זער גיבילדעט א קאמיטעט וואס פאראייניניקט אלע מנינים וואס גיהערין ניט צו דער קאנסוסטוַאַר, און מר מערקין שי' איז דער פארזיצער פון קאמיטעט, דער קאמיטעטאט אינטערעסירט זעך זייער מיט דער רבנות פראגע, און ויהל זייער וסין צו קאן מען ריידין וועגין דער רבנות קאנדאטור פאר דיר חתני יקירי הרב רמ"מ שי'. איינער א חבר פון קאמיטעטעס פון די פני החרדים דפרנקפורט, א גוויסער ארטדוכס, אינזשינער מר פייסט שי', האט וידער גיפרעגט בא ידידנו הנעלה מר רייניין שי', און ער וייס ניט וואס צו ענטפערין. א מאהל האט ער בא אייך ליבע קינדר גיפרעגט, און וי גיווינלעך איז ער גיבליבין אהן א ענטפער.

ידידינו היקר מר רייניין שי' פרעגט בא מיר צו איז דאס פאסיג אז מיינער א איידעם שליט"א זאהל זאיין א רב אין פאריז, וו קוק איך אויף דעם. ער זעהט אז מערקין און פייסט יחיו ואלטן זייער ועהלין. איך האב גיענטפערט לידידנו מר רייניין שי' אז איך ויהל וסין פערישידענע פרטים – ועלכע איך פרעג אים אין דעם בריף – וואס איך בעט אים אמשנעלסטין באענטווארטין.

קינדר ליבע איך האב גאר קין ווערטער ניט ארויס צו זאגין און וואס פאר א שמחה מיר האט די פראדלאזשעניע גימאכט, און וי גליקלעך איך ואלט גיוען, ועהן איהר ואהלט דעם פארשלאג אנגינומען, און השי"ת ואהלט געהאלפן און די זאך ואלט זעך בשעה טובה ומוצלחת אויסיגיפירט"."

the Rebbes of Lubavitch, but one that was otherwise generally uncommon even amongst chasidim, and needless to say amongst the Parisian intellectuals of his day. Why had the Rebbe undertaken this act of piety? Once again, the only way this can be explained, according to Heilman and Friedman, is against the backdrop of his childlessness: "Mendel's piety was directly attached to his and probably (sic) Moussia's longing for a child"[161].

They suggest that a letter that Rabbi Levi Yitzchak wrote to his son on this occasion indicates that the Rebbe's reason for adopting this practice – which Rabbi Levi Yitzchak "encouraged" – was based on his son's anxiety about children.

As for Rabbi Levi Yitzchak's letter, it is evident that Heilman and Friedman read it only in part and interpreted it arbitrarily. From his letter it is clear that Rabbi Levi Yitzchak was not enamored with the idea of wearing four pairs of *Tefillin* (something that he apparently did not do himself), but only suggested that, despite his own qualms, the practice may generate G-d's blessing for children, an idea that he explained in mystical terms. An examination of the letter implies that Rabbi Levi Yitzchak was not identifying his son's motivation, as much as offering his own possible 'justification' for this supererogatory initiative[162].

Moreover, if it is true, (as the authors suggest[163]), that the Rebbe's older brother-in-law, Rashag, who was not childless, also adopted this practice, and since (as the authors do not seem to be aware) the Rebbe adopted this practice at the advice of Rayatz[164], it is unlikely that it had anything to do with fertility issues. If anything, it displays the Rebbe's

---

[161] Heilman and Friedman page 129.

[162] Rabbi Levi Yitzchak's letter is published in *Likuttei Levi Yitzchak–Igrot*, pages 422-423. It has been reproduced in Figure 16 at the end of this book.

[163] Heilman and Friedman chapter 4, note 117.

[164] See *Likuttei Sichot* vol. 2, page 507 and *Reshimat HaYoman* page 296. (The requisite caution in relation to wearing four pairs of Tefillin is also reflected in a letter from the Rebbe published in his *Igrot Kodesh* vol. 5, page 128). See also Rayatz, *Igrot Kodesh* vol. 15, page 226 (letter dated 3rd Nissan 5696). From these sources it is clear that the Rebbe began wearing the additional pairs of *Tefillin* several years before 1939 - the year in which he apparently wrote about it to his father.

deep religiosity (and bond to Rayatz) – even when in Paris, something which Heilman and Friedman are unwilling to acknowledge.

Heilman and Friedman are consistent in their pattern of rationalization. They have made a decision that the Rebbe was leading an essentially secular life; whenever they choose to 'discover' an item that is not reconcilable with their thesis they explain it away as an anomaly. Even when they find him doing something that exhibits extra-ordinary religiosity, they attribute it to some 'irregularity' (in this case infertility) that 'must' have been the cause for the Rebbe's unexpected 'holy behavior'.

12. An Alternate Hypothesis

Given the Rebbe's Torah output (unexplored by our biographers as described above) and Chasidic piety (which we will yet have occasion to return to) during the years he spent in Berlin, it is reasonable to suggest that the Rebbe's sojourn in Berlin was not due to the lure of "reform Judaism, Jewish enlightenment, and neo-Orthodoxy against which the Lubavitchers had fulminated"[165] or the temptation of the secular and the profane. Rather it was likely based on a conscious decision, fully in keeping with his spiritual sensibilities, to lead a life of synthesis between that which is intrinsically sacred and the sanctification of the mundane[166].

In this light we can understand how the Rebbe would invest much of his time and energy whilst he was in Berlin to his Torah correspondence, writing a commentary on Tanya (with taxing attention to detail), authoring a variety of indexes to the classical works of Chabad Chasidism and to many of the discourses of his predecessors[167], and laying the

---

[165] Heilman and Friedman page 97.

[166] See the letter written by members of the Schneerson's community in Dnepropetrovsk in anticipation of the Rebbe's wedding (*Michtavei haChatunah* page 29) in which they describe him:

"אמנם כן יודעים אנו להוקיר את חין ערך בנך שמלא את כרסו בתורה ויחד עם זה קנה חכמה ומדע במדה גדולה, אך הדת והדעת, האמונה והתכונה אינן צוררות אצלו אשה את רעותה, תמים הוא עם אלקיו ויראת ה' היא אוצרו".

[167] See *The Early Year Supplement* (JEM 2009), testimony of Rabbi Sholom Ber Levin, chief librarian of the Library of Agudas Chasidei Chabad.

groundwork for an encyclopedia of Chasidic doctrines that he had anticipated authoring[168].

We can also understand, in this light, how the Rebbe could attend university courses in Paris, and at the same time keep personal commitments to daily Torah study and teaching[169], compose scholarly Torah essays in his personal files, edit Rayatz's Torah writings for

---

[168] See letter of the Rebbe to Rabbi SY Zevin, dated 11th Nissan 5731, *Igrot Kodesh* vol. 27, page 132ff. See also excerpt of letter of the Rebbe cited in the preface to *Sefer HaMafteichot LeSifrei uMa'amarei Chasidut Chabad* (Kehot Publication Society: Brooklyn, 1966), page III and the interview with Rabbi Dr. Nissan Mindel published in the *Kfar Chabad* magazine, 15th Cheshvan 5746.

[169] See the testimony of Rabbi Professor Eliav Shochetman (JEM, *The Early Years* vol. 2, 2006) in the name of his father, who studied Talmud regularly with the Rebbe in Paris before moving to Israel in 1936. Shochetman testifies that already by then the Rebbe was involved in arranging after-school Torah classes for Jewish children in Paris, a claim that is **independently corroborated** by Yoel Reitzer (JEM, *The Early Years* vol. 3, 2007) in the name of his own father, who was engaged by the Rebbe to teach a group of these boys during the late 1930s. Neither Shochetman nor Reitzer were Chabad Chasidim.

This negates the authors' contention on pages 126-127 that the Rebbe had little to no interest in the spiritual welfare of the Jewish refugees living in pre-war France.

Regarding the Rebbe's concern for the refugees even after the war started – when his and his wife's personal survivial should have been of even greater concern to him – see JEM's *The Early Years* vol. 4 (2008), testimonies of Young Israel of Kew Gardens Hills Rabbi Fabian Schoenfeld, Queens College Professor Joseph Sungolowsky and Rabbi Menachem Teichtel, who speak of the Rebbe's public Torah discourses, and his efforts to supply an Esrog for Sukkos and Matzah for Passover to the Jewish refugees in Vichy France.

In their response to me on the Seforim blog, Heilman and Friedman dismiss Schochetman's testimony on JEM's video on account of the fact that in *Yemei Melech* (vol. 1, page 380ff), Schochetman's father is quoted as having said that he helped the Rebbe gain enrollment into the **Sorbonne** in 1933, when in reality, the Rebbe started his studies in 1933 at **ESTP**.

However, the reason for this error is reasonably explained by Schochetman's son (in an unpublished section of his JEM interview), that many Jews who lived in Paris at that time often referred to the university area in Paris collectively as "the Sorbonne." ESTP is in fact just a few blocks away from the Sorbonne.

Indeed, at least one aspect of Schochetman's testimony has since been corroborated by independent evidence. For example, Schochetman's reference to the half-year trial period the Rebbe was given before official acceptance into the school (*Yemei Melech* ibid. page 381) is confirmed in the Rebbe's ESTP records.

publication[170], manage many of Rayatz's financial and medicinal affairs[171] and give a regular Talmud class at a synagogue in the pletzel[172]. All this had to be achieved in addition to the taxing requirements of his academic courses.

Granted that "Mendel managed to switch easily from one mind-set to the other", could a discordant soul have achieved all of the above?

It makes, I believe, much more sense to suggest that it is precisely on account of the internal harmony that the Rebbe had achieved, and the sense of oneness with which he viewed his diverse tasks – all being part of a wholesome existence, that he was able to synchronize his multifaceted duties and achieve success in all of them[173]. Indeed, man's service to find harmony between the sacred and the mundane would be a central theme of his forty-year leadership.

---

[170] For dozens of examples of Torah writings which his father-in-law sent to him to edit for publication, see Rayatz, *Igrot Kodesh* vol. 15..

[171] See Rayatz, *Igrot Kodesh* vol. 15, which reveals that Rayatz consulted the Rebbe numerous times for advice pertaining to his medical condition, and the Rebbe managed many of Rayatz's financial affairs. See also the testimonies of Mr. Bernard Lax and Rabbi Meir Greenberg in *The Early Years* vol. 3 (JEM: Brooklyn, 2007) that the Rebbe would obtain specially prepared medicines in Paris for Rayatz in Poland.

See also *Likuttei Levi Yitzchak-Igrot Kodesh* (Kehot Publication Society: Brooklyn, 2004), page 406, letter dated Ellul 5697:

"לפי הנראה ממכתבך יש לך טרחא לא מעטה בהשגחתך על בריאות חותנך שליט"א, למה לא הודעתנו מה מצב בריאותו ומה אומרים הרופאים, ה' ישלח לו רפו"ש במהרה בתכי"א".

[172] See the testimonies of Rabbi Asher Heber in *The Early Years* vol. 2. (JEM: Brooklyn, 2006) and of Mrs. Rivkah Marelus in *The Early Years* vol. 3 (JEM: Brooklyn, 2007). Eliav Shochetman testifies to the same in an unpublished section of his interview with JEM.

[173] Professor Elliot Wolfson, who is no chasid, has shared with me his own view according to which: "Based on the available documents (including the early letters and the reshimot of Menachem Mendel Schneerson), I see little evidence that Menachem Mendel was not fully engaged by the ideas and practices of Chabad, nor do I accept the notion of the "double life" theory – advocated by Heilman and Friedman. My sense is that he was exploring and expanding his horizons in Berlin and in Paris but not in a duplicitous way. On the contrary, the written sources from that period offer a different portrait, one of a man for whom the Chabad worldview encompassed everything including secular knowledge and cosmopolitan culture."

Section III

1. A Word About Sources

Before I commence this section, I pause, somewhat hesitatingly, to address the issue of 'sources'. An inspection of the (endnotes of the) book reveals that most of the negative stories about the Rebbe are based on interviews held with the late Mr. Barry Gourary, a nephew of the Rebbe. Some of these interviews were conducted by one of the authors of the book, Menachem Friedman, and others were conducted by Shaul Shimon Deutsch[174].This is particularly evident in the sections of the book that deal with the Rebbe's courtship, his relationship with his father-in-law, his life in Berlin and the Rebbe's ascension to the leadership of Chabad. In these sections they also tend to add a good deal of conjecture to the material gleaned from these interviews.

It is my considered opinion, that whilst the information allegedly gleaned from these interviews may contain grains of truth, they cannot seriously be seen as a *bona fide* source of historical information. This is for four reasons:

(a) the interviews with Gourary all took place during the 1980s or later. Gourary had become estranged from his uncle, the Rebbe, since 1950 and, as Heilman and Friedman tell us, Gourary did not even invite his uncle to his wedding in 1954. During the 1980s Gourary was involved in an acrimonious legal battle with his uncle and the Lubavitch movement in United States Federal Court. The case was prompted by the clandestine removal of books from the Lubavitch library by Gourary. As the defendant, Gourary solicited the services of professional witnesses, including Menachem Friedman who testified in his favor, but proceeded to lose the case[175].

---

[174] Many of the latter's reports were published in Shaul Shimon Deutsch, *Larger than Life: The life and Times of the Lubavitcher Rebbe Rabbi Menachem Mendel Schneerson*, vols. 1 and 2 (Chasidic Historical Productions: Brooklyn, 1995; 1997) .

[175] Incidentally, one must ask why Heilman and Friedman did not reveal that one of the authors (Friedman) was employed by Gourary to work as a professional witness on his side of the trial? These types of disclaimers are quite common and represent normative ethical practice. Perhaps it is because had the authors informed their readers of Friedman's role as witness on behalf of Mr. Barry Gourary, the reader

The prolonged conflict and legal battle dealt a fatal blow to any remnant of positive feelings that Gourary may have still harboured towards his uncle. During the case, Gourary was responsible for the pub-

---

may have suspected that the book does not reflect unprejudiced scholarship. Arguably, it is for this reason that they chose not to disclose Friedman's involvement in the above-mentioned legal battle. Indeed, Friedman may have suffered embarrassment by lawyers acting on behalf of the Rebbe's interest when they subjected him to cross-examination on the witness stand. Further, Friedman must have spent, during the course of the extensive legal battle, much time in conversation and dialogue with Gourary. On the other hand, Friedman never spent any time with the Rebbe nor did he ever meet him face to face (nor did Heilman). It is therefore fair to presume that he had ample opportunity to develop his own personal prejudices against the Rebbe, and needless to say, he would have had naturally absorbed (if only subconsciously) and internalized Gourary's subjective image of his rival in the feud, namely his 'Uncle Mendel'.

[Indeed it appears that a not-so-subtle bias in favor of positions held by the defendant may be evident in Heilman and Friedman's book. For example, on page 54 they write: "Rabbi Yosef Yitzchak's eldest daughter and only grandson were denied this final resting place and consigned to lie for eternity is separate cemeteries in New Jersey". As one who has spoken (several years ago) to persons with first-hand knowledge of the matter, I can write with confidence that it was they – the eldest daughter and grandson – who did not want to be buried in the Old Montefiore Cemetery. For details of the entire saga surrounding this burial, see Rabbi Moshe Bogomilsky's *Hey Tevet-Didan Natzach* (Hebrew edition, Brooklyn, 2007), page 6.

Some readers may be puzzled by the fact that the Rebbe had the dispute litigated in a federal court rather than a Jewish court (see Heilman and Friedman page 218: "Ironically, the main arena in which the Lubavitchers sought to do battle ... was the federal courtroom of Judge Charles P. Sifton ... The fact that these litigants were using the secular courts rather than their own was not lost on people who were used to thinking about their Rebbe in purely religious and spiritual terms"). I therefore deem it appropriate to mention that, in actual fact, Chabad wanted to bring the legal case for adjudication in a religious court, and their initial recourse to a secular court was only to obtain a temporary restraining order and injunction, which Jewish courts do not have the authority to impose. Once however the matter was brought to the federal court, the defendant's party – that is, Barry Gourary and his mother – insisted that the case be actually tried there. See the testimony of the lawyer, Mr. Nathan Lewin, recorded on http://www.chabad.org/454552.

Regarding the Rebbe's understanding of the significance of the Lubavitch library that was the subject of the lawsuit, see, for example, the letters of the Rebbe dated 16th Iyar 5739 and 17th Shevat 5740 published in *Letters from the Lubavitcher Rebbe* vol. 4, pages 160-163 and 174-175.

lication of tabloid style mudslinging broadsides against his uncle, and the vindictive bitterness that overtook him then did not completely fade until the day he died. It is extremely unlikely that Gourary's recollections of events that occurred fourty years prior would not have 'soured' and that his biases would allow him to present objective facts untainted by the acrimony that had engulfed him.

(b) Many of the tales that Gourary told were clearly based on hearsay, because at the time that the alleged events occurred, he was either an infant or a child under the age of seven. The inaccuracy of his reporting is underscored by Heilman and Friedman themselves who cite a story that Gourary related about the Rebbe and the Rebbetzen at a time that he was only three years old[176], commenting in an endnote[177] that their own enquiries actually demonstrated that the story could not have been completely true.

It is also for this reason that Gourary's (unpublished) memoirs in which he states that he "never remember[s]...Mendel...studying seriously" in Berlin, cannot be treated as credible. These memoirs relate to the time when Gourary and his mother lived near the Rebbe and Rebbetzen in Berlin in 1929-1930, while Rayatz and Gourary's father, Rashag, were in the United States. At the time Rayatz and Rashag left for America in September 1929, Gourary was five years old. He was six years old when they returned in July 1930. It appears to be highly unreasonable to attribute much weight to 'recollections' of this kind that go back to an age of infanthood and were penned over fifty years later, especially when they contradict documented evidence.

(c) All the above is further compounded by the fact that Gourary evidently told different people different things at different times. For example, Mr. Zalman Alpert, the Judaica librarian at the Mendel Gottesman Library at Yeshiva University, who spent many hours with Barry Gourary and was extremely close with him, wrote to me that the information Gourary shared with him (on more than one occasion) differs substantially from that which Menachem Friedman claims to have heard from Gourary in relation to family members and related

---

[176] Heilman and Friedman page 79.

[177] Heilman and Friedman chapter 3 endnote 29.

events[178]. For example, whilst Friedman claims that Gourary was not interested in inheriting his grandfather's leadership in 1950, Alpert claims that Gourary indicated, that were he offered the position of Rebbe in 1950 he may have accepted it. Indeed, Alpert's version matches Gourary's testimony in the context of the above-mentioned legal battle, according to which he did want to succeed his grandfather.

(d) Finally, and most importantly, some of the stories reported (in this volume) by Friedman in the name of Gourary stand in sharp contradiction to stories reported by the same Friedman in other publications.

For example, the authors refer[179] to the view of Mr. Gourary, as conveyed in an interview with Menachem Friedman, that although Rayatz died "intestate", in actual fact, he had left a will in which he named none other than Mr. Gourary himself as his successor. In their words: "Barry suggested there was one [a will] that gave him the crown but that that will had been made to disappear". Yet in a previously published interview[180] Menachem Friedman stated that by 1950 Barry Gourary "had renounced religion and became a secular computer businessman". This in itself would seem to contradict the notion, allegedly communicated by Gourary to Friedman, that Rayatz had left a will appointing Gourary to be his successor[181].

---

[178] Incidentally, Alpert relates that, as a young child, Barry spent time with his uncle and aunt in Berlin, and it was the Rebbe who used to take him to the synagogue for services.

[179] Heilman and Friedman chapter 2, endnote 10.

[180] Ha'aretz 30th May, 2007.

[181] We are informed, in the authors' own words (page 33), that even during Rayatz's lifetime people were already gossiping about the fact that "in America his grandson [Barry] was choosing another path that departed from CHaBaD Lubavitch" and that he would have been "unacceptable as a leader to most of the community" (page 34). [Whilst the authors suggest that Rayatz was protected from this knowledge, it is unlikely that this was the case; Rayatz was an extremely perceptive and astute person, and if it is true that (as they say) Barry had an extremely close relationship with his grandfather, it is unreasonable in the extreme to suggest that he, or anyone else for that matter, could pull the wool over his grandfather's eyes]. We also know, that as the authors say (page 34), Barry "was not interested in becoming a Rebbe ... he did not want to lead that sort of life" but rather he wanted a "hard science life" for which reason he had been studying in university.

Moreover, in that same interview Friedman stated, in no uncertain terms:

(a) that Rayatz did not even want his older son-in-law (Rabbi Shemaryahu Gourary, Rashag) to succeed him as Rebbe because his son, Barry, had rejected religion which, Friedman claims had "transformed" – not only Barry but even - Rashag "from an asset to an impediment".

(b) that Rayatz had actually decided in favor of appointing his younger son-in-law, Ramash, as his successor.

These statements blatantly contradict the narrative told in the book, co-authored by Friedman (published some three years later), and also mean that the alleged claims of Mr. Gourary are irreconcilable with the facts as presented by the very same author. Consequently, the claims of Friedman or Gourary's testimonies smack of (to paraphrase the authors) the stuff of "myth, mystery and reconstructed memory".

In light of the above, and considering the fact that there is no evidence whatsoever that Barry was ever involved in **any** aspects of Rayatz's **communal** work or that Rayatz ever referred any queries in **Torah, Chasidut** or **institutional matters** to him – and unlike his two sons-in-law, Rashag and Ramash, he had never appointed him to stand in on his behalf, speak or teach in any capacity – I find it hard to believe that Rayatz, who was a very wise man, would have wanted to impose the community on to Barry, or Barry on to the community (even if he had, during Barry's younger years, harbored hopes that he would succeed him).

For these reasons alone it is difficult to accept Barry's claim that his grandfather actually "gave him the crown".

Moreover, it is clear, again by the authors' own account (in chapter two) that neither Barry's parents, nor his grandmother (Rayatz's wife) believed that he was the one that Rayatz would have wanted to succeed him. If Barry had seen the will, would they not have also seen it? After all, they lived in the same house as Rayatz and had an even more intimate relationship with him than Barry; would they have not supported Rayatz's chosen one? Is it conceivable that they, who one may presume were ardent 'chasidim' and devoted wife and children, would have made the will "disappear"? And, if not they, who else would have made the will disappear? Surely, by all accounts Rayatz was surrounded by loyal family members and trusted confidants and aides twenty four hours a day; which one of them would have been party to such a heinous crime? Since, even on the authors' account, there was no one outside of Rayatz's loyal family that was 'competing' for the position, why would anyone else have had an interest to make the will disappear?

At any rate, these conflicts undermine the reliability of the reported interviews, and, in light of all the above, I venture to say that the contents of these alleged exchanges cannot be treated with any more credibility than fanciful hagiographical tales which have no place in a history book of academic value[182].

---

[182] **In their response to this argument (on the Seforim blog) Heilman and Friedman ask**: "What did they [the Gourarys] do to become the subjects of such enmity?" They add that by casting aspersions on the authenticity of the Gourary testimonies, I have made "an ad hominem attack" on "the Gourary son and mother ... after their death"; this, they say constitutes an "indictment of the truthfulness of the Sixth Rebbe's oldest daughter and son-in-law". My arguments constitute in their opinion "an act of partisanship masquerading as serious criticism".

They then argue that: **(a)** it is unreasonable to suggest that Gourary had a jaundiced view of his uncle, because in actual fact he "had a genuine admiration for his uncle"; **(b)** "Barry heard his parents repeat stories and facts over the years" and therefore even when he spoke of events that occurred during his infancy he is reliable.

To these allegations I responded: As sociologists, Heilman and Friedman are undoubtedly aware of the socio-psychological facts that: **(a)** people often lose their impartiality as a result of feuds and fissures, within the family unit in particular; **(b)** in case of prolonged quarrels, the combination of bad-blood, bitterness and even vindictiveness can cause a person to see and remember things in a way that, whilst may appear true to the individual himself, does not really reflect historical reality (this is actually akin to the way some chasidim come to believe that their hagiographical images, often developed from a kernel of historical truth, actually reflect historical reality); **(c)** In the case of hostility festering over many years, how much more so decades, especially when combined with the process of aging (in addition to the physical and existential alienation between the parties), the 'recollections' of an aggrieved family member often undergo a process of internal 'modification', if not radical metamorphosis, thus yielding an image that, whilst true to the imaginative faculties of the individual concerned, are remote from factual history, sometimes 'as east is far from west'. [It must be emphasized that these factors are not based on any presuppositions about Gourary's general integrity. Granted, for arguments sake, that Gourary was, generally speaking, the personification of piety, this would not mean that he was immune to the all-too-natural dynamics of human psychology]. **(d)** All the above factors become ever more pronounced when **repetitive** feuds occur, leading to painful and protracted legal battles; the individual permeated with resentment and animosity, 'justifiable' or otherwise, often loses all sense of proportion. All the above-mentioned socio-psychological facts are relevant, by the authors' own account, to the person of Mr. Gourary. Consequently they should be able to appreciate that the 'recollections' that

2. Entering the Court

All the above behoves me to preface my remarks about the Rebbe's relationship with his father-in-law with some basic documented facts about the 'match' between the Rebbe and Rayatz's daughter – facts that were either unknown, dismissed or ignored by Heilman and Friedman, often in favour of sleazy substitutes.

In the year 1923, long before the Rebbe met his future wife, Moussia, Rayatz told one of his close chasidim, Rabbi Eliyahu Chaim Althaus[183], that he wanted his daughter to marry the Rebbe. Rabbi Althaus was instrumental in bringing the Rebbe from his hometown to meet Rayatz[184] [185].

---

they have gleaned from interviews conducted with Mr. Gourary (may inform us about certain aspects of his internal life, but) tell us little about the subject of their biography.

As for their claim that Gourary admired his uncle; that may indeed have been the case (at least I am not in a position to deny this), but it is likewise clear that since 1950, and to a much greater extent during the 1980s, family fissures took over, and any admiration, if it still existed, was overshadowed by negative, acrimonious sentiments.

Finally, I address the authors' suggestion that Gourary may have heard things from his parents that occurred during his infancy. This may or may not have been the case. Two things are however clear: (a) that we are now also relying on reports that they heard from Deutsch (who is the tradent of many of the interviews) who heard from Gourary, who in turn may have heard from his parents. This is the type of evidence that they themselves dismiss as 'hearsay' or hagiography; (b) that at least one item of Gourary's testimony that he allegedly heard from his parents was proven to be inaccurate by the authors' own admission. I rest my case.

[183] Althaus was an assistant and confidant of Rayatz. See, for example, R. Shalom Dovber Levin, *Toldot Chabad BeRussia HaSovietit* (Kehot Publication Society: Brooklyn, 1989), on pages cited in the name index, under אלטהויז, אלי' חיים.

[184] A section of Althaus' letter has been published in *BeOr HaChasidut* (Heichal Menachem: Brooklyn, 1998), issue no. 56 (Kislev 5759), page 15:

"אני הראשון אשר זכיתי ... כי כ"ק אדמו"ר [מוהריי"צ] שליט"א גלה לי ביחידות בהיכלו בקיץ תרפ"ג את מצפוני לבבו הטהורה ... כי ברצונו ליתן את בתו היקרה והחביבה [חיה מושקא] שתי' לאיש ההוא [הרבי] אשר בו אדבר עתה".

[185] See Heilman and Friedman chapter 3 endnote 18, where they report finding absolutely no corroborating documentation of any visit made by the Rebbe to Rayatz in 1923. See, however, *Reshimat HaYoman* page 258. See also Rayatz, *Igrot Kodesh* vol. 15, page 31, where Rayatz writes from Rostov to his daughter, Moussia,

There may have been an untold number of reasons for the delay in their marriage especially given the backdrop of the tumultuous times in which they were living. Chief amongst these were of course the Rayatz's multifaceted campaign to keep Judaism alive under Communist oppression, a campaign that ultimately led to his imprisonment and his eventual departure from the Soviet Union and relocation to Latvia.

It is also evident from a letter of Rayatz's most personal confidant that the lack of the requisite funds was certainly a contributing factor to the delay[186], especially since Rayatz clearly wanted to celebrate this 'royal wedding' with abundant ceremony[187] (Heilman and Friedman

---

in the summer of 1923, about having spent the week "getting to know Mendel" in the vacation town of Kislovodosk.

It must be emphasised that although the Rebbe was first introduced to Rayatz and his daughter Moussia in 1923, there is no evidence that he was actually involved in an ongoing 'courtship' with her from that date on (as the authors suggest). At any rate, the available evidence indicates that the Rebbe spent the majority of his time between 1923 and 1927 in his parent's home, not in the court of Rayatz.

[186] See the letters of Rabbi Yechezkel Feigin published in the preface to the *Igrot Kodesh* of Rayatz vol. 2, page 8ff.

"אודות המצב בבית חיינו, הנה לא תוכל לשער דוחק המצב, נשארנו בע"ח גדולים מהמאורע ל"ע וכן מההכנות להנסיעה ומהנסיעה"; "המצב דחוק לע"ע ביותר לא תוכל לשער ... מובן לך שבמכתב א"א לכתוב הכל אבל לו יכולתי לספר לך דברים כאלו מדוחק המצב אשר בעצמו דבר עמדי ממש תסמר שערות הראש ... התבונן נא וואו דאס האלט ה"י, ברוסלאנד המצב הולך ודל מיום ליום".

With specific reference to the Rebbe's wedding Rabbi Feigin writes (on page 10ff):

"הנני כותב לך בסוד בבל תאמר, עד כמה מגיעים הדברים ... אף שלע"ע לא אמרו לי מזה, אבל סוף כל סוף, פריער מיט א חודש שפעטער מיט א חודש, חתונה דארף דאך זיין, ובמה?"

[187] See Heilman and Friedman pages 95-97.

[Incidentally, in this section of the book they theorize that Rayatz wished to hold a grand wedding in Warsaw for the self-serving purpose of showing the Jewish world the strength of his court, and to introduce to them his new son-in-law, his potential successor ("... a large wedding celebration could serve as a sign of its return to strength and life ... a celebration that would remind the world of the prestige and importance of the Lubavitcher Rebbe ... if the new bridegroom was to be a new leader, if not the face of the court, this wedding would be the most suitable opportunity to present him to the court and the Jewish world"). On the very same pages, however, the authors continue with a contradictory assertion, namely, that Rayatz saw the bride and groom as actually being dangerously embarrassing to his reputation, which is why he tried to 'hide the bridegroom' from the participants at

dismiss this possibility flippantly[188]).

Additionally, Rayatz writes clearly in a letter to the Rebbe's father, Rabbi Levi Yitzchak, dated 27th Sivan 5688 (15th June 1928), a full six months before the Rebbe's wedding on 14th Kislev 5689 (27th November 1928), that he had already postponed their children's marriage at least until Ellul of that year (5688), in the hope that Rabbi Levi Yitzchak and his wife, Chanah, would be able to obtain permission from the Russian government to attend the wedding in Poland[189].

What we do know is that long before the formal *Tena'im* ceremony (at which the wedding and its date were confirmed), which took place only a week before their wedding, Rayatz referred to the Rebbe in writing as "*ha-meyuad liheyot chatani*" "the one who is designated to be my son-in-law"[190].

Heilman and Friedman not only ignore the evidence, they write:

> In all the internal Lubavitcher hagiographies, before his marriage and during what might be called a courtship, Mendel is always referred to as 'the one intended to be the groom' (*sic*), a title that has no precedent in Jewish tradition and law[191].

Once again they exhibit their ignorance in the rabbinic vernacular, for the phrase "*ha-meyuad liheyot chatani*" was coined long before the

---

the celebration! The reader is left confused: Did Rayatz think that this wedding would bring him coveted glory or irreparable shame?]

[188] See also *Larger than Life* (above note 174), vol. 2, page 209, where he states that "lack of sufficient funds to make a wedding fit for a major chasidic dynasty had been the chief reason for the delay". Deutsch proceeds to prove this.

[189] See Rayatz, *Igrot Kodesh* vol. 16, page 198.

[190] See letter of Rayatz (and facsimile thereof), dated 17th Ellul 5688 (published in the *Kfar Chabad* magazine issue no. 850, page 39, and in Rayatz, *Igrot Kodesh* vol. 15, page 48, in which he writes:

"אל המיועד להיות חתני הנכבד והנעלה מר מנחם מענדיל יחי' ... והנני המיועד להיות חותנו הדו"ש מברכו בכוח"ט."

See also Rayatz, *Likuttei Dibburim* vol. 4, page 1246:

"ומה נעשה עם המיועד להיות חתני מר מנחם שהלך אל מעונו של מזכירי מר ליבערמאן, האם חס ושלום לא נתפס בכף."

[191] Heilman and Friedman page 91.

Lubavitchers and their hagiographies were invented and it appears often in rabbinic writings[192].

At the Rebbe's wedding which was held with great fanfare in Warsaw, Rayatz said: "'I have given my daughter to this man'; he is fluent in the Babylonian and Jerusalem Talmud and knowledgeable in the entire corpus of rabbinic literature"[193].

Rabbi Yitzchak Dovid Groner[194] testified (in the presence of this writer; his testimony was also video published by JEM[195]) that Rayatz made a similar declaration when the Rebbe arrived on the shores of the USA. In his words:

> On Sunday night I was standing with my father ... ready to go in to the Frierdiker Rebbe (Rayatz) for *Yechidus* because on that night ... I officially became a student in *Tomchei Temimmim*. As we were standing outside ... waiting to go in, Rabbi [Yisroel]

---

[192] See, for example, Rabbi Yosef Katz (1520-1591), *She'eilot uTeshuvot She'eirit Yosef* (Cracow, 1590), no. 2:

"נשאלתי ... על אחד שכתב בתנאים שעשה מצד בתו ובין המיועד להיות חתנו סך נדן ... ובתוך הזמן נתבקש האב לישיבה של מעלה והחל"י".

See, for example, Rabbi Joseph Yuspa (1570-1637), *She'eilot uTeshuvot Rabbi Yehudah Miller* (Jerusalem, 1993), no. 99:

"מנאי תלמידו המיועד להיות חתנו".

In the reponsa literature of the past hundred years the expression is found hundreds of times.

[193] Although the exact words used by Rayatz are only known from anecdotal evidence (see *Yemei Melech* vol. 1 page 273 note 33), the fact that Rayatz gave an outstanding accolade to the Rebbe (along these lines) is evident from a letter the Rebbe's father, Rabbi Levi Yitzchak, wrote to him not long after the wedding (*Michtavei HaChatunah* page 15):

"ת"ח לך בעד כותבך בפרטיות, אמנם קצרת במקום שאמרו להאריך. חפצי לידע מה היו הדברים, בפרט כשאמר שיכול הוא לאמר את בתי נתתי לאיש, וסיימת וכו' וכו' הכל לטוב, הפירוש של וכו' וכו' איני יודע, ותודיעני הדברים כמות שהן, ואין בזה כל כך משום גאוה לפניך, הלא לא אתה אמרתם, חפצי לידע מזה בפרטיות. כן מכל הדברים אשר דיבר במשך ימי החתונה בהנוגע אליך".

This letter, once again, shows how uncomfortable the Rebbe was in those days with occupying the stage and being the centre of attention.

[194] Rabbi Yitzchok Dovid Groner (1925-2008) became a leading Chabad rabbi in Melbourne, Australia, and the director of the Yeshivah Centre, which includes a boys' school known as Yeshivah College, a girls' school known as Beth Rivkah Ladies College, and other institutions.

[195] *The Early Years* vol. 4 (2008).

Jacobson עליו השלום came out from the Frierdiker Rebbe and he
goes over to my father and he says:

רבי מרדכי, דער רבי האט געזאגט אז די ישיבה זאל ארויסגיין מקבל פנים זיין מיין
איידעם; מיין איידעם איז קלאר ש״ס, תוס' רא״ש און ר״ן און אלע חסידישע געדרוקטע
ספרים.

It was on account of his deep appreciation of his son-in-law's
scholarship that he would refer learned enquiries and all matters that
required the scrutiny of a Torah scholar to his erudite son-in-law[196].

---

[196] See, for example, Rayatz, *Igrot Kodesh* vol. 6, page 185 (letter dated 8th Shevat
5702):

"נשען על שיחתנו אדות החומר בשביל הקוה״ק לחוברת אדר הבע״ל הנני מבקשו להתדבר עם חתני הרב
רמ״מ שליט״א שניאורסאהן להזדמן יחדו ולקרא את המאמרים ולשכללם כהצעות חתני שי' למען נוכל
לגשת להדפסה במועדה".

Rayatz, *Igrot Kodesh* vol. 9, page 5 (letter dated 7th Tishrei 5706):

"וכשבא הנה חתני הרב רמ״מ שליט״א שניאורסאהן בקשתיו לבקר את הספר ולהגיד לי את חוו״ד ...
כעבור איזה חדשים הגיד לי ...".

ibid., page 129 (letter dated 1st Sivan 5706):

"השו״ת מהרה״ג מוה״ר יעקב ישראל שליט״א זובער אחר שביקר אותה חתני הרה״ג הרמ״מ שליט״א
שניאורסאהן והגיד שבחו בסברות נכונות אמרתי לשלחה להרב פרדס שי' להדפיסה".

ibid., page 130 (letter dated 1st Sivan 5706):

"השו״ת ששלח ע״י הרב יעקובסאן שי' מסרתי לחתני הרה״ג מוהרמ״מ שליט״א ונראה בעיניו וצויתי
לשלחו להפרדם להדפיסו".

ibid. page 139 (letter dated Rosh Chodesh Tammuz 5706):

"במענה על מכתבם מי״א אייר הנה כללות ענין הוצאת עלון של תורה והתעוררות בעניני לימוד ועבודה
בעריכת תלמידי ישיבת "תורת אמת" הוא דבר נכון אבל הכל צריך להיות מסודר כנהוג בעדת חסידי חב״ד
מאז ומקדם ובטח יענה להם כבוד חתני הרה״ג והרה״ח הרמ״מ הרמ״מ שליט״א והשי״ת יהי' בעזרם ויצליחם
בלמוד התורה ובהנהגה בדרכי עבודה בהגברת הצורה על החומר ויעזרם הגשמיות וברוחניות".

ibid. page 475 (letter dated 5th Ellul 5708):

"אודות שאלתו בהמאמר בראשית תש״ב מסרתי מכתב שאלתו לחתני הרה״ח הרה״ג הר״ר מנחם מענדיל
שליט״א ובודאי אי״ה יענה".

Rayatz, *Igrot Kodeh* vol. 10, page 114 (letter dated 8th Adar 5709):

"סידור השיעורים להלכות טהרת המשפחה דבר מועיל הוא ובאם ישתמשו בספרים הכתובים באנגלית
צריכים לעיין מקודם היטיב בתוכן שלהם וטוב שישאל בזה חוות דעת חתני הרה״ג הרממ״ש שליט״א".

ibid. page 280 (letter dated 15th Marcheshvan 5710):

"אודות הצעת הרבנים שי' דבר סידור קיצור דיני טהרה בודאי בעזרתו ית' אתענין בזה ויעריכו מכתב
בקשה והצעה לחתני הרה״ג הרמ״מ שליט״א הרמ״מ אמנם עד אז צריכים להניח כל מרצם בהשתדלות מרובה
ובכחות של קירוב ודיבור ברבים".

See also Rayatz, *Igrot Kodesh* vol. 9, page 7 (letter dated 7th Tishrei 5706).

[The Rebbe may have assumed the role of 'court scholar' even before his marriage.
The following episode is noteworthy in this regard. In late 1925 a Russian Professor
named Alexander Vasilyevich Barchenko (1881-1938) came to consult Rayatz with
regard to various religious and mystical matters, including the significance and

A letter written to Rabbi Yisroel Noach Belinski[197] illustrates Rayatz's typical response in all such circumstances:

> I have handed these to my son-in-law, *ha-rav ha-gaon ha-rav ha-chasid*, Rabbi Menachem Mendel *shlit"a* ... He has shown me his detailed response which addresses all aspects of your enquiry. I trust that his written response will be studied with the attentiveness it deserves[198].

---

meaning of the *Magen David*. Rayatz received the professor warmly and agreed to help him, saying that he would ask his "relative, Rabbi Menachem Mendel Schneerson who will soon be arriving from Yekaterinoslav, to find the material that Barchenko required from kabbalistic literature and translate it into the Russian language . . . for he . . . is well versed in the kabbalistic vernacular and also has the ability to translate the material into another language". Barchenko sent a large sum of money to Rayatz to cover the expenses of the Rebbe's travel as well as the work that Rayatz would commission him to do. The Rebbe indeed spent a considerable amount of time in Leningrad on this work, corresponding with Barchenko in writing as well as meeting with him in person at the behest of Rayatz. The episode is described in some detail in Rabbi Eliyahu Chaim Althaus' letter (dated 24th Iyar 5688) published in *Likuttei Dibburim* (Hebrew edition, translated by R. Avraham Chanoch Glitzenstein, Kehot Publication Society: Brooklyn, 1990), vol. 5, page 1375ff and *Di Yiddishe Heim* (cited above note 35), page 6. [See also Rayatz, *Sefer HaSichot* 5680-5687 (Kehot Publication Society: Brooklyn, 2004), page 281-282]. Finally, see Rayatz, *Igrot Kodesh* vol. 16 (Kehot Publication Society: Brooklyn, 2011), pages 80-81:

"הנני להשיג על יסוד ראשית דבריי אשר הגדתי להחכם בארצעענקא בהתראותינו הראשונה (ביום 14 או 15 אקטיבער העבר [=כ"ו-כ"ז תשרי תרפ"ו]) ... דכאשר יואיל וימצא לנכון לבאר לי, בהרצאה מפורטת, עבודתו המדעית, ובמה איפוא יכול להיות השתתפותי, אז לכשאתבונן בזה, ואתייעב בזה עם חבריי המתאימים לדעתי והשקפתי המדעית, וארה אשר מדעתינו (כלומר שלו ושלנו) מתאימים המה, אז אוכל להגיד דבר בזה בשלילה או בחיוב. כל מרבית חלופי הדברים אשר הי' בין החכם בארצעענקא, ובין המלומד מר מ. שניאורסאהן (אשר נבחר למזכיר קבוצתינו המדעית), ואחרי אגרות המדע והתבונה אשר הואיל החכם בארצעענקא לכבדנו, באתי לידי הכרה כי דבר אין לנו במדעתינו אם כי באיזה יסודות יש להם איזה יחס זיו מדעי".

[Reference to this episode is also found in *Sefer HaSichot 5748* vol. 2, page 629, note 54].

[197] Belinski (1883-1983) was an outstanding chasid and Torah scholar; see S.Z. Berger, *Yisroel Noach HaGadol* (Israel, 2006).

[198] Rayatz, *Igrot Kodesh* vol. 14, page 405 (9th Ellul 5708):

"את מכתב שאלותיו בענייני דא"ח מסרתי לחתני הרה"ח הרה"ג הר' מנחם מענדיל שליט"א אשר יעיין בשאלותיו ויסדר המענות כפי אשר ימצא לנכון. וזה איזה זמן אשר הראני את מכתב תשובתו המפורט בכל עניני שאלותיו ולא אפונה אשר ילמדו את מכתב תשובתו בעומק הראוי לו והשו"ת יהי' בעזרו בגשמיות וברוחניות".

Indeed, the first three volumes of the Rebbe's *Igrot Kodesh* (and volume 21 of the same series) contain dozens of letters, all written during the lifetime of Rayatz, in response to queries posed to the Rebbe by the elite of Chabad scholars[199] and the crème de la crème of devout chasidim[200] in addition to Torah scholars and rabbis of other communities[201].

Rayatz clearly derived great delight from his son-in-law's outstanding knowledge and, even at the wedding ceremony, asked him to engage the great Torah scholars that were present in learned conversation[202]. The Rebbe, a natural introvert and a man of extreme modesty,

---

[199] These include such scholars as Rabbi Shlomo Yosef Zevin (1886-1978); Rabbi Moshe Dovber Rivkin (died 1977) and Rabbi Alter Hilvitz (1906-1994). [Hilvitz had already become acquainted with the Rebbe in pre-war Leningrad; see his *Chikrei Zemanim* vol. 2 (Mossad Harav Kook: Jerusalem, 1981), page 5, note 2.]

[200] These include Rabbi Yerachmiel Binyominson (1885-1955); Rabbi Yitzchak Dubov (died 1977) Rabbi Shlomo Chaim Kesselman (1894-1971) and Rabbi Nissan Nemenov (1894-1984).

[201] Many of these rabbis, such as Rabbi Ephraim Eliezer Yolles (1891-1989) had a close connection with Rayatz.

Rabbi Yolles, a scion of a distinguished rabbinic family, and a man steeped in Torah and mysticism, had corresponded with the Rebbe at least since 1942 and had developed a close relationship with him many years before the passing of Rayatz. After the passing of Rayatz, Rabbi Yolles urged Chabad chasidim to persuade the Rebbe to assume the mantle of leadership. In a letter penned thirty days after the passing of Rayatz, Rabbi Yolles wrote:

"במשך הזמן, שעה וחצי, שהייתי בצל קורתו של עטרת חסידי חב"ד, צדיק אמת הרמ"ש שליט"א, נתאמת אצלי הרושם שלי, מן דיבורים קדושים וטהורים שיצאו מפי קודש הקדשים אדמו"ר נ"ע הכ"מ, ביחוד בליל הושענא רבה תש"ו, בעת שאמר לי כי יתן עבורי את ההושענה בידי הרמ"ש שליט"א, כי 'ידו כידו', ובמילא פיו כפיו הקוה"ט. אתפלא עליכם צעירי צאן קדשים, למה תתעצלו להתקשר באותו צדיק קדוש וטהור, הגם שהבנתי מדבוריו הטהורים והנאמנים של הרה"ק הרמ"ש שליט"א כי אין רצונו עכשיו לנהל את העדה הקדושה, אבל עליכם צעירי חסידי חב"ד, להתגבר אפילו על רצון צדיק, באתערותא דלתתא, למען כבוד השי"ת. לא רבי אנוכי, אבל תלי"ת הנני בן ותלמיד של רבי, וגם לרבות נכדו ותלמידו של רבי וצדיק הדור, איש אלוקים קדוש ונורא זכי"ע. ויש לי ב"ה הרגשה באוירא דרבי. אותו צדיק שליט"א מנחם שמו, וכן הוא: לנחם את הלבבות הנשברים והנדכאים, והוא 'משיב נפש', להשיב נפשו הקדושה של רבינו נ"ע לתלמידיו ואנ"ש שי'. ש"ב אוהבך המצפה לישועה ונחמה שלימה, אפרים אליעזר במו"ה שלום הכהן זצ"ל".

A facsimile of this handwritten letter is published in, S. D. Wolpe, *Shemen Sasson MeiChavirecha* vol. 2 (Tel Aviv 1998), page 161.

[202] See the Rebbe's remarks on *Shabbat Parshat Tzav* 5731 (*Sichot Kodesh* 5731, vol. 2, page 41).

was, as he later recalled, reluctant to do so, but in light of his father-in-law's request 'stole' himself to enhance his father-in-law's joy.

[The Rebbe's discomfort in occupying the limelight finds expression in a letter written to him by his uncle Rabbi Shmuel Schneerson of Nikolaev, wherein the latter writes to his nephew that he understood that he (the Rebbe) would have preferred a wedding without all the attendant fanfare ("*ha-ra'ash ha-gadol ha-zeh*")[203]].

It is noteworthy that in addition to the 'spiritual' pleasure that Rayatz enjoyed from the Rebbe, the Rebbe was also an outstandingly caring son-in-law and his exceptional devotion to his father-in-law in matters of health and medical care was deeply appreciated by the latter[204].

Indeed, if there was something that bothered Rayatz about the Rebbe, it was his habit of shying away from public acknowledgment and his inhibiting tendencies; his unwillingness to allow his greatness to be exposed. Thus we find that when Chabad chasidim in Chicago asked Rayatz whether the Rebbe would come and address them, he warned them that his son-in-law was "by virtue of his natural inclination and his mode of conduct, extremely hidden". Although he hastened to add: "To be sure, he is exceedingly great in knowledge of Torah, both nigleh and chasidus, with outstanding expertise"[205].

---

[203] Note the respect with which the uncle writes to his nephew. After informing him the details of the celebrations that took place back in the Ukraine he goes on to say:

"אם חסרתי דבר ולא בארתי היטיב מאת כל הנ"ל הסליחה אתכם. ואם תאמרו זה מעשי נערות לכתוב דברים כאלו ובסגנון כזה ובפרט לרב בישראל, אולם האמת ניתן להאמר כי לא יכולתי התאפק מלדבר עמכם בעידן זה ואקוה כי לרצון יהי' לפניכם ולכן כתבתי מה שכתבתי".

[204] See, for example, Rayatz's letter to his daughter Moussia dated 24th Tevet 5693 (*Igrot Kodesh* vol. 15, page 130):

"בא אישך חתנינו הרב רמ"מ שי' האט זעך ענטוויקילט גרייסע ווירטששאפטליכע קענטענעשין, ער בעזארגט מיך מיט אלעס, זאיין אופמערקן[ז]אמקייט איז פאר מיר קין נייס ניט, נאר אזייפיל איז שיים צופיהל, ניט נאר ויא א טרייער איידים נאר ויא א גוטע טאכטער".

See also the references in the editor's footnote (*Igrot Kodesh* ibid.).

[205] See Rayatz, *Igrot Kodesh* vol. 9, page 134 (letter dated 20th Sivan 5706), in which he writes:

"בדבר בקשתו כי חתני הרה"ג הרב רמ"מ שליט"א שניאורסאהן יבקר את מחנם הט' יכתבו בקשתם ישר אליו. אינני יודע עד כמה שיפעלו בבקשתם כי בטבעו ודרכו איז ער זייער באהאלטען כי באמת הוא גדול בידיעת התורה בנגלה וחסידות בבקיאות נפלאה".

In several letters written by Rayatz he expresses his displeasure with the Rebbe's 'concealment' which he acknowledges is a symptom of his humility, and encourages him to allow himself to shine, if only so that others should benefit from what he has to offer[206]. Rayatz's quest was not fully fulfilled until after his passing, when despite his original unwillingness, the Rebbe ultimately accepted his role as leader of the Chabad movement, and transformed his conduct in this regard. In order to be true to his destiny as Rebbe, he pushed himself, to the maximum possible degree, to let down his guard and occupy the communal stage, to meet with masses of people both privately and publicly, and engage in the type of self-exposure, outreach and the dynamics of public-relations that were foreign to his nature and usage.

Yet even in the lifetime of Rayatz, he found other ways in which he could assist his father-in-law, which did not go against his grain. We have already mentioned his voluminous correspondence, in which he was able to serve as the 'scholar of the court'. In this capacity he also became the editor of Rayatz's *ma'amarim*. Indeed, a large number of his father-in law's *ma'amarim* were edited, to one degree or another, by the Rebbe. On many of them he added references and substantial scholarly notes.

In the year 1941, Rayatz appointed the Rebbe as the head of the three organizations he established as the pillars of Chabad upon his arrival in the US: Machaneh Yisroel[207], Merkos L'Inyonei Chinuch[208] and

---

[206] See, for example, Rayatz's letter to his daughter Moussia dated 9th Ellul 5693 (published in his *Igrot Kodesh* vol. 15, pages 171-172):

". . זייעדיק אין מאריענבד, זונטיג פאר אונזער אפפאהרין, איז באמיר גיוען מיט א בעזוך מר סופר שי' פון
פאריז, ער איז גיוען אין קרלסבד, איז ער גיקומען זעהען זיך. איז גיקומען צו רייד, האב איך אים ערצייילט
מכח חתני יקירי וחביבי הרב רמ"מ אישך הנכבד שי', **איז ער גיוען אין וילדע התפעלות**, ער ויל זער זייער
בעקאנען . . . איך ואלט זייער ועהלין מי זאל בעקאנט וערין, נאר מיט ריידין ניט מיט שוייגין.
דער אויסבעהאלטין זעך פון מענטשין ברייינגט צו קיין זאך ניט, איך וויס ניט, מיר פארשאפט דאס פיל
עגמ"נ, אדרבא מי דארף ועלין זאיין בעקאנט . . . ".

[207] For details see Rabbi Shalom Dovber Levin, *Toldot Chabad beArtzot HaBrit* (Kehot Publication Society: Brooklyn, 1988) chapter 61 (page 304ff).

See also Rayatz, *Igrot Kodesh* vol. 7, page 387 (letter dated 15th Ellul 5703):

"קבלתי את החוברות שהעתיקו ומסרתי לחתני הרה"ג רמ"מ שניאורסאהן שליט"א אשר יתדבר עמהם
דבר סידור מחנה ישראל באה"ק ת"ו כסניף למחנה ישראל שבפה."

[208] See also Rayatz, *Igrot Kodesh* vol. 8, page 592ff (letter dated 13th Iyar 5705):

Kehot Publication Society[209]. Testimony to his work in these three institutions, much of which did require a degree of self-exposure, can be found in his published letters and the published letters of Rayatz[210]. As the one responsible for the publication of holy books, the Rebbe not only did his utmost to disseminate the teachings of all the Rebbes of Chabad, he published dozens of books in English and in children[211] (micromanaging all the details of such publications), and, most significantly in our context, he published a number of his own works including the Lubavitch *Haggadah* with his commentary[212].

Characteristically, Heilman and Friedman mention none of the above scholarly achievements for which there exists ample documentation and first-hand evidence. The only booklet authored by the Rebbe that they mention (from this era) is his Chasidic manual entitled *HaYom*

"הצליחה עבודת המרכז לעניני חנוך המייסד בתי ספר לנערות ומוציא לאור חוברות לנוער באלפי אכזמפלארים וכן המוסד מחנה ישראל העובד בחיזוק היהדות ושניהם תחת הנהלת חתני הרב רמ"מ שליט"א שניאורסאהן והודו לה' כי טוב אשר המוסדות הללו מצליחים."

[209] For details see *Toldot Chabad beArtzot HaBrit* (above note 207) chapter 64 (page 316ff).

See also Rayatz, *Igrot Kodesh*, vol. 14, page 418 (English letter dated 23rd May 1949): "My son-in-law Rabbi Menachem Mendel is responsible for the publishing division known as Kehot as well as development of youth educational programs".

[210] See also Rayatz, *Igrot Kodesh* vol. 9, page 101 (letter dated 9th Adar 2 5706):

"חתני יקירי הגאון הרב רמ"מ שליט"א שניאורסאהן סבל צער רב מהמוסדות".

[211] See, for example, Rayatz, *Igrot Kodesh* vol. 7, page 336 (letter dated 29th Tammuz 5703):

"מדפיסים שמועטען באידיש ובאנגלית ויסדו בתי ספר לילדים וילדות. העמסתי על חתני הרב הגאון הר' מנחם מענדיל שליט"א שניאורסאהן שיסדר לוח באנגלית ויסדר הברכת המזון עם העתקה אנגלית מדויקת ויסדר לוח היום יום לאנ"ש שי'".

See also Rayatz, *Igrot Kodesh* vol. 9, page 101 (letter dated 9th Adar 2 5706):

"ובהתבונני במצבו הרע של החנוך אשר אלפים ורבבות ילדי אחב"י ילידי הארץ אינם יודעים מאומה לא מתורה ולא ממצוות התיעצנו להוציא לאור לוח לילדים בשפת המדינה להכיר את ילדי ישראל עם עיקרי הדת המצות והנהגות טובות וכבוד חתני הרה"ג ר' מנחם מענדיל שליט"א שניאורסאהן טרח ויגע לסדר את הלוח".

[212] Rabbi Shlomo Yosef Zevin published a review of this *Hagaddah*, which he described as "a scholarly work of the first order". See his *Soferim uSefarim* vol. 3 (Tel Aviv, 1959), page 270ff. According to R. Zevin:

"הגדה חבד"ת מיוחדת במינה היא: 'הגדה של פסח' עם 'לקוטי מנהגים וטעמים' של הרמ"מ שניאורסון (עכשיו הרבי החבד"י) . . הרי זו הגדה נפלאה שמעטים דוגמתה, ומתאימה לכל אדם מישראל, כחסיד כאשר איננו חסיד . . עבודה מדעית ממדרגה ראשונה . . פינה בספרות ההגדית".

Yom[213], which was not even a composition of his own thoughts, but rather a collection of aphorisms and anecdotes of his father-in-law.

It is not clear whether Heilman and Friedman were unaware of the Rebbe's intensive involvement in Rayatz's affairs and the mutual admiration and affection the two had for each other, or whether they simply chose to ignore these facts. If indeed they were unaware of the above, it would explain why they found it incomprehensible that the Rebbe, who was the younger of the two sons-in-law of Rayatz, was chosen to be his successor.

Indeed, in their discussion of the succession saga Heilman and Friedman argue: "To an outsider the contest might have seemed uneven from the start, favoring Shemaryahu Gourary ... The Rebbe Yosef Yitschak had described him as a man 'gifted with deep understanding' and 'a man of intelligence and intellectual stature'"[214].

Evidently, Heilman and Friedman were not able to find any accolades that Rayatz bestowed upon his younger son-in-law, the Rebbe, for whilst they return more than once to re-quote the praise that Rayatz gave to Rashag, they seem to have been unaware that the only one Rayatz describes as "*HaGaon HaAmitti*", the true genius, was his younger son-in-law, the Rebbe[215].

---

[213] See Rayatz, *Igrot Kodesh* vol. 15, page 370. See also Rayatz, *Igrot Kodesh* vol. 7, page 22 (letter dated 13th Cheshvan 5703):

"איר האט זיכער געקראגען דעם בוך 'היום יום' ... השי"ת האט אן עין הרע בעגליקט חתני הרב הגאון ר' מנחם מענדיל שליט"א צו קענען אויפשטעלן אזא גראנדיעזען חסידות היכל מיט חדרים וואס יום יום יביע אומר".

[214] Heilman and Friedman page 38. In endnote 28 they refer (as is often the case) to a secondary source. The primary source is Rayatz, *Igrot Kodesh* vol. 4, page 368.

[215] See Rayatz, *Igrot Kodesh* vol. 5, page 368 (10th Sivan 5701):

"אדות הרה"ג הרי"ד [=הרב יוסף דוב סולוביציק] שי' במהותו העצמי הנני יודעו ומכירו זה שנים רבות עוד בהיותו בברלין, וחתני הרב **הגאון האמיתי** הרה"ח **איש האשכולות** מוה"ר מנחם מענדיל שליט"א שניאורסאהן סיפר לי הרבה אדות גודל מעלותיו בלימוד ומרץ ומאד נהניתי מהתקרבותו אלי כי הנני רואה בו כח בר פועל בעסקנות צבורית בחיזוק הדת הנחוץ במדינה זו כאויר לנשימה".

See also *Igrot Kodesh*, ibid., page 401 (2nd Tammuz 5701):

"כבוד ידידי הרב הגאון האדיר הנודע לשם תהלה בתוככי גאוני יעקב עה"י פטה"ח כו' וכו' מוה"ר ישראל שליט"א הלוי ראזענבערג ... לרגלי ביאת בתנו הכבודה תחי' וכבוד **חתנינו הגאון האמיתי** גזע תרשישים הרב החסיד מוה"ר מנחם מענדיל שליט"א שניאורסאהן להצלחה בגשם וברוח".

They also seem to have been unaware that time and again when mentioning the two sons-in-law in tandem, Rayatz mentioned the older one first, but referred to the younger one with greater esteem[216].

3. The Beard Libel

Pictures of the Rebbe from the 1920s and the 1930s demonstrate that he did not sport a long beard. Throughout their book, Heilman and Friedman visit and re-visit the Rebbe's "trim-looking beard"[217], which they claim was a constant source of agony for Rayatz:

> For Rabbi Yosef Yitzchak, a long beard was a badge of honor and belonging. That his new son-in-law lacked one was no small matter[218].

---

216 See, for example, Rayatz, *Igrot Kodesh* vol. 4, page 288 (18th Adar II 5698):

"בעמוד הראשון יהי' כתוב המכתב תהלה ... ומקום לחתום עבורי עבור **חתני הרש"ג** שליט"א ... וכאשר יוגמר החתימות בבקשה לשלוח לכאן על אדרעס **חתני הרה"ג** הרמ"מ שליט"א ש"ס עבורי".

Igrot Kodesh ibid., page 554 (2nd Menachem Av 5699):

"ובטח כתב **להרה"ג הרמ"ש** שליט"א ... הייתי חפץ אשר חתני **הרש"ג** שליט"א יקבל משרה – המתאימה לפני – במוסד הדזוינט".

Rayatz, *Igrot Kodesh* vol. 8, page 606 (19th Iyar 5705):

"המוסדות מרכז ישיבות תת"ל שמתנהל ע"י **חתני הרב רש"ג** שליט"א, ומרכז לעניני חנוך ומחנה ישראל אוצר החסידות הוצאת קה"ת מתנהלים ע"י **חתני הרה"ג הרמ"מ** שליט"א שניאורסאהן ודורשים סכומים עצומים וקנאת המתנגדים ושנאתם אין לשער והשי"ת יהי' בעזרי ויצליחני בגשמיות וברוחניות.

Rayatz, *Igrot Kodesh* vol. 9, page 118 (Rosh Chodesh Iyar 5706):

"סדרי המוסדות המתנהלים ע"י **חתני הרב רש"ג** שליט"א **וחתני הרה"ג הרממ"ש** שליט"א שהם מנהלים כפי הבנתם".

Igrot Kodesh, ibid., page 267 (8th Sivan 5707):

"אל אחוד האדמורי"ם והרבנים הגולים בצרפת ... ובודאי אקבל מאתם ידיעות מפורטות ... ע"י חתני הרבנים **הרב ר' שמרי'** שליט"א גורארי' **והרה"ג הרמ"מ** שליט"א שניאורסאהן".

Rayatz, *Igrot Kodesh* vol. 13, page 431 (25th Iyar 5707) wherein he writes:

"חתני **הרב רש"ג** שליט"א נסע עם כמה תעודות מרבי הממשלה לפעול העברתם למדינה זו ... חתני **הרה"ג הרמ"מ** שליט"א שנסע לבקר את מחותנתי כבוד אמו הרבנית תחי' ולהביאה בעזה"י לפה הנה יסד שם בתי לימוד לנערות בשם בית רבקה ובית שרה ... כבר בעזה"י החלטתי וכתבתי לחתני **הרב רש"ג והרה"ג הרמ"מ** שליט"א להתענין בזה".

The distinction between the two is obvious.

217 On one occasion they even refer to the Rebbe as the "son-in-law with the **trim** beard" (page 102).

218 Heilman and Friedman page 103.

They write about the "beard - too short for Rabbi Yosef Yitzchak's preference but too long for the Americans" - alluding also to the contrast between the Rebbe's pre-war beard and to those of his post-war Shluchim who would wear "snap brim fedoras and untamed beards, the trademark look of the group"[219].

But this leads us to another quandary based on the premise posited by Heilman and Friedman that the Rebbe had become a devout follower of his father-in-law during the 1940s. Judging by the pictures of the Rebbe, even as he had ascended the throne of Chabad leadership in the 1950s, his beard was still far from looking long or untame. Moreover, examining the many photographs[220] of the Rebbe taken during the 1940s and 1950s, his beard often looks even shorter and more spruce than it does on some of the photographs taken earlier in Europe. Could it be that the Rebbe would still publicly sport a short, neat and 'tame-looking' beard that was abhorrent to his beloved predecessor, even after arriving in America and becoming a devout follower of Rayatz (according to the authors' timeline).

Furthermore, in the early 1950s, if not before, we find the Rebbe writing[221] to people, advising them not to trim their beards[222], yet at this time his beard still appears short. Is it really plausible that, even when standing on the world stage, he would not mind being perceived as a hypocrite, preaching one thing and practicing another? Would not

---

[219] Heilman and Friedman page 1.

[220] There are a number of published albums which contain numerous photographs and depictions of his beard between 1941 and 1955. For an exhibition of numerous photographs taken during this period, from a variety of angles and in a range of different settings, see the album *Mekadesh Yisrael: Talks and Images at Wedding Celebrations* (Kehot Publication Society: Brooklyn 2000) and the historical biography *Yemei Bereishit* (Kehot Publication Society: Brooklyn 1993). For some examples see Figures 17, 18, 19, 20, 21 and 22 at the end of this book.

[221] See the Rebbe's letters penned in 1953, published in *Igrot Kodesh* vol. 7, pages 251-252 and vol. 8, pages 87-89. See also his *Igrot Kodesh* vol. 9, pages 235, 247 and 265; vol. 10, pages 311, 365 and 395; vol. 12, page 241; vol. 14, pages 127 and 290.

[222] See also *Letters from the Lubavitcher Rebbe* vol. 3 (Brooklyn, 1998), page 178 (letter dated 12th Tevet 5739). See however *Letters from the Lubavitcher Rebbe* vol. 4, page 189 (letter dated 5th Iyar 5719).

his authority as a Rebbe have been challenged if he did not exhibit the trademark of the union?

The answer to all these questions is simple: Neither the Rebbe, nor his predecessor, Rayatz, had any problem with tame-looking or trim-looking beards. Indeed, until this day, some of the most devout chasidim have extremely neat beards. They achieve this, as did the Rebbe, by combing their beards thoroughly, folding them and pinning them up under their chins, creating thereby a more groomed countenance.

Therefore, the whole beard issue, which runs like a spinal column throughout the biographical section of the book (and evidently contributed to their choice of pictures) is a storm in a teacup. Never did Rayatz insist that people have long or wild looking beards; he was against (as was the Rebbe) the practice of cutting one's beard. This the Rebbe never did, as is evident from a close look at the wide-spread pictures of him during the 1920s and the 1930s[223]. Consequently, there is no reason to accept the beard-libel and its ramifications.

It is also noteworthy that in 1932, Rayatz asked his son-in-law, the Rebbe, to give his unbiased opinion concerning a Halachic essay he

---

[223] See, for example, Figures 17, 18 and 19 at the end of this book.

Whilst on the subject of the Rebbe's external appearance in general, it is noteworthy that the photographs available to us from the European era illustrate how the Rebbe was careful to observe the Chasidic tradition whereby one's jackets and coats must be tailored in a manner that the right side of the garment overlaps the left when buttoned up (see, for example, the above mentioned Figures at the end of this book). Many great Chasidic Rabbis were evidently not so particular about this. See, for example, the image of Rashag in Figure 8 of Heilman's and Friedman's book.

For record of the practice see, for example, Rabbi Avraham Chaim Naeh (1890-1954), *Ketzot HaShulchan* vol. 1 (Jerusalem 1926), 3:4. See also Binyomin Kluger, *Min HaMakor: HaYishuv HaYashan al Luach HaModaot* vol. 2 (Jerusalem 1980), page 117, for an old Jerusalemite 'ban' on suits that are not tailored in the right over left style.

See also Rabbi Yitzchak Isaac Liebes, *She'eilot uTeshuvot Beit Avi*, vol. 3 (Brooklyn, 1980), *Even HaEzer* 145:4 and Rabbi Moshe Sternbuch, *Teshuvot veHanhagot* vol. 1 (new ed., Jerusalem 5752) 453 (end).

For the Rebbe's concern about this practice see the following of his addresses: 12th Tammuz 5723 (*Sichot Kodesh 5723*, page 352); Shabbat *Parshat Emor* 5744, *Hitva'aduyot 5744*, vol. 3 (Lahak Hanochos: Brooklyn, 1984), page 1672. See also *Sefer HaSichot 5750* vol. 1, page 193 and *Torat Menachem-Menachem Tziyon* (above note 124), vol. 1, pages 148-149.

had authored in his youth concerning the cutting of the beard[224]. The Rebbe wrote back to his father-in-law and provided a scholarly analysis of, and annotation to, the lengthy responsum of the third Rebbe of Chabad known as the Tzemach Tzedek[225], in which the latter forbids trimming beards[226]. A close reading of the Rebbe's letter and his published lengthy notes on the above-mentioned responsum show that the Rebbe treated the words of (his great-great grandfather and namesake) the Tzemach Tzedek on this matter as authoritative, and related to them with the deference and humility typical of a chasid[227] [228].

Finally, as Heilman and Friedman recall, the Rebbe met dozens of chasidim as he travelled from Berlin and Paris to Rayatz's court and back several times a year; some of these chasidim (including a few who are still alive) 'scrutinized him externally and internally'[229] and found him to be "complete" in his fear of Heaven. Would they have written this had he committed what in Chabad is considered a cardinal act of rebellion against the Tzemach Tzedek?[230]

---

[224] Rayatz, *Igrot Kodesh* vol. 15, pages 114–115, 117.

[225] See *She'eilot uTeshuvot Tzemach Tzedek* (Kehot Publication Society: Brooklyn 1964; 2004), *Yoreh Deah* no. 93.

[226] See *Igrot Kodesh* vol. 1, pages 3-13.

[227] Heilman and Friedman (page 109) are aware of this, but would have us believe that by giving his son-in-law the task of studying and commenting on the Tzemach Tzedek's responsa, Rayatz was perhaps trying to "cause young Mendel to recognize the religious importance of growing his beard longer". They ignore the fact that the Rebbe's treatment of the subject illustrates that he accepted the Tzemach Tzedek's authority in this regard.

[228] It is noteworthy, however, that the Rebbe (*Igrot Kodesh* vol. 21, page 273) acknowledged that:

"כמה חרדים מאנשי אשכנז ועוד הם בלי חתימת זקן."

[229] See the testimony of Rabbi Eliyahu Chaim Althaus referred to below (note 415).

[230] In this context it is noteworthy that the Rebbe's nephew, the above-mentioned Barry Gourary, spent many hours sharing his memories with the above-mentioned Mr. Zalman Alpert. According to Alpert (personal communication), even Gourary whose relationship with his uncle had soured, sometimes to the point of vindictive bitterness, described the Rebbe in his pre-war days as "a worldly person, but he never claimed that his uncle was not a devout Hasid". According to Barry's recollections as told by Alpert, "the Rebbe did not trim his beard".

4. The Rebbe's Leadership: Noble Altruism or Cheap Opportunism

A recurring feature in Heilman and Friedman's psychological analysis of Rayatz, the Rebbe and the Rebbetzen, is the assumption that their decisions and actions were often driven by uncomplimentary motives.

I submit three random examples (one involving each of the above-mentioned persons) working backwards in time:

(a) The Rebbe spoke on several occasions about Israel's 1976 rescue mission in Entebbe[231], and declared that the success of that operation was nothing short of a miracle. Since some of his talks on this subject were delivered at farbrengens (public gatherings) that took place on Lubavitch commemorative occasions (such as the 19th of Kislev and the 12th of Tammuz), the authors interpret this to mean that he was claiming the success of the so-called Entebbe campaign as a Lubavitch victory[232]; another accomplishment for him to boast of![233]

This patently false theme, namely that the Rebbe attempted to boast of victories that were not his (for which they do not bring a shred of evidence), is central to the authors' vision of the Rebbe's relationship with Israel, at least from the period of the six-day-war and onward. It is in this vein that they write[234]: "...the gulf war was over...and the Rebbe

---

[231] This was a hostage-rescue mission carried out by the Israel Defense Forces (IDF) at Entebbe Airport in Uganda on 4th July 1976, in response to the hijacking of a passenger aircraft by Palestinian terrorists.

[232] See Heilman and Friedman page 208: "[I]n August 1976 he combined ChaBaD celebrations of the fiftieth anniversary of the freeing of Rabbi Yosef Yitzchak from soviet imprisonment and the freeing of the Alter Rebbe ... from his second imprisonment by the czar (which had actually taken place on October 7, 1800) with the success of the daring raid a month earlier that freed Israeli hostages from their imprisonment in Entebbe, Uganda. It was as if all these miracles were G-d's victories that Lubavitchers had instigated".

'Incidentally', the Rebbe spoke about the successful raid on the Uganda airport and its theological ramifications on several other (non-Chabad related) occasions from when the event occurred in the summer of 1976 through the end of that year.

[233] See also Heilman and Friedman page 175: "For him it was critical to persuade his followers and the world that *his* ideas were the crucial elements in the triumph of the Jews over their adversaries, and that they **alone** were bringing the Messiah".

[234] Heilman and Friedman page 228.

could claim perhaps his greatest victory...The message was unmistakable: when the Israeli army fought battles, there were casualties, but when the Rebbe 'fought' as he had now, no Jews died. ... No doubt this victory, for which he and his followers took credit, increased his hubris".

Yet there is nothing in any of the Rebbe's printed or recorded teachings that supports such outlandish accusations! The authors provide no sources for their claims.

As for the occasions on which the Rebbe chose to speak about the Entebbe Campaign, those who have even a superficial familiarity with the Rebbe's talks will know that he often spoke about religiously significant current affairs at the first possible opportunity, or whenever his message would be heard live across the globe. More often than not, this coincided with a Lubavitch occasion, or another weekday holiday, which had no intrinsic connection to the issue at hand. Thus, for example, the Rebbe spoke about the theological challenges inherent in Transcendental Meditation on the anniversary of Rayatz's liberation from Soviet persecution (12th Tammuz); his concerns about the conservation of world energy in a pre-Pesach address (11th Nissan); a Gay Rights bill on Purim, and so on and so forth[235]. The idea that the Rebbe was claiming credit for the miracles of Entebbe because he spoke about these on Lubavitch anniversaries, could only be suggested by someone who lacks basic knowledge about the way the Rebbe conducted his public addresses[236].

---

[235] In this context, it is noteworthy, that the authors' statement (page 210) that the "*farbrengens* that before the [heart] attack [in 1977] he had carried only once a month (and on Lubavitcher festivals and Jewish holidays), he now carried out weekly" has no basis in reality as a simple consultation of the Rebbe's transcribed talks (*Sichot Kodesh* and *Hitva'aduyot*) will illustrate.

[236] In their response to this critique on the Seforim blog, the authors wrote: "On the matter of the Entebbe raid and Lubavitcher claims on it, we are not the only ones to have shown these connections. The late Jerome Mintz in *Hasidic People* made a similar point (p. 58)".

To which I responded: To be sure, even were Mintz to have "made a similar point" it would in no way justify the authors' baseless accusation. In actuality, however, Mintz makes no such point at all. On the contrary, in that book (*Hasidic People: A Place in the New World*, Harvard University Press: Cambridge, 1992) Mintz discusses

As for the Rebbe's response to the rescue from Entebbe airport, in his address on the 20th Menachem Av 5736 (16th August 1976)[237], he applauded the courage and selflessness of the soldiers, particularly of the young "newly-weds, or those preparing for marriage, who flew for thousands of miles, putting their lives in danger, for the sole purpose of possibly saving the lives of tens of Jews ... their portion in the Hereafter is guaranteed". On that occasion the Rebbe also protested vehemently against those who sought to undermine the motivations, roles and actions of the soldiers. It has been well documented that the Rebbe was actually vilified by some non-Chabad rabbis for publicly praising the bravery and courage of the irreligious, Zionist soldiers and for suggesting that G-d chose these people as a medium through which He would send deliverance to the Jewish People.

Yet the authors chose to ignore this body of evidence. Publishing the Rebbe's factual response would undermine the impact of their provocative remark that the Rebbe simply "took what he could to sustain Lubavitcher needs, but wherever possible he undermined the Zionist enterprise[238]" and other references they make regarding the Rebbe's "belligerent attitude towards the Zionist state". So instead they chose to 'compose' on the Rebbe's behalf a different response to the miracles of Entebbe.

(b) The authors report that the Rebbe's wife, Rebbetzen Moussia Schneerson, "treasured the few objects and mementos she had from her sister Sheina" who lived in close proximity to her in Paris and who, together with her husband, Mendel Horenstein, had been killed in the gas-chambers of Treblinka. Why did Moussia hold dear the items she

---

the relationship between Satmar and Lubavitch chasidic movements and their respective approaches to the State of Israel and the Entebbe victory. On page 58 he writes: "Relationships [between the two movements] deteriorated even further after the raid on Entebbe. Again the Rebbe said it was a miracle. G-d performed miracles through the Israeli soldier. To the Satmar this was totally unacceptable". Indeed, Mintz represents the Rebbe's views accurately and makes no reference to the authors' offensive suggestion. See Figure 23 at the end of this book.

[237] See the Rebbe, *Sichot Kodesh 5736* vol. 2, pages 625-626. One can listen to this address online and hear the Rebbe's words loud and clear at www.chabad.org/therebbe/sichoskodesh.htm

[238] Heilman and Friedman page 197.

had inherited from Sheina? Heilman and Friedman suggest that Moussia would have preferred that her husband be an engineer living in the non-Jewish quarters of Paris rather than a Chasidic Rebbe living in the heart of the Lubavitch community. This is why she was so fond of her sister's heirlooms, "because they reminded her of an earlier life and all its exciting promise"[239].

In this case the authors' reading is particularly grotesque. Any humane person would cherish items that they had inherited from a sibling they loved and who had perished in the Holocaust. Does one really need to resort to highly speculative conjecture in order to appreciate why the Rebbetzen felt attached to such memorabilia? The authors take a straightforward human emotion (longing for a perished sister) and crassly twist it to suit their agenda[240].

---

[239] Heilman and Friedman chapter 6, endnote 79.

[240] In general, the authors are unable to find anything complimentary to say about Moussia, and they go to great lengths to hide anything that might compromise the narrow image they have created of her (based, to a great degree, on hearsay or the conjectural writings made by people who did not know her in person. See, for example, the foot of page 92, top of page 93, and endnote 7 thereon).

For example: (a) on page 93 of their book, Heilman and Friedman assert: "Indeed, from an early age, Moussia's attachment to the broader culture could be seen in her embrace of the Russian language. When her father, while on a brief trip abroad, wrote a letter to his then twelve-year-old Moussia, he did so in Russian" (and based on *HaRabanit*, Brooklyn 2003, page 18 which refers to a single letter written by Moussia to her parents in Russian they assert that "she would generally write to her parents in Russian rather than Yiddish"), yet in an endnote they acknowledge that he also wrote to her in Yiddish. In fact the vast majority of published letters sent by father to daughter were written in Yiddish. See Rayatz, *Igrot Kodesh* vol. 15.

(b) On page 81, they write: "Rabbi Yosef Yitzchak was 'exiled' for just ten days with Shmaryahu Gourary and one of his daughters to Kostroma...". The same source that informed them that Rabbi Gourary accompanied Rayatz into exile also reveals the identity of the specific daughter who joined him, namely his middle daughter, Moussia (See Rayatz, *Igrot Kodesh* vol. 2, page 66), but they chose to conceal her identity. Why?

(c) On page 40, regarding Moussia's life in New York, the authors write: "Though she was a rebbe's daughter and wife, Moussia did not attend celebrations, farbrengens, or Lubavitcher womens' group gatherings; indeed, throughout her life she referred to herself as 'Mrs. Schneerson from President Street,' almost as if to emphasize an identity that separated her from ChaBaD and the Lubavitcher court of her father."

The implication is that she shunned certain expected communal obligations traditionally performed by the wives of the rebbes of the Chabad Chasidic movement. The fact is that there are virtually no reports of any of the wives of the first six Chabad rebbes attending farbrengens of their fathers/husbands/sons or leading any parallel "women's group gatherings." There is no definitive role for the 'first lady' in Chabad and some played more public roles than others. Moussia was undoubtedly much more reserved than her predecessors and clearly shunned all publicity and fanfare. Unlike her predecessors in Europe, her husband's court was not adjacent to her own house, and she did not have children, factors that probably contributed to her relative isolation. The fact that her mother was alive for the first two decades of her husband's leadership, and most importantly the fact that she enjoyed an excellent relationship with her older sister Chanah Gourary which would have been jeopardized had she assumed any public role (see below Appendix Two note 500), probably contributed to her decision to play a low profile (see the remarks of Moussia's cousin, Mrs. Leah Kahn, in her interviews with JEM conducted in 2007).

To be sure, Moussia joined her husband at her parents' table regularly, and when her father held farbrengens in his apartment upstairs at 770, Moussia often manned the front door, deciding how many visitors to allow in so as not to overcrowd her father. According to eyewitnesses at the time, Moussia visited her parents' home almost every day during the 1940s and 50s. (JEM Archive, interviews with Rabbi Dovid Edleman, 2008, and with Moussia's cousin, Mrs. Hadassah Carlebach, 2007). Yet, like her mother and sister she did not attend the farbrengens or lead any parallel gatherings for women.

It is beyond the scope of this essay to even attempt a minimal sketch on the Rebbetzen's life. However it would be remiss of me not to mention the fact that the decades of single-minded service her husband gave to the international Jewish community would not have been possible were it not for the robust encouragement, unyielding support and assistance that she provided for him.

Her dedication and devotion are clearly outstanding virtues when one considers the personal sacrifice she had to make to facilitate her husband's commitments, especially given the fact that she had no children of her own.

The authors allude to her sacrifice, but, characteristically, they seem to assume that this was imposed on her against her will and she resigned herself to this fate.

However, whilst many aspects of the Rebbetzen's life remain an enigma, the evidence of those who were in daily contact with her between the years 1950 and 1988, as indeed the Rebbe's own remarks about her, suggests that she actually encouraged the Rebbe to assume the role he did and she may well have considered her sacrifice to be a true privilege and a source of ultimate merit.

(c) The authors quote a talk (delivered by the Rebbe on the 9th Sivan 5747 (6th May 1987)[241] in which he recalled an episode that took
place at his wedding. Here is their paraphrase:

> In his own account of the day, Mendel would many years later
> report that 'my father-in-law stood up from his place to give
> l'chaim [make a toast] to everyone. When I saw him doing this,
> I could not sit in my place while my father-in-law was going
> around giving out Vodka. I stood up in order to go and join
> him, at least to hold the bottle or the cups'. But the Rebbe Yosef
> Yitzchak would have none of that. 'Immediately he turned to
> me and motioned that I should remain seated", a gesture he
> repeated when Mendel tried to ignore him and rise. When the
> Rebbe Yosef Yitzchak insisted the groom remain seated, the
> latter did so reluctantly, later reporting that he remained 'oyf
> shpilkes', a Yiddish expression that denotes the nervousness of
> pins and needles[242].

The authors raise the question: "What was he so nervous about?"
and why did Rayatz not want the Rebbe to assist him? They
acknowledge that "this encounter can be explained as evidence of the
solicitude of a father-in-law for the new groom". But they prefer:

> an alternative explanation. As he went around from table to
> table, the Rebbe Yosef Yitzchak ... was clearly seeking out those
> guests that were important to him, perhaps the distinguished
> among the rabbis ... To walk around with a son-in-law at his
> side who sported a short looking beard, fashionable
> appearance ... would occasion at each stop a chat about the
> groom, his plans and his past – questions that Yosef Yitzchak

---

Readers who may be interested in exploring more than the authors' one-
dimensional image of the Rebbe's wife are referred to *The Rebbetzin* vol. 1 published
by Jewish Educational Media (2008) which provides illuminating video testimonies
of those who actually knew her.

[241] See *Hitva'aduyot* 5747, vol. 3 (Lahak Hanochos: Brooklyn, 1989), page 464.

[242] Heilman and Friedman pages 100-101.

might not have been terribly comfortable exploring at this time. Perhaps the groom was nervous as well about that.

It is striking that once again they ignore the facts: (a) that in the very same talk (6th May 1987) the Rebbe offered the reason for his father-in-law's insistence that he remained seated. It was, he said, because at the wedding the groom and bride are supposed to be waited on and should certainly not serve as assistant waiters for others, however senior. Nevertheless out of his deference for his esteemed father-in-law and Rebbe, the groom felt compelled to assist his father-in-law and remained in a situation of unease "until my father-in-law returned to his place and sat down"; (b) according to the Rebbe's own recollections[243], Rayatz urged him to make conversation with those very "distinguished among the rabbis" that the authors suggest Rayatz wanted to shield from him![244]

---

[243] See his *Sichot Kodesh 5731*, vol. 2, page 41. See also the Rebbe's conversation recorded in *BeTzel HaChochmah* (Kollel Avreichim Chabad: Kiryat Malachi 1987), page 109.

[244] Heilman and Friedman (page 101) continue the above wedding story as follows: "Indeed, when at last Yosef Yitzchak arrived at the section of the hall where the *temimim*, the Lubavitcher yeshiva students, were, he asked that vodka be distributed to all of them and then turned to them and said, 'The Torah remains only with those who give their life for it. Diligence in studying the depths of Torah is what causes that Torah to remain in a person's mind.' And he added that they need 'to suppress themselves' **and all their other career aspirations** (emphasis added) in favor of such labor in the Torah. Did he want to make such a toast with a son-in-law standing with him ... who was headed back to the university in Berlin, who was at that point not apparently 'giving his life' and suppressing himself **and all his other career aspirations** (emphasis added) to a life of Torah?"

The authors would have us believe that Rayatz was lambasting against people gaining qualifications for a career or working for a livelihood, perhaps espousing the ethos currently popular in the (Israeli) 'Lithuanian' *yeshivot*.

However, whilst he would have undoubtedly not wanted the boys who were still studying in Yeshivah to be distracted from learning by their concerns for a livelihood, there is no evidence whatsoever that Rayatz would not want people in their late twenties (and after their marriage) to be concerned with a career. (We have already noted – above note 149 – that Rayatz was evidently quite comfortable with his older son-in-law's business enterprises, even as he was in his early twenties).

Yet what are we to make of the dogmatic stance Rayatz conveyed to the *temimim* at the wedding ceremony?

This style of 'psycho-analytical' interpretation that flows freely through the veins of the book, serves likewise as the spinal column of their psychological portrait of the Rebbe from the day that (in their terms) 'he decided to give up his career as a mechanical engineer and embark on a new career as a spiritual engineer' and throughout his life. In what appears to be an attempt to mirror neo-Freudian theories, they depict the Rebbe as a self-centered individual, obsessed with a desire for power and engaged in a web of manipulative tactics.

Thus they explain that when the Rebbe wanted to "reinvent" himself upon his ascendancy to leadership, he utilised a tool-bag of underhanded schemes to get his way.

One method he resorted to was "mystification". In order "to enhance his charisma and the charisma of his office - audiences with him began at 10 p.m. and ran into the wee hours of the morning, so that people who came to see him had to walk through abandoned streets when the rest of the world was asleep and specially prepare themselves and remain awake for the encounter"[245].

Let us explore the source for this (part of the) narrative as given by the authors (Heilman and Friedman, chapter 4 endnote 30). It is to be found in the personal diary of the "university-bound" student, the Rebbe himself (*Reshimat HaYoman*, pages 440-441):

"כבוד קדושתו הלך סביב השולחנות ויחלק משקה לכאו"א בברכה. בגשתו למקום עמידת תלמידי הישיבה ציוה להמשגיח ר"א שימחאוויץ לחלק משקה לכ"א מהתלמידים ויאמר: תמימים אין התורה מתקיימת אלא במי שממית עצמו עלי', קיום התורה בא ע"י היגיעה דוקא. לימוד התורה בכלל הוא ע"י היגיעה, דמי שמתיגע בא על עומק הדבר דגם מי שיש לו שכל טוב שכל דק ובהשקפה ראשונה לוקח הענין בטוב מ"מ מי שאין שכלו טוב כ"כ אבל מתיגע על השכל בא על העומק יותר, לפי שהתורה היא חכ' פי' אלקות דגם שכל הנגלה שבתורה הוא אלקות. ובשביל זה הוא מה שבאים בגלות. הגלות הוא בישראל בכלל ולומדי תורה בפרט ואתם תמימים בפרט, יש בזה אריכות דברים נאר ניט דא איז דער ארט פון דעם און ניט יעצט איז דער זמן דערפון, ועיקר קיום התורה הוא במי שממית עצמו עלי', תדעו תמימים שעליכם לבטל עצמכם מכל וכל, און אויף דעם גייט איהר ביגיעה, תלמדו תורה ביגיעה גם בנגלה, וכן תלמדו חסידות ולא שתשאר רק ההשכלה לבדה רק תבוא לידי פועל, הפי' במדות טובות, ואז הנני מברך אתכם איהר זאלט גיהאלפען ווערען בכל הענינים הנצרכים לכם ותאריכו ימים ושנים כו'".

The only phrase that Heilman and Friedman could have possibly misconstrued and understood as a reference to the suppression of career aspirations is שעליכם לבטל עצמכם מכל וכל, but (particularly in the Chabad vernacular) this expression simply means that **those who are in Yeshivah** must completely subordinate themselves to toiling in the service of G-d. There is no mention whatsoever of the negation of career aspirations.

245 Heilman and Friedman page 147.

(Even the facts are wrong: Audiences began at 8.00p.m[246]).

At a later stage in his leadership, when the Rebbe reached the age of 70, he declared that he wanted to establish 71 institutions. In this context the authors write: "To eliminate any insecurities his shluchim might have about their ability to succeed in this, he took repeatedly to quoting the prophet Malachi (3:10), saying, 'test me now in this'. His use of the expressions of Malachi whose name means 'My G-d's messenger" and who some call the last of the ancient biblical prophets, subtly identified the Rebbe as the one who continued in that prophetic line"[247]. (For the record, the Rebbe never mentioned the words of Malachi in this context[248], and the ostentatious intimations of grandiosity that they read in to such statements are completely fanciful).

When the Rebbe was ill he did not want to go to hospital. Why? The authors suggest that: "Hospitals were places where one becomes

---

[246] It is difficult to understand how Heilman and Friedman could have erred in this regard, because they were clearly familiar with an interview with the Rebbe conducted by Israel Shenker, and published in the *New York Times* on March 27th 1972. In this article, entitled, *Lubavitcher Rabbi Marks His 70th Year with Call for 'Kindness'*, Shenker states explicitly: "The rabbi receives visitors twice a week - Thursdays and Sundays beginning at 8 P.M. and often continuing till dawn or later. He explains that after 8 P.M. it is difficult to reach people at their work, so time is available for visitors".

[For other reasons for the night-time audiences see the article of (former Israeli journalist and politician) Geulah Cohen in *Ma'ariv* (19th Tevet 5725/2th December 1964), reprinted in the album *Shloshim Shenot Nesiut: HaRebbi* (Kfar Chabad 1983), vol. 1, page 68ff].

It is noteworthy that in their citations from the New York Times article, Heilman and Friedman omit the segments of Shenker's interview with the Rebbe that demonstrate his humility. Shenker writes: "How can he [the Rebbe] possibly reply to such a range of concerns? 'I am not afraid to answer that I don't know', he replied. 'If I know, then I have no right not to answer. When someone comes to you for help and you can help him to the best of your knowledge, and you refuse him this help, you become a cause of his suffering ...' ... The faithful consider him a *tzaddik* (holy man), but that is not the way the rabbi sees himself – 'Because I am not a tzaddik', he explained. He continued: 'I have never given any reason for a cult of personality, and I do all in my power to dissuade them from making it that'.

[247] Heilman and Friedman page 208.

[248] Indeed Heilman and Friedman cite no source for this.

passive, loses control, and is defined as sick; none of these roles or identities suited the leader of messianic redemption"[249].

A more reasonable explanation is that the Rebbe generally viewed hospitals as a mixed blessing, and sometimes advised people to avoid them – if only possible. He believed that the psychological and spiritual welfare of the patient played an enormous role in his bodily vitality and in his potential for recovery. Therefore, when he was ill, he wanted to remain in 770, because it was there, in close proximity to his chasidim and in the sacred ambiance of his spiritual home, that he felt most relaxed and comfortable, spiritually supported and morally fortified. Perhaps he wished to spare his chasidim the anxiety and worry they would inevitably experience with his unprecedented absence from his synagogue and study. Most importantly, it was there that he was able to maximize his meaningful and fulfilling contribution to his People, which, in the course of time proved to be the most therapeutic treatment, if not an elixir of life, for a man of his chemistry.

Considering Heilman and Friedman's reductionist analysis of the Rebbe's motives and personality, it is no wonder that the authors' biography neglects key features of the Rebbe's life-story. They do not discuss the Rebbe's many efforts to enhance the level of traditional Torah study even within the Chabad community, not to mention his contribution to the in-depth studies of the classical writings of Rashi and Maimonides. They do not discuss his unique dedication to helping the troubled and the disturbed; the countless hours that he spent empathising with troubled souls, guiding, advising and encouraging them, and the many days he stood at the *Ohel*, without having eaten, in the heat and cold, praying for the myriads of people who had requested his blessing – for recovery, for livelihood, for domestic peace, for material and spiritual success.

Indeed, the impression one gains from Heilman and Friedman is that the time that the Rebbe spent at Rayatz's gravesite was dedicated to holding 'conversations' with his father-in-law[250].

---

[249] Heilman and Friedman page 209.

[250] For example, on page 148, Heilman and Friedman write: "Rabbi Menachem Mendel Schneerson ... would be the channel of the late Rabbi Yosef Yitzchak ... with

The fact of the matter is that all the evidence demonstrates that his primary activity at the gravesite of his father-in-law was prayer on behalf of individuals across the globe that had asked him to implore, on their behalf, for G-d's compassion.

This leads me to another dimension of the portrait presented by the authors. They describe the Rebbe as one who travelled to and from the gravesite of his father-in-law, claiming to hear messages from beyond the grave and transmitting them to the community[251]. This grandiose image of a person who presents himself as one who is engaged in constant communion with the celestial spheres and has access to the secrets of Heaven is contrary to the unpretentious demeanour in which the Rebbe spoke about himself and which was noticed by all who came into personal contact with him. He never claimed to have supernatural powers and sometimes even asserted the opposite. When he gave a blessing he was anxious to assert that he was only an intercessor and people should not confuse him with the true source of blessing: the Almighty[252].

---

whom he would hold frequent 'conversations' at the *tsiyen*". In the endnotes (chapter 5 note 76) they provide their source for this statement. It is a letter of the Rebbe published in his *Igrot Kodesh* vol. 4, page 297 which they translate as follows: "when I visited the Ziyyun of my father-in-law ... I mentioned all of them **and I know** (emphasis added) that he has aroused G-d's mercy to help every one of you". Presumably the phrase "I know that he has aroused" is intended to illustrate their premise that the Rebbe claimed to have held frequent conversations with his father-in-law, for otherwise how would he have known?

In reality the text reads (emphasis added):

"ווען איך בין געווען פאריגן ל"ג בעומר אויפן ציון ... האב איך אייך אלעמען מזכיר געווען, **און געוויס** איז ער מעורר רחמים אז השם יתברך זאל העלפן יעדערען פון אייך".

The accurate translation here to anyone somewhat coversant in Yiddish is: "When I visited the Ziyyun of my father-in-law... I mentioned all of them, and **he is surely** arousing G-d's mercy to help every one of you". Heilman and Friedman's deduction is dubious to put it mildly.

[251] See for example, Heilman and Friedman page 62: "More important, he could *hear* and receive replies. That capacity to serve as the channel or emissary for his father-in-law's messages would become a cornerstone of Menachem Mendel's leadership".

[252] See for example, New York Times journalist Israel Shenker's testimony in note 246 above. See also *Nine-and-a-Half Mystics* (Touchstone publications: NY, 1997), by reform rabbi Herbert Weiner, pages 173-177, 190-195.

[When a couple once asked the Rebbe why his blessing for children was not effective, he wrote that one of the reasons was "because they forgot that it is G-d Who is the source of blessing and the One Who gives it etc. They placed their trust in the 'son of man', in 'flesh and blood' alone – in me"[253]].

They fail to mention his sterling humanitarian efforts to provide critical material assistance for thousands of individuals who needed food and shelter, warmth and care. Examples of such work include his work to send provisions for Jews that were trapped behind the Iron Curtain and sustain those who had emigrated to Israel or the USA; or, more recently, his projects to rescue children during the Iranian revolution and to save the physical lives of the children of Chernobyl.

Since none of these facets of the Rebbe's leadership support the portrait that they wish to paint, Heilman and Friedman take the easier path of simply avoiding discussion of them, or describing them in a manner that contributes to the caricature of the Rebbe that they have spent their years constructing.

Parenthetically the authors' predisposition towards less than complimentary insights is not restricted to the Rebbe himself. This tendency seems to be reflected in their treatment of other figures in the Rebbe's family such as his parents Rabbi Levi Yitzchak and his wife Rebbetzen Chanah Schneerson.

One random example: It is common knowledge that the Rebbe had a younger brother, Dovber, who evidently suffered from some health condition, quite possibly acute depression. At some stage in his life, possibly when his parents were sent into exile by the communists, he was sent to be cared for in an institution.

The authors have occasion to address this issue as well, gratuitously assuming that "Bereke, the middle son, suffered from some form of mental retardation" from his childhood.

In this context they write:

We do not really know the attitude the Schneersons took to Berel's diminished mental status. We know that he spent most of his life in an institution. In perhaps a cryptic hint of the way

---

[253] The facsimile of this response is published in his *Igrot Kodesh* vol. 29, page 19.

Berel was viewed, we find that in April 1911, the Schneerson family gave donations in honor of their sons in the following amounts: 18 kopeks (18 is a number that is equivalent to the Hebrew word for 'life') in honor of Leibel, and 27 kopeks (a life and a half) for Mendel and Berel. Who was the half? See *Ha'Ach* (a Lubavitcher monthly published in Lubavitch, Belarus) 16 Nissan 5611[254] (April 14, 1911) last page[255].

The authors seem to be suggesting that Rabbi Levi Yitzchak and his wife Chanah, considered Dovber's life as less valuable than the lives of his brothers and therefore only donated half the amount of kopeks in his honor. Whatever the exact meaning of the authors'proposition is, it has not the slightest basis in reality. For as is clear from the very publication that they refer to[256], it was the children themselves, not the parents, who made these donations: Mendel and Dovber (Bereke/Berel) – the older brothers - contributed 27 kopeks independently of each other and Leibel, the youngest child, donated 18 kopeks. Once again one is forced to conclude that it is either inadequate skills in deciphering the simple meaning of a newspaper text or a particular propensity towards creating undue sensationalism (if not a combination of both) that led these professors of sociology towards such an ill-conceived hypothesis[257].

---

[254] The date they give is wrong and could have not been right because Chasidic monthlies would naturally not be issued on the second day of the festival of Pesach. The contributions they refer to are recorded in *HeAch* issue no. 26 page 8 (a facsimile of which was published in the *Kfar Chabad* magazine issue no. 907, page 84 and *Yemei Melech* vol. 1, page 151).

[255] Heilman and Friedman page 70 and footnote thereon.

[256] See Figure 24 at the end of this book.

[257] Sometimes the authors do not actually articulate a derogatory thesis per se. Rather their approach is to present the 'facts' in such a way that almost forces the uninformed reader to arrive at the wrong conclusions himself. Thus even as they extol the virtues of the Lubavitch 'emissaries', ostensibly underscoring the nobility of their cause, the authors write (page 5):

"These emissaries feel that their power comes not from themselves alone but from the one whom they represent. Their boundless confidence has been characteristic of the movement since its early days. Consider, for example, the case of Abraham

5. The Rebbe's Relationship with Israel

I should state at the outset that the Rebbe's position regarding the State of Israel is a nuanced one[258], and it is beyond the scope of this essay to attempt a full-scale appraisal of his multi-faceted teachings on this topic. I have heavily footnoted my comments in this section so as to benefit future researchers on this topic, which admittedly, deserves a lengthier treatment than afforded here.

I have chosen to hone-in on four particular topics in the hope that they are instructive to the reader.

Heilman and Friedman depict the Rebbe as a virulent anti-Zionist, because:

Hecht, one of the first ten students in the Lubavitcher yeshiva Tomekhei Temimim in America, who in 1939, on the eve of the Nazi conquest of much of Europe, was sent on a mission by Yosef Yitzhak Schneersohn, the sixth rebbe, to the Lubavitcher Yeshiva in Poland. When the mother of one of those who joined him said she was frightened to send her son on a mission to a place where the Nazis were attacking Jews and Jewry, she was told by the Rebbe, 'He has nothing to fear. He's going to go and he's going to come back and everything will be alright'." In endnote 9 they provide their source: "Abraham Hecht speaking on the video The Early Years III (Jewish Educational Media)".

The implication here is that Rayatz sent a young American *Tomchei Temimim* student away from Rayatz's own safe haven in New York into a war zone in Europe and was therefore willing to risk the life of a concerned mother's precious son for his own purposes. The truth however is that *Tomchei Temimim* in America was not established until the arrival of Rayatz on American shores in March 1940. Up until the outbreak of the War in September 1939, Rayatz lived in Otwock, Poland, in close proximity to the central *Tomchei Temimim* Yeshivah. It was thus while Rabbi Yosef Yitzchak was still living there that he had invited Abraham Hecht and a handful of other American boys who had been studying with his emissary to New York, Rabbi Yisroel Jacobson, **to come to Otwock in order to study there and be near him**. Germany did not actually invade Poland until a few weeks after they had arrived there. As testified by many of those very students, one of the first measures Rayatz took after the Nazi invasion was to personally arrange for the American boys' safe return **back** to America through the coordinated efforts of his chasidim in Poland, Latvia and Sweden (JEM Archive, interviews with Rabbis Abraham Hecht and Mordechai Altein, 2005, and Rabbi Meir Greenberg, 2007).

[258] See also the Rebbe's letter to Menachem Begin from the summer of 1967 published here: http://www.shturem.net/index.php?section=news&id=49729.

(a) The Rebbe "argued [that] Judaism's greatest danger lay in Israel, where Zionists 'have invented substitutions and replacements' for religion ... that in reality only fostered a base desire to be no different from the Gentiles"; "the State of Israel was an entity that had inserted the 'feeling of exile' into the land of redemption"; the Rebbe asserted that the secular State of Israel "brought exile to Tel Aviv and Jerusalem" because instead "of acting according to the statutes of the Torah" the Zionists "sought to be like all the other nations"[259].

(b) "Unlike the religious Zionists, he refused to see it as in any way *askhalte digeule*, the beginning of the redemptive messianic age"[260];

(c) He said that "'Zion and Jerusalem are not ours. This is not the Zion for which we yearned'. Indeed, he would never refer to the State of Israel"[261].

(d) Like all other haredi Jews "he took what he could to sustain Lubavitcher needs, but wherever possible he undermined the Zionist enterprise"[262].

Perhaps the most insulting feature of Heilman and Friedman's description of the Rebbe's association with Israel is their oft-repeated assertion (touched upon earlier in this essay) that the Rebbe constantly sought to seize the credit and honor from those who deserved it and attribute Israel's accomplishments to himself.

When discussing the Six Day War they write:

> When after six days the unanticipated military triumph of the Israelis led not only to survival but also to their regaining the ancient Temple Mount in Jerusalem and the biblical lands of what would be called Judea and Samaria, the Rebbe could claim the victory as his, arguing that it was the sight of soldiers

---

[259] Heilman and Friedman pages 197-198. The source for the citations in quotation marks are to be found (as they state in their endnotes, chapter 7, note 2) in the memories of a journalist from "more than thirty years earlier".

[260] Heilman and Friedman page 198.

[261] Heilman and Friedman page 198. Strangely, once again, they offer no source for this, although it is true that he did not refer to Israel as the "State of Israel".

[262] Heilman and Friedman page 197. Again no source is given. This time however, the statement is unquestionably false, as will be explained.

donning *tefillin* that had miraculously frightened the enemy. Now Israel, once the product of Zionist accomplishments, could be reclaimed by ChaBaD, and its rebirth after 1967, stronger and bigger than ever, could be portrayed as the result of the Rebbe's campaign and the Lubavitcher plan for redemption[263].

Their description of the Rebbe's relationship with Israel is, once again, typical of their overall style. They select certain quotes and facts and omit others; remove at least some of the quotes and facts from their original context; coin phrases on the Rebbe's behalf and offer the most outlandish interpretations for things he did or did not do in relation to Israel. All in all, they manage to present a completely distorted image of his stance.

There are four undeniable facts, readily appreciable to any student of the Rebbe's teachings:

(a) The Rebbe did not accept the notion of the secular State of Israel[264] as the fulfillment of the Jewish people's destiny. He believed (as do for that matter 'religious Zionists') that the Torah and the Mitzvot are the life-line of the Jewish People, and that were the State to be established on the principles of Torah, its potential would have been far greater. In general, the Rebbe believed that one's material wellbeing does not operate in its own orbit, and is profoundly affected by one's spiritual welfare. All the more so with regard to the collective Jewish community in Israel; he was convinced that the overall spiritual health of the People was indispensable to the physical stability of their country; and most particularly, the safety and success of the country's soldiers may be positively affected by their religious conduct , and that of Jewish people everywhere [265].

(b) The Rebbe believed (as I assume do many religious Zionists) that inasmuch as secular Zionism offered people a substitute for tradi-

---

[263] See Heilman and Friedman pages 187-188. "In place of the Israeli army he would send his *shluchim* to do the work" (page 188).

[264] As envisaged in Theodor Herzl's *Altneuland* (Leipzeig, 1902).

[265] See, for example, *Igrot Kodesh* vol. 30, page 80, 131ff, 171 and 246.

tional Judaism and drew them away from the observance of the Mitz-vot, it posed a significant challenge to Torah Judaism[266].

(c) The Rebbe emphatically objected to the theology, popular amongst many religious Zionists, that the establishment of the State constituted 'the beginning of the Final Redemption'[267].

(d) Unlike virtually all Zionists he insisted on using the Biblical term *Eretz Yisrael* (the Land of Israel) rather than *Medinat Yisrael*, in or-der to assert that our relationship with, and our rights to, the Land are anchored in the Torah rather than on the Balfour declaration, the UN partition plan, or international consensus[268].

It is clear, therefore, that the Rebbe did not subscribe to classic Zi-onist ideology, whether Secular Zionism or Religious Zionism. Does this mean that, as Heilman and Friedman assert, the Rebbe "took what he could [from the State] to sustain Lubavitcher needs, but wherever possible he undermined the Zionist enterprise"?

Let us enumerate another four facts that are equally undeniable, and perhaps even more appreciable to any student of the Rebbe's teachings:

(a) The Rebbe believed that the entire Land of Israel belonged to the Jewish People and that those parts that were under the governance of the State of Israel should remain in Jewish hands.

(b) Inasmuch as the State secured a homeland for the Jewish People in the Holy Land, he considered it a blessing. Notwithstanding his con-

---

[266] See, for example, the Rebbe's letter in *Igrot Kodesh* vol. 15, pages 440-441.

[267] See, for example, the Rebbe's remarks in *Likuttei Sichot* vol. 5, page 149 note 51 and *Igrot Kodesh* vol. 5, page 121; vol. 10, pages 122 and 334; vol. 13, page 77; vol. 17, page 75.

[268] See the letters of the Rebbe in *Igrot Kodesh* vol. 16, pages 215-216; vol. 26, page 167ff.

I have only found one occasion in which **Rayatz** employs the term *Medinat Yisrael*. This is in a letter dated *Shushan Purim* 5709 (*Igrot Kodesh* vol. 14, pages 412-413):

"פילע פון אונזערע חב"ד פליקטלינגע שטראמען יעצט קיין מדינת ישראל פון די די. פי. קעמפּס און
אנדערע פלעצער אין אייראפע. די מדינת ישראל איז זייער אינטערעסירט אין די לאגע פון דיזע
אומגליקליכע אידישע פליטים ... די ישראל רעגירונג איז גרויט צו געבען איין טויזענד ישראל פונטען ...
נעמענדיג אין אנבאטראכט דאס דיזע חב"ד פליטים זיינען א חומר מיוחד און זייער ווינשענסווערט אלס
קאלאניסטן וועלכע וועלען זיין פון גרעסטען ווערט פאר די נייע מדינת ישראל, דאריבער האט אט די
רעגירונג פון ישראל אויסגעדריקט איהר אינטערעס און גרייטקייט צו העלפען עטאבלירען אזא חב"ד
קאלאניע ווי איך האב שוין אויבען דערמאנט".

cern about the secular nature of the State, he considered the establishment of a homeland in Israel as a miraculous, life-saving phenomenon;
a Divine gift[269] for the Jewish People[270]. He likewise considered the victories that the Israeli forces have enjoyed over the years as manifestations of special Providential and miraculous intervention, which call
for our acknowledgment and gratitude[271].

(c) He did whatever was in his power to support the infrastructure
of the State[272], and advance its success. He was concerned with the ag-

---

[269] The Rebbe was distressed by those who did not recognize the hand of G-d in all
these cataclysmic events. See, for example, *Igrot Kodesh* vol. 11, page 85 (letter dated
11th Iyar 5715) and vol. 25 page 257 (letter dated 5728).

[270] See, for example, the Rebbe's address on 11th Nissan 5736 (*Sichot Kodesh 5736*, vol.
2, page 53) regarding "the events of **1948**":

"דאָס איז געוואָען אַן ענין פון פיקוח נפשות, הצלה פון כו"כ אידן משעבוד צו אַ חירות בערך פון אַ שעבוד
שלפנ"ז, און ביי כו"כ, הצלה ממיתה לחיים".

[271] See, for example, the Rebbe's talks on 12th Tammuz 5727 (*Sichot Kodesh 5727* vol.
2, page 76); *Shabbat Parshat Pinchas* 5727 (*Sichot Kodesh* ibid. page 299); *Shabbat
Parshat Matot-Masei* 5727 (*Sichot Kodesh* ibid. page 307ff); *Shabbat Parshat Matot Masei*
5736 (*Sichot Kodesh 5736* vol. 2, page 444); 20th Menachem Av 5736 (*Sichot Kodesh*
ibid. page 125); *Simchat Torah* 5737 (*Sichot Kodesh 5737* vol. 1, page 172ff); 19th Kislev
5737 (*Sichot Kodesh* ibid. page 340ff).

Regarding the miracles of the Six Day war, see also *Igrot Kodesh* vol. 24, pages 341,
345, and 370; *Igrot Kodesh* vol. 26, page 483.

See also a letter of the Rebbe (dated 1974), in *The Letter and the Spirit* (page 282) in
which he discusses the miracles of the Yom Kippur war: "As a matter of fact, there
was no shortage of miracles, quite obvious ones, in the last war. The underlying
miracle, which has now been revealed, although not overly publicized, is the plain
fact of survival after the first few days of the war... The greatest miracle was that the
Egyptians stopped their invasion, for no good reason, only a few miles east of the
Canal. The obvious military strategy would have been to leave a few fortified
positions in the rear, then, with the huge army of 100,000 men, all armed to the
teeth, march deeper into Sinai, where at that point in time there was no organized
defense of any military consequence. This is something that cannot be explained in
the natural order of things, except as it is written, 'The dread of the Jews fell upon
them' [Esther 8:17] – in the face of their intelligence reports about the complete
unpreparedness of the Jews in Eretz Yisrael at that time...".

[272] Note also his concern for the welfare of the new immigrants and their
acclimatization in the country in a manner that would be beneficial both for
themselves and for Israel. See, for example, *Letters from the Lubavitcher Rebbe* vol. 4
page 127 (letter dated 24th Tammuz 5733).

ricultural[273], industrial and overall economic welfare of Israel[274]. He sought to promote its scientific achievements and enhance Israel's standing in the international community[275].

See also "To Israel's Labor Party, with Love", testimony of Rabbi Menachem Hacohen (former rabbi of Israel's Moshavim movement and the Histadrut), on Living Torah Disc 79, Program 315, My Encounter (http://www.chabad.org/1280192).

[273] The Rebbe followed the developments in this arena with attention to detail. See, for example, *The Letter and the Spirit* pages 251-252. See also his *Igrot Kodesh* vol. 19, pages 444-445.

His positive appraisal of the pioneers initiatives in the agricultural rejuvenation in Israel finds expression in his talk on the eighth day of Passover 5728 (*Sichot Kodesh 5728* vol. 2, page 83):

"אזוי אויך דאס וואס בזמן קיבוץ גליות וועט זיין אז מען וועט ברײַנגען אידן מירכתי צפון (יחזקאל לח, טז; שם לט, ב), וואס דאס וועט דאך זיין ערשט נאך בנין בית המקדש כפס"ד ברור של הרמב"ם (הל' מלכים פי"א ה"ד), **איז אבער אויך אין דעם פאראן דער ענין פון 'טוּעמי' חיים זכו', אז א חלק פון זיי זיינען ארויסגעגאנגען און געקומען אין ארץ ישראל זיך מתעסק זיין בעבודת אדמה** ... דערווײַלע שטייט מען טיף טיף אין גלות, עס איז מערניט וואס 'חשף הוי' את זרוע קדשו' (ישעי' נב, י) ..."

[274] See, for example, the Rebbe's remarks regarding the propriety of *aliyah* in a letter (dated 1981) published in *The Letter and the Spirit* page 324ff: "There must be a set of priorities as to what kind of *aliyah* should be concentrated on. Several basic factors must be taken into account: 1) That the new immigrant arriving in Eretz Yisrael should be able to contribute towards the development and well-being of Eretz Yisrael; and certainly not to be detrimental to it. 2) The new immigrant should be able to integrate into the economy of the land, and not add to the excessive burden already placed on it. 3) Even where the said conditions (1) and (2) are met, the gain of a new immigrant, or group of immigrants, should be weighed against the loss that their immigration from their present country will cause to the local Jewish community... Far too long have those who are concerned with *aliyah*, with all good intentions, considered only the immediate gain and ignored the loss in the longer run ... Needless to say, it is not enough to get someone to be an *oleh*; it is necessary to make sure, to the extent that this is possible, that the *oleh* will not, sooner or later, become a *yored*... Yet, it is a matter of record, that all too often *aliyah* activists have ignored this basic principle, either through wishful thinking or, more deplorably, setting up for themselves "quotas," to be fulfilled by all means, in order to justify and maintain their positions as successful recruiting agents".

See also "Turning the Wheels", testimony of Israeli industrialist, Efraim Illin, in Living Torah Disc 75, Program 300, My Encounter (http://www.chabad.org/therebbe/livingtorah/player_cdo/aid/1203590/jewish/Turning-the-Wheels.htm).

[275] See also *Letters from the Lubavitcher Rebbe* vol. 5, page 234 (letter dated 11th Shevat 5740).

He taught his followers (many of whom he sent to settle there[276]) to be loyal citizens of the State[277]; he instructed them to travel (whenever possible) with the Israeli Airline[278]; and at least on one occasion sent a personal delegate to offer the Rebbe's financial contribution to the Israeli Prime-Minister, which he had earmarked for *binyan ha-aretz* (the building of the land)[279].

Indeed, the Rebbe often advised Jews in the Diaspora to focus their investments in Israel[280].

(d) Most importantly: The Rebbe's passionate concern for Israel's security is indisputable[281]. He consistently expressed enormous recog-

---

[276] Incidentally, the Rebbe emphasized that *aliyah* (emigration) to geographical Israel (or even a temporary visit thereto) must be accompanied with an *aliyah* (elevation) in the behavior of the tourist or immigrant – as befitting the Holy Land. See also the letters of the Rebbe dated 18th Shevat, 16th Adar 1 5738 3rd and Tammuz 5722 published in *Letters from the Lubavitcher Rebbe* vol. 2, pages 195-197. See also *idem*, vol. 1 page 3 and vol. 4 page 41.

[277] See for example his address to the residents of *Kfar Chabad* 29th Tishrei 5729, *Sichot Kodesh 5729*, vol. 1 page 486 (with regard to the payment of taxes), and the letters of the Rebbe (dated Cheshvan 5745), published in *Heichal Menachem* vol. 1 (Kehot Publication Society: Jerusalem, 1994), page 158ff with regard to honesty and integrity in relation to army service.

[278] See letter of the Rebbe's secretariat published in *The Letter and the Spirit* page 244: "As a matter of fact, far from discouraging Jews from traveling via El Al, the Rebbe favors this line as evidenced by the fact that this year too, the Lubavitcher Chasidim coming to visit the Rebbe from Kfar Chabad made their round trip via El Al". See also the Rebbe's letter to Rabbi Shlomo Yosef Zevin dated 23rd Tammuz 5716, *Igrot Kodesh* vol. 13, page 293:

"מובן שנסיעתם נסתדרה שבכל מקום האפשרי יסעו דוקא באל על וכדרז"ל עה"פ קנה מיד עמיתך".

[279] See http://shturem.net/index.php?section=artdays&id=1321 from the diary of Rabbi Mordechai Mentlik (the Rosh Yeshivah of the central Lubavitch Yeshivah in New York) 18th Shevat 5736:

"להיום בשעה 4:30 אחרי הצהריים נקבעה הפגישה עם ראש הממשלה בבנין הכנסת ... אמרתי שהרבי שליט"א שלח על ידי שיק על שם ראש הממשלה המיועד במיוחד לבנין הארץ. ישנם הרי ענינים כמו הגנה וכדומה, אבל שיק זה מיועד לבנין הארץ ... כל מה שדובר כאן הוקלט, וכן יש הרבה תמונות".

[280] See, for example, "Israel, the Safest Investment" on Living Torah Disc 24, Program 96, Eye to Eye (http://www.chabad.org/394470).

[281] See most recently, *Faithful and Fortified: The inside story of the Rebbe's involvement in Israel's security, as told by its defense and government leaders* vol. 1 (Conversations with Defense and Intelligence leaders, including Efrayim Halevi, Mossad Chief; IDF Major General Yossi Ben Chanan, Commander, Armored Corps IAF Brigadier

nition for the role of the Israel Defense Force. He stated that those who serve in the Israeli army perform a great *mitzvah*[282], and gave his utmost support for those who took part in the many military operations carried out by its soldiers. He spoke with deep admiration and appreciation about the courage and bravery of the soldiers[283] and accorded a special privilege to those who were wounded in their military capacity[284]. [It was, to a large degree, his deep concern for the welfare of the soldiers that inspired him to encourage them and those who care for their welfare to observe the *mitzvah* of *Tefillin* in particular[285]].

General Ran-Ronen Pecker, Commander, Tel Nof Airbase), Jewish Educational Media: Brooklyn, 2009. See also *Faithful and Fortified* vol. 2, Israel's Journalists (2010).

[282] He believed, however, that Yeshivah students should be exempted from such services. See, for example, his *Igrot Kodesh* vol. 20, pages 317-318. [Cf. Rabbi Moshe Feinstein, *Igrot Moshe, Yoreh Deah*, vol. 4 (Jerusalem, 1996), no. 33:

"אף שעניין צבא ההגנה הוא עניין גדול, אבל עניין לימוד התורה ללומדי תורה עוד יותר גדול גם מלהגין על המדינה ... ומי שלומד בישיבה גדולה ועוסק בתורה פטור מעניייני חיובי הצבא, ולכן ודאי מי שיש לו תשוקה ללימוד התורה ולהעשות ולהעשות גדול בתורה ובהוראה וביראת שמים, יש לו לילך לישיבות הגדולות, ויהי' ברכה לכלל ישראל והגנה גדולה לכל ישראל"].

[283] See, for example, the Rebbe's address on the 20th Menachem Av 5736 (*Sichot Kodesh 5736* vol. 2, pages 625-626).

See also the letter of the Rebbe (dated 1976) published in *The Letter and the Spirit* page 296: "Every Jew is grateful to, and admires the *mesirat nefesh* of, the brave rescuers" involved in the Entebbe campaign.

[284] See the Rebbe's special address delivered on the 23rd Menachem Av 5736 (*Sichot Kodesh* 5736, vol. 2, page 633ff). See also *Igrot Kodesh* vol. 29, pages 37-38; 62-63.

[285] See, for example, *Likuttei Sichot* vol. 6, page 271ff.

The importance of observing the mitzvah of Tefillin for anyone drafted in army service was already underscored by Rayatz in his *Igrot Kodesh* vol. 7, page 80 (letter dated 15th Tevet 5703):

"די מצוה פון לייגען תפילין, שטייט אין ספרים אז חוץ דעם וואס דאס איז א מצוה איז דאס אויך א שמירה. עס איז פון דער גרעסטער וויכטיגקייט פאר דער שמירה און הצלחה פון די זעלנער זיי זאלען פון דעם וויסען זיי זאלען לייגען תפילין יעדן וואכנדיגען טאג און האבן דעם דעם גרעסטן ערפאלג מיט א אמת'ן זיער".

See also Rayatz, *Igrot Kodesh* vol. 6, pages 71 and 72; vol. 8, page 527.

It is noteworthy that many senior non-Chabad Rabbis were supportive of the Rebbe's Tefillin campaign. See, for example, the documents reproduced in A. Y. Chananel, *Nesiei Chabad u Venei Doram* (Kfar Chabad 1972) pages 125–133.

For facsimiles of the correspondence between Rabbi Yitzchak Hutner (1906-1980) and the Rebbe regarding some aspects of the Tefillin Campaign (in which R. Hutner also expresses his support for the campaign and disassociates himself from the

In the context of the Six Day War, which according to Heilman and Friedman the Rebbe approached as an opportunist seeking to "claim the victory as his", the Rebbe actually made the statement (widely reported in the Israeli Press[286], albeit omitted from the authors' study) that the soldiers who fought in the Israeli army, putting their lives at risk for the security of the People of Zion, attained unparalleled merit![287]

His position on territorial concessions was based on his opinion that such compromises would lead, not to a lasting peace, but to increased bloodshed[288]. The Rebbe considered such concessions as ill-advised, dangerous and constituting a security threat to the population of Israel akin to *pikuach nefesh* - the hallachic designation of a life-threatening danger[289]. It was for this reason, and because of his con-

---

Rebbe's detractors), see Rabbi Shalom Dovber Levin, *Treasures from the Chabad Library* [The Central Chabad Lubavitch Library and Archive Center] (Kehot Publication Society: Brooklyn, 2009), Hebrew pagination, pages 88-97.

[286] See, for example, Gershon Jacobson in *Yediot Achronot* 24th July 1967 under the title:

"הרבי מלובאביץ': גדולה זכותם של לוחמי צה"ל מלומדי תורה".

[287] See the Rebbe's public addresses on 13 Tammuz and Shabbat *Parshat Masei* 5727 (*Sichot Kodesh 5727* vol. 2, pages 298 – 299 and page 306ff). In these addresses the Rebbe cited the famous teaching of the Talmud (Sanhedrin 49a) to the effect that were it not for those who are engaged in the study of the Torah, the military enterprises would not have achieved success; and conversely, were it not for the generals and the soldiers on the battlefield, no one would be able to study Torah. Nevertheless, he said, it was only the warriors who had participated in the battle in the literal sense of the word who had achieved the status and merit described by Maimonides in his *Mishneh Torah, Hilchot Melachim* 7:15. See also the Rebbe's *Igrot Kodesh* vol. 24, pages 404-405.

[288] See, for example, The Rebbe and Rabbi Jakobovits: 'A Correspondence between the Rebbe and Chief Rabbi Immanuel Jakobovits after the Six Day War', in Peter Kalms, Guidance from the Rebbe: Personal Recollections 1961-1993 (SHAMIR Publishing House: Jerusalem 2001) page 131ff.

[289] See also S.D. Wolpo, *Da'at Torah be-Inyanei ha-Matzav be-Eretz HaKodesh* (3rd edition, privately published: Kiryat Gat, 1981), esp. chapter 7 (page 89ff).

For a particularly impassioned and in-depth discussion concerning the repercussions of the Camp David Accords, the reader is referred to the Rebbe's hour-long public address on the 10th Kislev 5741-1980 (Sichah 5), at http://www.chabad.org/therebbe/sichoskodesh.htm

cerns for Israel's economy, that he was so adamantly opposed to the Camp David agreement to give the Sinai desert to Egypt.

These positions of the Rebbe were hardly ever a secret. He expressed them clearly and elaborately in numerous public addresses and in communications with Israeli leaders, and they were widely reported in the Israeli and diaspora anglo-Jewish media.

[All of this was apparently lost on Friedman and Heilman who perform a remarkable *volte face* when they invoke the Rebbe's position on territorial compromise. They matter-of-factly state: "As for Sadat's desire for the return of Sinai, the Rebbe readily gave his blessing for Israeli leaders to broker a deal, as he considered it devoid of religious and redemptive meaning"[290]].

Finally, a point to consider:

Throughout the years, the Rebbe received correspondence from, and was frequently visited by, senior officials in the Israeli government and Israel Defense Force. They came to meet with the Rebbe seeking his wise counsel on the widest range of issues affecting the State, including matters of diplomacy, economy, military, education, immigration, housing, etc. The visitors included Israel's Presidents and Prime Ministers (five of Israel's Prime Ministers – Menachem Begin, Yitzchak Rabin, Shimon Peres, Ariel Sharon, and Benjamin Netanyahu – visited the Rebbe in Brooklyn at various stages of their careers). In addition, there was a steady stream of visiting military and intelligence leaders, as well as ministers and Knesset members from the entire gamut of the Israeli political spectrum.

Moreover, these were not the typical political vote-getting meetings, but genuine consultations. These dignitaries saw the Rebbe as a repository of authentic Jewish wisdom combined with an abiding love and dedication to the welfare of Israel and its citizens that was untainted by partisan politics[291].

---

[290] Heilman and Friedman page 212. For obvious reasons they offer no source for this idea.

[291] In July of 1977 then Prime Minister Menachem Begin visited with the Rebbe. He spoke to members of the media: "I have come to … ask for and get from him his blessings before I go to Washington to meet with President Carter… Rabbi

Is it conceivable that all these ardently Zionist Israeli leaders would expend considerable time and effort to seek out the Rebbe's guidance if they thought for a moment that he had "a belligerent attitude toward the Zionist state" or that "wherever possible he undermined the Zionist enterprise"?!

As stated from the outset, the Rebbe's position regarding the State of Israel was nuanced, and it is beyond the scope of this essay to even attempt a full-scale appraisal of his multi-faceted teachings on this topic. However, I presume that the above will suffice to wean the thinking reader off of Heilman and Friedman's projection, according to which the Rebbe adopted an attitude of 'use and abuse' towards the Zionist State and resorted to cheap opportunism to 'usurp' the achievements of the State and its Defense Forces and attribute all its successes, military and otherwise, to himself and his chasidim.

6. Conclusion

I could continue with the endless task of demolishing one claim after another, but I hope that given the prototypical examples I have provided, it is no longer necessary for me to dissect the untold number of totally unfounded allegations and insinuations that Heilman and Friedman have woven their 'biography' around. Those who have spare time on their hands, and want to explore all their accusations and gratuitous insults, will discover themselves that neither history nor sociology is the hallmark of this biography. If they have made any insightful observations or written any scholarly sentences in this context, these are over-shadowed by the pervasive under-current of the volume, namely the sport of character assassination, a hobby which both Heilman and Friedman have proven themselves to be keen practitioners of, if not celebrated experts.

Schneerson ... is a great lover of the House of Israel. He has shown his deep sentiment and love for our children"

We get a hint at the significant nature of these meetings from Begin's response to a reporter's question about his ninety-minute audience with the Rebbe. Begin said: "This is not my first meeting with the Rabbi; we have met many, many times before. There is an old custom between us for many years: Whatever I say to the Rabbi and whatever he says to me is confidential and remains between us."

Section IV

1. Did the Rebbe Deny His Mortality?

One of the unsavory characteristics that Heilman and Friedman attribute to the Rebbe is an alleged obsession with power. Thus statements that the Rebbe made that illustrate his true humility and awareness of his human weaknesses, remain for the most part, unacknowledged. On the other hand, any turn of phrase that he said (selected from amongst tens of thousands of pages of transcripts), or that was said about him, that could be interpreted as boasting of divine-like independence, is seized and exploited with great excitement. Apparently, when it suits them, the authors are willing to embrace even hagiographic tales as admissible evidence.

Thus for example, they tell us that the Rebbe's wife once said: "He has no fear of pains". They then interpret the saying: "that is, he believed he could ignore his mortality"[292]. When, however, one consults the source they provide for the Rebbetzen's statement[293], it becomes readily apparent that their interpretation is demonstrably wrong.

One of the Rebbe's aides asked the Rebbetzen if he was suffering a lot from the physical pains he was experiencing. The Rebbetzen responded: "My husband is not afraid of pain; he is afraid of Rosh Hashanah" (=the Day of Judgment). The idea she wished to convey is that 'he can cope with a bit of pain; what really weighs on his mind are his concerns about his spiritual preparations for the holy day of Rosh Hashanah'. By omitting half the quote, Heilman and Friedman were able to invest the saying with a new meaning, one that suited their thesis perfectly but was far removed from its original intent.

Time and again segments of statements that could reflect a nobility of spirit are excised from their original context and subjected to a goal-oriented hermeneutic that turns them on their head and contributes to the furtherance of the biographers' agenda.

---

[292] Heilman and Friedman page 209.

[293] *Yemei Melech* vol. 3, page 1264.

Once they have 'established' the Rebbe's reluctance to acknowledge his human limitations, they are well positioned to psychoanalyze his messianic yearnings and their attendant consequences.

Heilman and Friedman, who pay much attention to the Rebbe's messianic impulse, believe that it was fueled, in part, by an internal psychological dynamic. Plainly stated, they argue that the Rebbe was reluctant to acknowledge his mortality and the finite nature of his power. In their words:

> This growing insistence on the imminence of the Messiah was also a denial of death. Ernest Becker has argued that to deny death is at its root 'to deny one's lack of control over events' and to reject any feelings of powerlessness or impotence in the face of reality. The suppression of awareness of impending death, Becker explains, plays a crucial role in keeping us functioning. The messianic campaign accomplished this both for the Rebbe and for his chasidim[294].

The denial syndrome was, in their opinion, compounded by the Rebbe's "hubris". In their words:

> 'Hubris' as Ernest Becker has reminded us, 'means forgetting where the real source of power lies and imagining that it is in oneself'. It tends to grow particularly in one who lives in an isolated human consciousness, a condition that seems to define the situation in which the aging leader, bereft of wife, family, and intimate friends, whose followers saw him as a messiah, increasingly found himself[295].

Whatever one makes of these psycho-dynamic theories, they are totally irrelevant to the Rebbe, because it was precisely when the Rebbe became "bereft of wife, family, and intimate friends" that he was actively preparing for his death more than ever before.

Once again, Heilman and Friedman subject their readers to an astounding disregard of well-documented and readily available evi-

---

[294] Heilman and Friedman page 220.

[295] Heilman and Friedman pages 228-229.

dence which decisively contradicts their depiction of the Rebbe. Seeking support in the psychological musings of Earnest Becker, they opt for unsubstantiated leaps of fancy, rather than availing themselves to the truth that is plainly within sight.

During the first week of mourning after the passing of his wife, Rebbetzen Moussia Schneerson, the Rebbe summoned Rabbi Chaim Yehuda Krinsky (a member of his secretariat), and informed him that he wanted to write a will. The will, which is on public record and was subsequently published[296], was executed by the Rebbe, witnessed and notarized. It reads as follows:

> The foregoing, consisting of 2 pages, including this page, the first page of which was initiated prior to the execution hereof by the Testator, MENACHEM MENDEL SCHNEERSON, was signed, published and declared as and for his Last Will and Testament in our presence and hearing, and we, at his request.
>
> I, MENACHEM MENDEL SCHNEERSON, of Kings County, New York, hereby make, publish and declare this to be my Last Will and Testament. FIRST: I revoke all wills and codicils previously made by me.
>
> SECOND: I request that my debts, my funeral expenses (including, but not limited to, the cost of a suitable monument), and my administration expenses be paid as promptly as shall be practicable.
>
> THIRD: The balance of my property, real, personal and mixed (of whatever kind and wherever situated, including, but not limited to, any books, manuscripts, objects d'art and all other property intended for personal or household use), in which I shall have any interest at the time of my death, and all property over or with respect to which I shall have any power of appointment, remaining after provision for the payments of my debts and my funeral and administration expenses, is referred to as my "Residuary Estate."

[296] Binyamin Lipkin, *Cheshbono Shel Olam* (Machon HaSefer, Lod 2000), pages 60-63.

FOURTH: I devise and bequeath my Residuary Estate to AGUDAS CHASSIDEI CHABAD (which presently has an office at 770 Eastern Parkway, Brooklyn, New York).

FIFTH: A. I appoint RABBI YEHUDA KRINSKY as my executor.

B. In the event of RABBI KRINSKY's death or his failure or refusal to serve as executor for any reason, I appoint RABBI ABRAHAM I. SHEMTOV and RABBI SHOLOM M. SIMPSON, to serve singly and in the order named, as alternate or successor Executor.

C. Each alternate or successor Executor shall have all of the rights and powers, and all of the privileges and immunities hereby granted to my original Executor.

D. I direct that no bond or other security shall at any time be required in any jurisdiction or any of the persons named as Executor for the faithful performance of his duties.

SIXTH: In the administration of my estate, my Executor shall have all the powers granted by law and all necessary powers.

I have executed this will this 14th day of February, 1988.

Menachem Mendel Schneerson

Is this the testament of a man who cannot face up to his mortality[297]?

---

[297] **In their response to my original review essay on the Seforim blog, the authors write:** "The matter of the Rebbe's signed will plays a large part in undermining what Rabbi Rapoport sees as our claim of the Rebbe's seeing himself as immortal. No doubt that when his wife died, this event made him aware of his own mortality in a way that nothing before had. It was so strong, we are told (*sic*), that during Shivah he met with his attorney and signed the will. But Rabbi Rapoport assumes that on the matter of his mortality the Rebbe was single minded and clear, as the will shows. We suggest the Rebbe's attitude toward mortality and messianism was far more complex and ambivalent... Rabbi Rapoport and his supporters have taken the very Rebbe they so revere and have reduced him to a simple rather than a complex Figure. We prefer a far more complex explanation that suggests that the Rebbe was torn on the essential matter of what messianism meant, and what his role in it was."

To which I responded:

Moreover, not long after the Rebbe got up from the seven days of mourning for his wife[298], he gave, on a Saturday night, an extraordinary speech which was broadcast worldwide to all his followers. This keynote address (recordings and transcripts of which are published and widely available[299]) was dedicated in its entirety to the subject of authority in Chabad communities upon his incapacitation and demise. He delineated a system whereby questions of personal nature should be addressed to mentors (*mashpi'im*), rabbis and empathetic friends etc. (depending on the nature of the question), and questions of

---

"a) If indeed you had wanted to project a more complex view you would not have failed to mention such **hard documents**. Why would you fill pages and notes with rumor conjecture and manipulative interpretations to prove that the Rebbe thought that he was not subject to mortal failings, and you omit even the slightest reference to such published documents? Is this the way you illustrate your 'complex' approach?

b) Even now you seem un-willing to accept that, in **addition** to the signed will, there are other documents and public messages (such as the keynote address he gave regarding authority after his passing, recordings and transcripts of which are published and widely available) that demonstrate the Rebbe's **ongoing** and **unambiguous** recognition of his mortality. Why?

[In case you are referring to the idea that after the arrival of the Messiah and the Resurrection of the Dead, G-d will grant mortal beings eternal lives, this of course has nothing to do with the Rebbe; it is a traditional and widely accepted Torah doctrine.]"

[298] It is noteworthy that during the same week of mourning, when someone brought up the subject of the forthcoming *Simchat Torah*, the Rebbe said that he anticipated that the Messiah would arrive before that festival. [See the Rebbe's remarks to Rabbi Moshe Rotenberg (Rosh Yeshivah of Gur) published in *VeHachai Yiten El Libo* (Va'ad Hanochos b'Lahak: Brooklyn: 1988) page 96, and in *Torat Menachem-Menachem Tziyon* (above note 124), vol. 1, page 227]. This demonstrates that even when the Rebbe expressed himself about the imminence of Moshiach's arrival in terms that would seem to indicate absolute certainty, he was in actually acutely aware that nothing is guaranteed!

[299] See http://www.chabad.org/therebbe/article_cdo/aid/554605/jewish/3-Adar-5748-Sicha.htm

See http://www.chabad.org/554605

A recording of this *sichah* can be heard on http://www.chabad.org/therebbe/sichoskodesh.htm

115

a communal nature should be presented before a panel of three chasidic rabbis who should constitute the final authority in such matters[300].

Neither the Rebbe's legal will that related to the intimate details of his burial nor the Rebbe's public will that clearly illustrates the Rebbe's concern for times in which he will no longer be available to guide his flock are mentioned by Heilman and Friedman. Indeed, between the passing of his wife and the devastating stroke that he suffered in 1992 the Rebbe was engaged in a host of preparatory activities and assignments related to his departure from this world.

The details of these preparations are described in detail in a published and available volume entitled *Cheshbono shel Olam*[301] which contains much of the documentary evidence for all the above. Even a perfunctory glance at the material in this volume will suffice to convince the skeptic that the Rebbe acknowledged and confronted his own mortality in a manner befitting the humble and dignified person he was[302].

---

[300] According to Heilman and Friedman, after the Rebbe's passing "Lubavitcher Hasidim refused to formally make the transition to a new leader, for there was no alternative for them – after all, the Rebbe had promised his would be the first generation of the final redemption. To ensure continuity, they simply denied the finality of death and continued to see Rabbi Menachem Mendel as their Rebbe" (Heilman and Friedman page 14).

This is sheer nonsense. There is no question that if the Rebbe would have had a son, or even a disciple who was worthy of succeeding him, he would have been appointed as Rebbe, and this would have been the best way to "ensure continuity". Alas, this was not to be.

I am inclined to agree with those who say that the Rebbe himself could not identify anyone on the horizon that would be able to stand in his shoes, and it is for that reason that he sought to consolidate the administrative side of the establishment and instructed his Chasidim to follow the leadership of rabbinic mentors and courts rather than appoint a Rebbe.

[301] Binyamin Lipkin, *Cheshbono Shel Olam* (above note 296).

[302] One wonders what Heilman and Friedman would say about the 'haughtiness' and perceived 'immortality' of the very humble Rabbi Moshe Feinstein, if they were ever to discover that (a) when he had a heart attack he would not stop in the middle of a Torah lecture or allow the doctors to examine him until he had finished his lesson; (b) he anticipated serving as a member of the Great Sanhedrin (a significant factor in his dental treatment!), and (c) he did not leave instruction with regard to

Those who wanted to see this at the time, and there were few who did, could detect signs of withdrawal and even disengagement. When he was asked questions he referred the questioners, ever-increasingly, to rabbis, mentors, friends and doctors. As *Cheshbono shel Olam* accounts in great detail, he designated substantial time to 'clearing his desk', both literally and figuratively. He spent many hours organizing books and papers, letters and documents. He consigned some to his drawers and bookshelves, some for various archives, others for the library and others still for the incinerator[303].

He likewise issued directives for the restating and amending of the corporate documents that dictated the legal constitution and administrative bodies of his umbrella organizations, a critical procedure in the event that his life-long dream did not come to fruition, that is, if the Messiah did not come in his time – as much as he yearned for his arrival.

All the above information, which is easily verifiable, gives lie to those with fertile imaginations who, with the help of misquotes and half-quotes, assert that the Rebbe spoke with an omniscient and omnipotent confidence in his 'power' to save the cosmos, and that he somehow considered himself immortal.

---

his desired place of burial because he expected that he would not die before the arrival of the Messiah when all Jews would merit immortality.

See the biographical tract entitled *Man Malchei Rabanan* published at the beginning of the eighth volume of his *Igrot Moshe* (above note 78) which contains the following information:

"באמצע דרשת שבת הגדול תש"מ לקה רבינו באיזו הפרעה בליבו. הוא החוויר כסיד, אבל המשיך את הדרשה עד תומה" (עמוד 29).

"מאוחר יותר הושתל בליבו קוצב לב – רק לאחרי שהתברר לו כי אין בהשתלה זו משום הטלת מום בגופו שתפסלנו מלכהן בסנהדרין לכשיבוא גואל צדק במהרה ... רבנו הקפיד שלא יוטל בגופו מום כדי שיהי' ראוי לישב בסנהדרין. בשנת תשל"ט הי' צורך לעקור כמה משיניו ולהתקין לו שינים תותבות. הוא דרש שישאירו בפיו לפחות שתי שיניים כדי שלא יהי' בגדר מי שניטלו שיניו (בכורות מד, ע"א) שהוא בעל מום משום מראית העין" (שם עמוד 29 ועמוד 34).

"רבינו לא הותיר כל צוואה מפורשת באשר למקום קבורתו, ומהתנהגותו עלה תמיד בטחון שיזכה לקבל פני מלך המשיח" (שם עמוד 35).

[303] See *Cheshbono shel Olam* chapter 9, page 135ff.

Yet, simultaneous to the preparations for his passing, the Rebbe intensified his prayers to G-d Almighty[304] and his endeavors to do (and encourage others to do) whatever it is possible for people to do so that we may merit G-d's redemption with the coming of Messiah. He spoke incessantly about his yearnings for the redemption of the Jewish people and of all mankind, but his focus was always on the pragmatic: what good deeds could be added to generate more merit and tilt the balance of the scales in our favor so that we may enter the utopian era in which peace shall reign and 'death will be swallowed up forever'.

Even during these twilight years, as his physical health declined and his sight was partially impaired by the growth of cataracts, his diabetes accelerated and his loneliness became increasingly painful, the Rebbe continued to do whatever he could do for the benefit of his followers and his people. He still stood for hours on end every Sunday, offering blessings and words of encouragement for the multitudes who sought his advice, support and intercessory prayers. In a sense he sublimated his personal suffering by giving more to others.

2. On the Meaning of the Word *Mamash* in the Chabad Lexicon

In chapter seven the authors describe the honours President Ronald Reagan bestowed upon the Rebbe on the occasion of his eighty-first birthday (in the year 1983). They then write:

> When he accepted these honours from President Reagan via satellite, he assured his followers, 'Our Messiah is coming soon'[305]. Then he pointedly added the word **mamesh**, which

---

[304] See Rabbi Meir Leibush Weiser, the Malbim (1809-1879), *Chazon Yeshayahu* on Isaiah 63:6-7 that it is G-d's will that the righteous in every generation pray passionately and incessantly for the Redemption:

"כל היום וכל הלילה תמיד לא יחשו ... המזכירים את ה' אל דמי לכם, אל תשתקו רגע רק תצעקו ותזכירו אותו וגם ואל תתנו דמי לו, בל תניחו אותו שהוא ישתוק ובל תשתקו עד יכונן ... ועד שישים את ירושלים לתהלה ולשם והשומרים האלה הם הנביאים והצדיקים שבכל דור".

[305] In the endnotes they refer (without providing any bibliographical details) to a talk delivered by the Rebbe a year earlier (in 1982) on the 22nd Nissan (5742). Perhaps they meant to refer to the talk he delivered on the 22nd Nissan (which, by the way, is the eighth day of Pesach 5743 (1983). I have explored that talk again, and I have found no such assurances.

means 'in fact'. His Hasidim interpreted this last word as an acronym for Menachem Mendel Schneerson and as a hint that he would reveal himself soon[306]. The Rebbe knew this was their interpretation, and afterward he used the phrase often, once adding that he meant *mamesh*, 'with all its interpretations'.

They do not cite any sources for their claims and I therefore assume that they must have gleaned these ideas from anecdotal evidence or hearsay. Were they to have had an even peripheral familiarity with the sources, they would have realised how outlandish these claims are.

Let me explain:

The expression '*mamash*' is found hundreds of times in Chabad discourses and books, from the writings of the founder of the movement and throughout. It is a frequent expression in the writings and talks of Rayatz (see, for example, the degree of his usage of this term in his *Igrot Kodesh* and *Sefer HaSichot*) and he used it particularly when he expressed his fervent prayers for, and confidence in, the imminent arrival of the Messiah.

It occurs thousands of times in the talks and writings of the Rebbe, starting long before the Rebbe's ascendency to leadership (see, for example, the degree of his usage of this term in the first three volumes of his *Igrot Kodesh*), and long before any chasidim could have possibly dreamt of the acronym for 'Menachem Mendel Schneerson'.

A perfunctory inspection of his *Igrot Kodesh* as well as his *Likuttei Sichot* and *Sichot Kodesh* (the unedited transcripts of the Rebbe's public addresses) will reveal that, just like his predecessors, he also used this term in relation to a whole variety of issues, especially with regard to prayers for the redemption. One only needs to listen to a few recordings of the Rebbe's discourses[307] to be convinced of the frequency of his usage of this term throughout his leadership and to realise that it did

---

[306] The authors cite no source for this, and whilst there may have occasionally been a few radicals who dabbled in 'acronyms' of this style, this was by no means a mainstream trend.

[307] Recordings of all the above talks can be found in http://www.chabad.org/therebbe/sichoskodesh.htm.

not creep in to his vernacular in the year 1983, as the authors have suggested.

Most importantly, the term *mamash* 'with all its interpretations' "ממש עם כל הפירושים", was used by the Rebbe specifically in contexts that could not possibly have anything to do with the above-mentioned acronym. See for example, the Rebbe's public address on 6th Tishrei 5745[308] in which he said[309]:

מכיון שכל יהודי הוא 'חלק אלקה ממעל ממש' (לקו"א תניא רפ"ב) **עם כל הפירושים ד'ממש'** הרי כאשר לומד תורה צריך להיות ניכר גלוי לעיני בשר הענין ד'הלא כה דברי כאש' (ירמי' כג, כט).

See also the Rebbe's address on 19th Ellul 5748[310] in which he said:

וכל יהודי מקבל **כתיבה וחתימה טובה** לשנה טובה ומתוקה תיכף ומיד ממש **עם כל הפירושים** ובהצלחה הכי גדולה.

3. The Rebbe's Messianic Fervor

Yet what are we to make of the Rebbe's references that the Messiah would come in his/our day, and the insinuations that some, including Heilman and Friedman, saw in his talks that he, or his late father-in-law[311], would be the Messiah?[312] It is beyond the scope of this essay to

---

[308] *Hitva'aduyot* 5745 vol. 1 (Lahak Hanochos: Brooklyn, 1985), page 140.

[309] As the editors of *Hitva'aduyot* (ibid.) note, the phrase 'with all the meanings of the word *mamash*' probably refers to an explanation the Rebbe had given two days beforehand, in his public address on 4th Tishrei (the Fast of Gedaliah) 5745 (*Hitva'aduyot* ibid. page 91), wherein he said (in explaining the virtues of giving charity to the poor):

"מכיון ששטר זה הוא באופן של 'ממש', שטר גשמי שיכולים למששו בידים, ובפרט שע"ז נפעל העניין ד'החיית את נפש העני' כאשר העני מחליף את השטר וקונה בו דבר גשמי ממש, הרי זה פועל וממשיך את ברכותיו של הקב"ה גם באופן ד'ממש' היינו שהמשכת הברכות מלמעלה למטה היא ללא כל שינוי ח"ו ברכה בלי מיצרים הנמשכת למטה מטה בטוב הנראה והנגלה בכל המצטרך".

[310] *Hitva'aduyot* 5748 vol. 4 (Lahak Hanochos: Brooklyn, 1991), page 300.

[311] On page 204 Heilman and Friedman write: "The ultimate promise, of course, was the fulfillment of a plan for redemption, in which the Moshiach would lead all Jews into the Promised Land. And who would that be? As he would repeat **always** (emphasis added), it would be none other than 'his honor, my teacher, my father-in-law', the man to whom he was inextricably linked and whom he could channel, 'will lead us to the **complete and true** redemption'. In the endnotes (chapter 7, note 16) they refer to "Hisvadus Parshat Shlach 5710 (1950), 106".

In actuality, on that occasion (as on most occasions that the Rebbe mentioned his father-in-law in connection with the Messiah) the Rebbe said that his predecessor:

"will lead us **towards the righteous Messiah**". The substantial difference between the Rebbe's words and those which Heilman and Friedman put into his mouth hardly needs to be explicated.

In a similar vein, on page 215, Heilman and Friedman recount how the Rebbe once admonished a chasid who publicly called upon the Rebbe to "reveal himself"; The Rebbe responded: "Do not talk like that for you will force me to leave the room". This report is essentially true; however the authors place this exchange in "1970 or even earlier", suggesting explicitly that in his later years the Rebbe encouraged such talk. This is blatantly false, because although such an episode did occur in the 1970s it occurred a second time in **1991** in the height of the messianic anticipation (only months before the Rebbe suffered a terrible stroke). See the Rebbe's talk on Shabbat Parshat Noach 5752, *Sichot Kodesh 5752* (Va'ad Kitvei Kodesh: Brooklyn, 1993), vol. 1, page 259ff.

312 Parenthetically, it is a shame that Heilman and Friedman do not mention the Rebbe's categorical position regarding the identity of the Messiah which is available even in English. See, for example, *The Letter and the Spirit* page 273, where the Rebbe quotes Maimonides' formulation: ["*There will arise a king from the House of David, studying the Torah and practicing the mitzvot like his father David, according to the Written Torah and the Oral Torah, and he will induce it all the Jewish people to walk in its ways and strengthen its repair, and he will battle the battles of G-d - it may then be assumed that he is Mashiach. If he did so and was successful and built the sanctuary in its place, and gathered the dispersed of Israel - then he is Mashiach with certainty* (Rambam, Hil. Melachim, ch. 11(end)], and deduces from it: "We see clearly that **even after** he induces **all** of the Jewish people to walk in the path of Torah, etc., it may only be *assumed* that he is Mashiach, but it is **not yet certain**, and it could in fact turn out that he is not. In other words, there is still a possibility that even this development will not necessarily spell the end of the *Galut*. As a matter of a fact, the Rambam mentions in the previous *halacha* the fact that there was a time in Jewish history when it appeared that Mashiach *had* arrived, in the person of Shimon ben Kuziba, yet it later became quite clear that he was not. Only when – as the Rambam says – he will build the Sanctuary in its place and will gather the dispersed of Israel, **only then** will it be certain that he is Mashiach beyond all doubt".

The Rebbe also dwelt on Maimonides' messianic criteria in a number of public addresses. He always insisted that Maimonides, who was writing in a legal framework, meant for these criteria to be understood in their literal sense, and that they constitute the ultimate authority on this matter. Moreover, the Rebbe stated that in addition to providing qualifications on whose basis the real Messiah may be identified, Maimonides sought to provide the Jewish people with foolproof ammunition against mistaken messianic claimants.

We see this, for example, in the Rebbe's insistence that Maimonides' phrase, "If there arise a king," refers, as it always does in Maimonides' code, to a monarch in the conventional sense of the term. The word king (*melech*) connotes a person who enjoys recognized autocratic authority over the Jewish people (albeit one who has

provide a comprehensive answer to this question, but there are two important points that must be taken into account and that will hopefully put things into a reasonable perspective.

Firstly, the Rebbe was an heir to the commonly-held traditional beliefs: (a) that life in 'exile' (as in contrast to redemption) is an untenable situation that had to be rectified[313]; (b) that the Jewish People are engaged in an ongoing and ever-accelerating journey toward bringing the entire world to a state of redemption; (c) that, in recent generations, the

---

not yet been appointed by the Sanhedrin), and who wields the political and military power to fight battles and to coerce noncompliant Jews to observe the Torah's commandments. Moreover, he prevails upon Israel (*ve-yakuf kol Yisroel*) to walk in the way of the Torah, namely by using his monarchical power to coerce recalcitrant Jews into abiding by Jewish law. The Messiah will thus succeed in bringing all Jews, willingly or not, back to full observance. Only once this has been accomplished will the king proceed to the next stage, namely fighting the wars of the Lord — i.e., bodily battles fought against Israel's foes, including the physical wars that he will fight against the people of Amalek. [The Rebbe noted that this may also include battles against anti-Jewish elements from within, but, he hastened to add, "this is merely a *phshetel*," i.e., a non-literal interpretation of the term]. If and when a king fulfills all of the above criteria — and only then — it is possible that he may in truth be the awaited Messiah.

Time and again the Rebbe reiterated that this was Maimonides' final word on the matter, and any claims to the messianic mantle that do not meet the latter's requirements **in their literal sense** must be vigorously rejected. On occasion, he added that, to date, there is no one that fits the bill. Clearly, then, according to the Rebbe's own stated position on the matter, he could not have entertained the idea that he himself was the Maimonidean messiah incarnate.

For all the above see the Rebbe's discourses dated 12th Tammuz 5727 (1967); Eighth Day of Passover 5730 (1970); Shabbat Parshat Vayeshev 5734 (1973); 13th Tishrei 5736 (1975) and Motza'ei Shabbat Parshat Ha'azinu 5739 (1978). See also *Likuttei Sichot* vol. 18, page 282 and vol. 24, page 19; *Igrot Kodesh* vol. 10, page 334ff; vol. 16, page 216; vol. 18, page 527; vol. 23, page 248 and vol. 24, page 366. See also *Likuttei Sichot* vol. 24, page 252. The published indexes to the Rebbe's works will enable the researcher to find more relevant sources.

[313] See, for example, *Likuttei Sichot* vol. 30, page 235:

"... אמנם מאידך, ביחד עם שלילת היראה מן הגלות, צריכים להרגיש את ה'מיצר' וצער של הגלות, היינו
שהיחס למצב הגלות לא יהי' ח"ו ברגש של שלוה ומנוחה, אלא אדרבה בתנועה של צער תמידי ע"ז שבנ"י
אינם נמצאים במקומם האמיתי, כי אם **כבנים שגלו מעל שולחן אביהם** (ברכות ג, סע"א), ולא רק הבנים
וכנסת ישראל נמצאים בגלות ובשבי' כו', אלא כדברי ה' ליעקב (בראשית מו, ד) 'אנכי ארד עמך מצרימה',
שכינתא בגלותא".

redemption was on the horizon, if not 'overdue'[314] [Rabbi Yisroel Meir
Kagan, the saintly Chafetz Chaim who passed away in 1933 used to
say: "Even a blind man can see that we are the generation of Moshiach.
All signs indicate that he is not far off"[315]]; (d) that a Jew ought to be
constantly motivated by an intense craving for immediate Divine redemption and must never allow himself to become passive, or worse
still, indifferent to the plight of an unredeemed world[316].

Indeed his predecessors had also expressed their anticipation of the
redemption in absolute terms, both Rashab[317] and Rayatz[318] had stated

---

[314] See, for example, Rabbi Moshe Feinstein, *Igrot Moshe Orach Chaim* vol. 5
(Jerusalem, 1996), no. 8:

"הרי עברו כל הקיצים שאמרו אף גדולי עולם . . שלכן מצד אמונתנו הטהורה יכול לבא בכל רגע ורגע".

[315] See his *ma'amar* entitled *Tzipita LiYeshu'ah* (Tel Aviv, 1929).

[316] See, for example, Rabbi Moshe Feinstein (above note 314) that we are obliged to
anticipate the arrival of the Messiah on any given day as a **near certainty**.

"דהחיוב בכל יום ויום לצפות **כעין וודאי** שיבא היום ... יש לנו לצפות כעין וודאי שיבנה בכל שעה ושעה
... שכן יש עלינו לצפות".

See also *Igrot Moshe, Yoreh Deah*, vol. 2 (New York, 1973), no. 153 where Rabbi
Feinstein criticizes those who, upon the death of one partner in a marriage (husband
or wife), prepare a double stone (*matzeivah*) designed to be placed, ultimately, on
the graves of both husband and wife. According to Rabbi Feinstein those who truly
anticipate the arrival of the Messiah every day would not do such a thing; it is he
says, "כעין **כפירה**" ('quasi heresy'), because, "even those who are of the opinion that
people will still eventually die after the arrival of the Messiah – after extreme
longevity – the death and the burial will take place in Israel" and the double stone
will remain redundant.

With regard to Rabbi Feinstein's assertion that when the Messiah will come people
will live forever, see also his letter to the Rebbe dated 5th Menachem Av 5742
(published in the beginning of the rabbinic festschrift produced in honour of the
Rebbe's eightieth birthday entitled *Vayehi Bi-Yeshurun Melech* (Philadelphia, 1982):

"בקשר לידידי וחביבי מעלת הוד כבוד קדושת הגאון הצדיק האדמו"ר מנחם מענדל שליט"א שניאורסאהן
מליובאוויטש ... הי' לי כמה הזדמניות להשתעשע עמו בעניינים מסובכים בין בתורת הנגלה ובין בתורת
הנסתר ותמיד החשבתיו כרום גדולתו וגאונותו ... לפיכך אני משתתף בשמחה להענין שנתקבל בהעולם
כולו שיש שמחה גדולה שהשי"ת האריך ימיו לשנת השמונים, ואין מספיק סתם לברכו לאריכות ימים
ושנים, שהיום לא מספיק ברכה זו שמקוים שמלך המשיח יבא מיד ובקרוב ויזכה אז האדמו"ר שליט"א
לעבוד לעולם ועד".

[317] Indeed Rashab had declared in 1907: "We are now in the last generation [of the
galut].... We are now in the generation of the Messiah...**This present generation is
the generation of Messiah, without any doubt whatsoever**" (See, Rashab, *Torat
Shalom* pages 73-74).

with confidence that the Jewish People would be redeemed in their life-times; whether it appeals to modern sensibilities or not, this was the religious vocabulary of some of the most illustrious Jewish leaders throughout the ages[319]. The Rebbe, like his predecessors, expressed these ideas in terms of certainty, arguably in order to increase anticipation and, more importantly, vigorous preparation.

This does not mean that the Rebbe was merely overindulging in hyperbole and rhetoric. Rather, from his vantage point, he did see that the redemption was a reality to be expected, more than ever before, in his generation[320]. Moreover, he believed that faith and messianic anticipation that is expressed in fervent prayer and manifest in the intensification of good deeds could actually evoke G-d's response, who would then hasten to send the Messiah[321].

---

[318] In 1927 Rayatz said: "We now enter a new era ... I do not refer to spiritual revelations. Rather I mean welcoming the face of the Messiah in the very literal sense of the word. It will not be long at all. It will happen in my lifetime, for I am not very old. I am about 47 years of age... during my lifetime the Jewish people will be saved...I together with the *Temimim* will be from the first to greet the Messiah" (Rayatz, *Sefer HaSichot* 5687, Kehot Publication Society: Brooklyn, 1988 pages 121-122). Some twelve years later, he said: "...We see clearly that the Messiah is already near, he is 'behind a wall'. One whose senses of hearing and vision function well can hear his voice and see . . ." (Rayatz, *Sefer HaSichot 5696-Choref 5700*, Kehot Publication Society: Brooklyn, 1989, p. 316).

[319] Cf. Rabbi Jonathan Eybeschutz, *Ya'arot Devash* (Karlsruh, 1779) vol. 2, sixth homily:

"התחכמו תמיד לקרב הקץ, לומר חזו דאתא, חזו דאתא, ובזה חיזקו ידים רפות וברכים כושלות אימצו. ותמיד בבוא עקא וגזירא לישראל, תלו אותו בחבלי משיח לומר, הנה מלכנו יבא ויושיענו . . . והנה לכך הנביאים וחכמי קדם התחכמו לתקוע בלבב ישראל כי קרובה ישועת ה' לבוא ובל יתייאשו מן רחמים".

[320] He was not the only one. See also Rabbi Sholom Shachna Zohn, *Pirkei Teshuvah uGeulah* (Brooklyn, 5730) page 177:

"וזה כב' או ג' שנים שאלתי את הגאון הגדול המפורסם מרן **הרב ר' משה פיינשטיין** שליט"א מה הוא אומר אודות ביאת המשיח, ואמר לי בזה"ל **'ער איז שוין געוויס דא'**. והבנתי ממנו שדעתו הוא שכבר נמצא בעולם ולע"ע פועל הוא מה שצריך לפעול באופן הסתר וכנ"ל וצריכין אנו להתחזק בתפלתנו ובתשובה כפי שאפשר לנו למהר השתלשלות של משיח צדקנו ונזכה להתגלותו **הגמורה**".

[321] See *Yalkut Shimoni* on Psalms no. 736 – cited in the classical 14th century commentary of Rabbi David Abudarham on the Liturgy (prayers for the Day of Atonement, end) and Rabbi Joseph Chaim David Azoulay (1724-1807) *Midbar Kedeimot* (Livorno, 1793) *Ma'arechet Kuf* no. 16; *Chomat Anach* (Pisa, 1803-4) on Isaiah 33:2. See also the discussion and sources cited in *Likuttei Sichot* vol. 30, pages 182-183.

Yet, as we have demonstrated, the Rebbe saw both the forest and the trees. He continued to lay the groundwork for the building of institutions in the Diaspora that would be useless in the event of the Messiah's imminent arrival. Likewise, he addressed other issues that would only be relevant in the event that (in the Rebbe's words[322]) "the coming of the Messiah will be delayed"[323].

Secondly, it cannot be overemphasized that the talks on the subject of the Messiah during these years were not typical discourses or sermons by any stretch of the imagination. As one who was present at many of these, and who has compared impressions of these unforgettable addresses with eminent chasidim, the best way to describe our experiences is that we were watching a man who was engaged in intimate dialogue with G-d, beseeching his Creator with impassioned pleas. As in the transcendental language of the Psalmist, the hopes for the future were sometimes couched in terms of achieved reality, even though on the very same occasion he made it abundantly clear that these hopes had not yet been realized. It is therefore meaningless to quote isolated phrases from within these talks, or even one whole talk from within a series of talks, because the talks that the Rebbe gave can only be appreciated as a whole[324].

On one occasion in 1992 (shortly before he suffered a devastating stroke), when a young woman in the community[325] was brutally murdered, the Rebbe described his own feelings of helplessness and an-

---

[322] See, for example, *Igrot Kodesh* vol. 27, page 118:

"אבל בטח [**באם ח"ו תתעכב ביאת משיח צדקנו**] כשיבוא זמן הבחירות ...".

[323] In this vein, the Rebbe explained on the last Rosh Hashanah before he suffered the stroke that left him speechless (1991), why it was necessary for the Tzemach Tzedek to leave a will; this he said was because, in the event of a delay he may die before the arrival of the Messiah! See *Sichot Kodesh* 5752, vol. 1, page 11:

"הצ"צ דאג בחייו שהוא [אדמו"ר מהר"ש] יהי' ממלא מקומו מפני שבאם ח"ו תתעכב ביאת משיח צדקנו וממילא יהי' הענין ד'ואל עפר תשוב' הי' עליו לדאוג לממלא מקום".

[324] In contradistinction to Professor Elliot Wolfson, who in his *Open Secret: Postmessianic Messianism and the Mystical Revision of Menahem Mendel Schneerson* (Columbia University Press: New York, 2009) appreciates that the language of Messianism is subtle and calls for sophisticated analysis, Heilman and Friedman treated all of the literature as if it were breakfast reading.

[325] Mrs. Pesha Leah Lapine הי"ד.

guish as he contemplated the fate of the orphans who will have to en-
dure much loneliness and pain in years to come 'if the Messiah does
not arrive'; he then went on to express the futility of the human effort –
his own particularly – to comprehend G-d's ways, and concluded with
the statement that enormous opportunity for redemption was on the
horizon ('in front of our very eyes, if only we would open them')[326]. To
this listener, the talk resonated with language styles used by the great
prophets: it was as if snippets from the reflections of a dejected Job, the
pessimistic musings of Ecclesiastes and the triumphant prophecies of
Isaiah all mixed into one.

In light of the mystical nature of the Rebbe's words, it is clear that
we are not in a position to make any definitive statements on how exactly he saw the messianic drama unfolding or what would be the exact
role that he, his predecessor, or anyone else, would play in the scheme
of things.

Finally, it is noteworthy that in 1992, not long before the Rebbe suffered the devastating stroke from which he never recovered, a journalist from Israel approached the Rebbe and said to him—in a video-
recording preserved by Jewish Educational Media—"We appreciate
you very much, we want to see you in Israel; you said soon you will be
in Israel, so when will you come?" The Rebbe responded: "I also want
to be in Israel." The journalist insisted, "So when, when will you
come?" The Rebbe responded, "That depends on Moshiach, not on
me." The journalist persisted, "You are the Moshiach!," to which the
Rebbe responded, "I am not."[327].

What is clear beyond any doubt is that the Rebbe's desire for the
Redemption, and his insistence that we have a pivotal role to play in
that redemption, was not based on any desire for self-aggrandizement
or delusional estimates of his own power. Rather it was grounded in
his firm belief that, paraphrasing the words of Maimonides that he
quoted incessantly: 'Every good deed (*mitzvah*) that a person does has

---

[326] See *Sefer HaSichot* 5752 vol. 2, page 404ff.

[327] See also my 'Chabad's Messianism', published in *Azure* Summer 5770/2010 (no.
41), page 3ff.

the capacity to tilt his own balance and indeed the balance of the entire world for the good, and thereby bring deliverance and salvation'[328].

4. Summary and Conclusion

We originally set out to appraise the methodology of authors Heilman and Friedman in their book, 'The Rebbe: The Life and After-life of Menachem Mendel Schneerson', their use of sources, their particular pre-suppositions, and attempt to judge the quality of this biography as a work of scholarly research and analysis.

This essay is not a biography of the Rebbe. It is an elaborate review essay on Heilman and Friedman's efforts. In this essay we have demonstrated that regrettably:

(1) Heilman and Friedman lack familiarity with, and appreciation of, the primary sources, customs and culture that are required for the type of project they embarked upon;

(2) they were either painfully unaware of, or have deliberately chosen to ignore, a whole host of documented material that were they to have examined honestly, would inevitably have guided them to entirely different conclusions;

(3) they have unfortunately adopted a variety of biases and prejudices that interfered with their pursuit of objective scholarship;

(4) they have exploited texts and manipulated events in a manner that has enabled them to create an image of their making in lieu of the historical truth;

(5) they have likewise relied more on unsubstantiated rumors and fanciful conjecture than on hard evidence and reliable documents;

(6) they have skillfully woven into their narrative a hefty measure of sarcasm and ridicule unbefitting of their professional demeanor;

(7) most sadly, they have made statements that exhibit a clear lack of integrity in a manner that makes a mockery of their readers' intelligence.

Rather than address the complexity and tensions of the Rebbe's life, both early and late, his strengths and weaknesses, his achievements and his failures in a manner befitting serious scholars, they have

---

[328] See Maimonides, *Mishneh Torah*, Hilchot Teshuvah 3:4.

unfortunately resorted to sensationalism. I am willing to anticipate that they will make corrections in future editions of their book; I fear, however, that the flaws are too many, too broad and too deep as to render this task nearly impossible.

To paraphrase Professor David Berger in the final remarks he made in his review essay of another book co-authored by Samuel Heilman[329]: The book is "marred by fatal conceptual confusions, it is more likely to mislead its readers than to enlighten them".

An objective study of the life of Rabbi Menachem Mendel Schneerson still remains a desideratum.

---

[329] David Berger, Modern Orthodoxy in the United States: A Review Essay, *Modern Judaism*, vol. 11, no. 2. (May 1991) page 271.

APPENDIX 1

The French Visa Affidavit (1937)

In their entire book, as well as on their website, the authors reveal precious little in terms of new, heretofore unknown documentation about the Rebbe's life. In fact almost all of the documents they present have actually already been publicized and published in Chabad works. These include the documents relating to the Rebbe's university studies in Berlin and Paris which JEM has already published in their five-part documentary series about the Rebbe's life, *The Early Years* (Brooklyn 2005-2009)[330].

There is, however, one exception: The Rebbe's sworn affidavit for French citizenship.

The authors, who publicized this document for the first time, cite many of its details and present them as if they constitute authentic history with unadulterated, undisputed and undeniable facts.

For the authors, the most significant elements of the affidavit that are used in support of their narrative are the following:

(a) Mendel attended high school (in Yekatrinoslav) and graduated in 1915 following which he performed Russian military service from March 1915 to August 1915, when he was discharged due to a student exemption (although they conclude "What he did during those six months of army service remains unknown")[331].

(b) Mendel apprenticed as an engineer from 1920 to 1922, studied at the Yekatrinoslav Polytechnic from 1923 to 1925; and then continued his studies in Leningrad from 1926 to 1927.

These last two points are clearly intended to underscore the secular nature of his occupations in his youth.

---

[330] The images of the Rebbe's Sorbonne registration documents were discovered and publicised by JEM in 2007. See also JEM, *The Early Years* vol. 3, (2007), testimony of Yoel Reitzer in the name of his father, who studied pharmacology at the Sorbonne and testified to having seen the Rebbe attend classes there. Note that many Sorbonne student records were destroyed during the Sorbonne student riots of 1968.

[331] Heilman and Friedman page 73.

(c) In 1926 when the Rebbe moved to Leningrad, "arrangements had been made for Mendel to live in the apartment of his cousins, the Schneersohns, on the third floor of 22 Mokhovaya Street. For the first time Mendel would live in the court of the Lubavitcher Rebbe. Here he met and actually lived in the same apartment with the Rebbe's middle daughter Chaya Moussia, whom in time he would marry"[332] (the authors base this on the fact that in the affidavit Mendel lists Rayatz's address in Leningrad as his own).

This third point is of sensational and somewhat scandalous import for the authors, who rightfully point out the anomaly of such a living arrangement in Chasidic circles.

(d) Mendel and Moussia never intended to leave Paris since they state in their affidavit their plan to make France their permanent residence, professing no desire whatsoever of returning to their countries of origin.

This final point is intended to illustrate the commitment of Mendel and his wife to live a long-term bourgeoisie existence in the City of Light [333].

The truth, however, is that there is a fatal flaw in their reliance on the affidavit. Indeed it is abundantly clear that this sworn legal affidavit would actually never even be admissible in a court of law!

The reason for this is that many of the details provided in the Rebbe's affidavit were deliberately falsified in order to guarantee his and his wife's physical safety (*pikuach nefesh*). Indeed this was done in the affidavits of many pre-war immigrants who were fleeing for their very survival and needed to secure immigrant papers in safe havens. Having left Nazi-occupied Germany the only country they had a natural right to return to would have been the Soviet Union and they would

---

[332] Heilman and Friedman page 75. The sensational nature of this 'finding' was not lost on one reviewer who paraphrased the authors' contention and certainty with the following phrase: "It is known that they lived in the same apartment before being married" (Elaine Margolin, 'The Man Who Changed Judaism', in *Jewish Journal.Com* 19th July 2010).

[333] See, for example, Heilman and Friedman pages 124 and 137 where the authors assert that the Rebbe and Rebbetzen harboured no hopes of returning to their countries of origin.

have faced imminent danger to their own lives had they gone back there[334]. As religious Jews they were obliged to seek relative safety and security even if this meant dispensing with the truth.

We have already demonstrated that it is clear beyond any shadow of a doubt that the date that the Rebbe gave for his birth was a false one. The Rebbe was born in 1902 and not in 1895 as it appears in the affidavit. Indeed the authors themselves concede that the 1895 birth-date provided in the affidavit was fabricated, most likely in order to save the Rebbe from military service (and the attendant dangers therein). Yet notwithstanding the fact that they reach this conclusion, they ultimately miss the implications of their own deductions. For if that were indeed the case the Rebbe's testimony regarding his six months of military service was presumably also fictitious: if the Rebbe was actually born in April 1902 then it would have been highly unlikely that he would have entered the Russian military in March 1915 at the tender age of twelve!

It is clear that the earlier birth-date of 1895 would have meant that biographical data needed to be filled in a manner that would have been amenable to achieving his desired goal (French citizenship)[335]. Consequently no credence can be given to the idea that he entered military service at the age of twelve or, for that matter, that he graduated from High School that same year (in 1915). Consequently it would be highly disingenuous to build a thesis regarding the Rebbe's life-long career aspirations and dream lifestyle based upon an alleged engineering apprenticeship that he reported having undertaken from age eighteen to twenty (1920 to 1922).

It is informative that the Rebbe and Rebbetzen lived in Paris for five years before applying for French citizenship. As the authors themselves acknowledge[336], the Rebbe and Rebbetzen's status as Latvian citizens was tenuous even before they ever set foot on French soil. If that

---

[334] Note the Rebbe's description of the escalating threats to Jewish survival in the USSR, penned already in 1930 (published in Rayatz, *Igrot Kodesh* vol. 15, page 79).

[335] It is also possible that the details he provided for the French affidavit mirrored those he had already provided in order to obtain a passport with the birthdate of 1895.

[336] Heilman and Friedman page 113 and in endnote 70 thereon.

were indeed the case, why would the couple have then waited until their Latvian papers expired in 1937 before starting the French immigration process?

The authors themselves were already aware of Moussia's own words on the matter[337], expressed in a letter written to her in-laws (the Rebbe's parents) in May 1938: "We want to live here as permanent residents, and we are trying with all our ability to get approval for this," for, as she concluded, "without permanence, life is very difficult".

These words clearly reflect the frustrations of a refugee who had suffered from years of statelessness and travel limitations and the attendant perils, who was finally hoping to gain permanent legal status, thereby giving her and her husband a semblance of normality and safety. They had already failed to gain Latvian citizenship when they had had a much stronger case to obtain it (by 1937 Moussia's family had anyway moved to Poland), so it seemed that the safest and most viable option would be to apply for citizenship in the country where they had lived and studied for five years, had learned the language and where they had developed relationships with upstanding citizens who could serve as references, that country being France.

In the light of the above it is clear that for the purposes of securing citizenship the Rebbe and Rebbetzen had to give their word that they had given up hope of ever returning to their country of origin and that they intended to make France their permanent home. Yet it is far from clear that in reality they considered France their final place of destination.

Finally with regard to the authors' contention that the Rebbe lived in the same apartment as Moussia and her family in Leningrad, even if we are to assume that this address was listed in the affidavit in all honesty, the authors have clearly over-stepped the bounds of both logic and propriety:

The apartment on Mokhovaya Street housed Rayatz and his wife, their three daughters (one of whom was married and had a child) and Rayatz's mother, Rebbetzen Shterna Sarah. One of the rooms served as Rayatz's private office (or *yechidut* room) and the apartment also

---

[337] Heilman and Friedman page 122.

housed his library[338]. Therefore bearing in mind the number of people already living there, it is highly improbable that they would have been able to dedicate a room as living quarters for the Rebbe, even if they had wanted to. Such an arrangement would not have been conceivable in any event, as the authors themselves would surely agree that Rayatz would never have sanctioned it.

It is therefore reasonable to suggest that the Rebbe gave the address of Rayatz rather than his own (if he did indeed have a fixed address in Leningrad), because that was the address of the Court of which he had become part and where he clearly spent much of his time even though it was not where he actually lived[339].

Indeed the authors themselves adequately demonstrated that the Berlin addresses that the Rebbe and Rebbetzen listed as their past places of residence in their French affidavit cannot be taken at face value[340]. It is therefore surprising that they do not apply the same reasonable approach when discussing the Rebbe's address in Leningrad.

---

[338] The regular services that took place three times a day in this apartment were held in the dining room (testimony of Rabbi Mendel Morozov in personal communication to this writer. Morozov lived in Leningrad as a child and frequented these services).

[339] According to Rabbi Raphael Newmotin who lived in Leningrad at that time (in an interview published in the *Kfar Chabad* Magazine issue no. 491 page 48) the Rebbe boarded with his family:

"באותה תקופה התגורר בביתנו הרבי שליט"א. הוא התאכסן בחדר שלי וכשהגעתי היינו שנינו באותו חדר ... קשה מאוד היה לדבר עם הרבי שליט"א בעת ששהינו יחד באותו חדר. הוא היה תמיד אדם מאוד מופנם, סגור מאוד בעצמו, וממעט לדבר ... האצילות שלו והרציינות הגדולה שלו זה משהו שאי אפשר לתאר. הוא היה עסוק תמיד. אף פעם לא היה אפילו שניה אחת שהתבטל, רוב הזמן למד או כתב. הוא היה מגיע כמעט תמיד אחרון לחדר, ועוזב אותו ראשון. הוא היה מכונס בתוך עצמו, עסוק בענייניו, ולא דיבר כמעט עם איש".

[340] See Heilman and Friedman page 107. See also Heilman and Friedman page 86, regarding the address the Rebbe listed on his Berlin University registration papers.

APPENDIX 2

The Ten Lost Years (1941-1951)

Heilman and Friedman dedicate substantial space in their volume to the story of the succession after the passing of the sixth Lubavitcher Rebbe, Rabbi Yosef Yitzchak (Rayatz). My analysis and critique of the narrative as presented in their book evolved into a relatively long essay in its own right. As a result, I have chosen to include it as an independent chapter.

This essay offers a fairly comprehensive review of the authors' treatment of the rise of Rabbi Menachem Mendel Schneerson (or 'Ramash' as he was referred to in the era under discussion) to leadership as the seventh Lubavitcher Rebbe. The authors' story is compared to accounts gleaned from published first-hand sources, the vast majority of which are readily available to all and many of which were used by the authors themselves, albeit selectively, as the basis of their narrative. The primary sources are:

1) *Igrot Kodesh* (Kehot Publication Society: Brooklyn, 1982-2011): The published letters of Rabbi Yosef Yitzchak Schneersohn and Rabbi Menachem Mendel Schneerson[341]. A survey of the content of the vast correspondence of two of the principle figures of the authors' work (Rayatz and Ramash) provides first-hand insight into their character, highlighting their attitudes, activities, interests and their sphere of influence.

2) *Yemei Bereishit* (Kehot Publication Society: Brooklyn, 1993): This volume includes a day-by-day account of the events which led from the passing of Rabbi Yosef Yitzchak to Rabbi Menachem Mendel's succession[342]. Most importantly this work includes many facsimiles of origi-

---

[341] As mentioned above (note 2), references to *Igrot Kodesh* always refer to those of Rabbi Menachem Mendel Schneerson (the Rebbe) unless stated otherwise.

[342] Although the authors do not refer to this important compendium of original sources, they do refer to many of the sources referred to therein, including *Shemuot veSippurim* (Heilman and Friedman, chapter two, endnotes 2 and 4) and the diaries of Eli Gross (ibid. endnote 67). The newspaper reports which they refer to are also reproduced in this volume.

nal letters and newspaper articles, providing first hand sources from which we can learn a great deal about the events as they unfolded.

3) Excerpts from the private letters of Rabbi Yoel Kahn to his father written during the early 1950s. Copies of these letters have been circulated amongst chasidim for decades and some of them have appeared in various publications. They were first published in instalments in the *Kfar Chabad* magazine and subsequently collected and published in *Yoman miMichtavim* (Buenos Aires: 1998).

A brilliant rabbinical student, Kahn arrived from Tel Aviv merely a few days after the passing of Rabbi Yosef Yitzchak, and was immediately plunged into the centre of the Lubavitch movement and the heart of its activities. He remained there throughout the interregnum period and beyond, witnessing the entire controversy surrounding the succession. His letters to his family in Israel provide us with an intimate perspective on what was happening in the court of Lubavitch, enabling us to tune in to the finer nuances of the transition period that only an insider could be aware of. Kahn comes across as an independent, perceptive and often critical observer, who carefully transcribes anything of interest and at the same time is not afraid to express his opinion.

Heilman and Friedman rightfully designate these diaries as an "important source" and claim that much of the information they provide came from them[343].

Although reference will be made to the flaws in the authors' methodology as the relevant sections of their work are summarized, the main object of this essay is both to fill in the glaring gaps in their version of the narrative, as well as to accurately describe the Rebbe's activities during the ten years from 1941 till 1951 (beginning with his arrival in New York). It will be demonstrated that many well-documented facts seem to have somehow been 'lost' in the process of the writing of their biography. It was only by mixing selected data with baseless conjecture and by carefully omitting facts that conflicted with their conclusions that the authors were able to present their thesis in a viable way.

---

[343] Heilman and Friedman refer to these excerpts in chapter two, endnotes 52 ("Kahan Diaries. Much of what follows... comes from this source"), 65 ("Yoel Kahan, "Excerpts from a Diary", *Kfar Chabad*... 1981"), 67 (an "important source"), and 94 ("Selections from a Diary", *Kfar Chabad*... 1981").

The relationship between Rabbi Menachem Mendel Schneerson
(Ramash) and his brother-in-law, Rabbi Shamryahu Gourary (Rashag),
will also be dealt with in full since this topic is a natural development
of the subject matter.

Part 1 – In the Shadow of His Father-In-Law

Rashag

As is evident from the subtitle of Heilman and Friedman's book,
'The Life and Afterlife of Menachem Mendel Schneerson', this work is
intended to be a biography of Rabbi Menachem Mendel Schneerson,
the seventh leader of the Chabad-Lubavitch Hassidic movement. At the
end of chapter one the authors inform us that in order to answer questions such as "who was this leader...? Where did he come from...?
...we must first go to the day his predecessor died."

Chapter two begins with a lengthy account of the passing of his father-in-law and predecessor, Rabbi Yosef Yitzchak Schneersohn, on
Sabbath morning, the 10th of Shevat 5710 (28th January 1950). However, rather than using that event as a platform to introduce us to the subject of their biography and his role in the Lubavitch hierarchy, instead
the authors discuss Rabbi Yosef Yitzchak Schneersohn's older son-in-
law, Rabbi Shmaryahu Gourary (known as Rashag).

The authors note (without any source reference) that, "the fifth
rebbe [Rabbi Shalom DovBer, Rashab] had great hopes for this marriage between Chana [his oldest granddaughter, Rayatz's oldest
daughter] and Shmaryahu, a descendent of the famous MaHaRaL Rabbi Judah Loew of Prague..."[344]. It is not clear why this lineage is
deemed so significant; no mention is made here (or, for that matter, anywhere else in their study) of the fact that the second son-in-law (Rabbi
Menachem Mendel) was also a descendent of the very same Rabbi
Loew.[345]. [Indeed, it is not until several pages later that we learn that

---

[344] Heilman and Friedman page 32.

[345] See the brief biographical sketches of the Rebbes of Chabad that are published in
the beginning of *HaYom Yom* (above note 8) where the lineage of the first Rebbe of
Chabad (of whom the Rebbe was a direct descendant) is traced to the Maharal of
Prague.

Ramash was "a blood descendent of the third Rebbe for whom he was named"[346].

Much is made of Rashag's presence at a reading of the fifth Rebbe's will, described as being "of great importance, since the question of continuity and leadership was implicit in that event..."[347]. It is unclear exactly what significance the authors ascribe to "that event", bearing in mind that the only individual who was a viable candidate for the leadership of Lubavitch at the time was Rashab's only son, Rabbi Yosef Yitzchak. It is unlikely in the extreme that Rayatz would have intended to imply who should ultimately succeed him, especially when one considers the fact that at that time the identity and characteristics of his other two sons-in-law were not yet known.

Furthermore, Rashag was not the only individual outside of the Rebbe's immediate family who had been allowed access to the entire will. According to the source[348] cited by the authors[349], Rabbi Yosef Yitzchak "showed the entirety of the will only to... Rabbi Shmuel Gourary[350] and his brothers... and also Rabbi Shmaryahu Gourary... he stood over each one of them while they read the will..." Rabbi Yosef Yitzchak also allowed Rabbi Dovber Rivkin[351] to read the entire will in

---

346 Heilman and Friedman page 39.

347 Heilman and Friedman page 32.

348 Rabbi M. D. Rivkin, *Ashkavta deRebbe* (New York, 1953). A second edition of this work was published twenty-three years later (New York, 1976).

349 Heilman and Friedman chapter 2, endnote 8.

350 He was a wealthy chasid who had been a close confidant and long time supporter of Rabbi Shalom Dovber and his family. See, for example, Rayatz, *Igrot Kodesh* vol. 1, page 194.

351 Rivkin, the author of *Ashkavta deRebbe*, was a yeshivah student at the time. He had tended to Rabbi Shalom Dovber during his illness, and became very close to his son, Rabbi Yosef Yitzchak. Rabbi Rivkin describes the event: "He [Rabbi Yosef Yitzchak] put the will into my hand and instructed me to enter the small office and close the door. I was there for more than an hour and read the will many times, until it was practically committed to memory and 'fluent in my mouth'. After more than an hour the Rebbe [Rabbi Yosef Yitzchak] entered and asked me if I had finished..." (*Ashkavta deRebbe* pages 120-121).

private and without supervision[352]. Finally, all three sisters appear to have been treated equally by their parents and grandparents. It is therefore reasonable to assume, that if the future husbands of Chaya Moussia and Sheina had been present in Rostov at the time they too would have been welcomed into the inner circle at that special moment.

In the next pages we are provided with many details of Rashag's role as Rabbi Yosef Yitzchak's "right hand man", his status as "a familiar presence in Lubavitcher circles", the praises that Rabbi Yosef Yitzchak had lavished upon him and his responsibility "for many of the administrative details of his father-in-law's leadership". "In Rostov," they write, "he had been the one who accompanied the then new Rebbe, Yosef Yitzchak, on the periodic visits to the tomb of his father"[353]. We are informed too that "he had been with the Rebbe on his pilgrimage to the Holy Land and had accompanied him on his visits to physicians and spas, and even on his first trip to the United States in 1929"[354].

Taking the authors introduction at face value, however, it will naturally come as a surprise to the reader of this chapter, that when news of Rabbi Yosef Yitzchak passing first emerged, Ramash, "who had seemed so distant...[355] was now evidently more openly broken up than Shmaryahu Gourary over the loss of their Rebbe"[356].

---

[352] A better illustration of Rashag's distinction is the fact that while on his deathbed, Rabbi Shalom Dovber blessed his three granddaughters and his son and "afterward called one of the *temimim* [Rabbi Shmaryahu Gourary], and blessed him as well, and also rested his holy hands upon his head" (*Ashkavta deRebbe* page 99).

[353] Incidentally, Rabbi Dovber Rivkin also accompanied the Rebbe on these visits.

[354] Heilman and Friedman pages 38-39.

[355] As shall be demonstrated below, this distance is "apparent" only if one does not take into account the large body of available documentation attesting to a very strong, deep and multifaceted relationship between Ramash and his father-in-law.

[356] Heilman and Friedman page 32. Indeed, the two words "evidently" and "openly" employed by the authors in the context of their narrative may have been intended to suggest the possibility that Ramash's sobbing may have been slightly contrived. It is perhaps in order to amplify this suggestion that no mention is made of the fact (recorded in the same sources from which the authors gleaned the rest of their story) that Ramash rushed to 770 as soon as he heard the tragic news, nor that

Ramash

Rabbi Menachem Mendel Schneerson's involvement in his father-in-law's activities and his status in Lubavitcher circles following his arrival in the USA are both dismissed by Heilman and Friedman in a solitary sentence: "Although in the years since his arrival, Menachem Mendel had sat at his left side on public occasions ...he remained a largely unknown figure to the rank-and-file Hasidim, especially the yeshiva boys"[357]. For corroboration of this statement they rather ambiguously refer to the thirty-two page long chapter five of their work.

They do make mention of "reports – many of them emerging later, after his star had risen... – that he had carried out some 'important' unheralded missions and tasks for his father-in-law during the preceding years", and they also concede that "Hassidim and others who had been exposed to him... in Marseilles in 1941... and in Paris in 1947... had been impressed...". Yet they seem not to have heard of the many activities that he conducted on his father-in-law's behalf in the United States. They admit somewhat grudgingly that "in New York he had been initiating a farbrengen... once a month" and conclude that consequently "he wasn't a completely blank slate". The most significant event of the ten years after Ramash's arrival in New York that they

---

he repeatedly entered the room where the Rebbe lay, as well as the room in which the rest of the family sat, throughout the Sabbath day. Several eyewitnesses noted that only with supreme effort did Ramash remain composed (see *Yemei Bereishit* pages 67-69 where it is also noted that Ramash prevented anyone who had not immersed himself in the *mikveh* that day from joining the group of chasidim who kept vigil, reciting Psalms throughout the day). [Much of the information in *Yemei Bereishit* is based on the same memoir that is published in Rabbi Raphael Nachman Hacohen, *Shemuot veSippurim* Vol. 3 (New York, 1990), pages 135-146 on which Heilman and Friedman, by their own admission, based their description of events "in a large measure" (chapter 2 endnote 2)].

Since the authors present only a partial description of the events, the reader might be forgiven for supposing that Ramash did not take much interest in his Rebbe's passing till after the conclusion of the Sabbath.

[357] Heilman and Friedman page 40. Ironically it was specifically the yeshivah boys who, perhaps more than anyone else, recognized Ramash's erudition and some of them interacted with him on scholarly matters on a very personal level. Ramash's office was on the same floor as the yeshivah study hall and he was a familiar figure to the students. See *Beit Chayeinu*, (Heichal Menachem: Jerusalem, 2004), page 129.

seem to be aware of is that "even in Brooklyn [Ramash] had remained in a separate residence", a point that they mention twice[358].

In chapter five too the authors seem blissfully unaware of Ramash's activities after his arrival in New York, blithely stating "what Mendel Schneerson did next is not altogether clear..."[359], as if there were not a scrap of documentation that could possibly provide any clues. A few pages later, however, they do seem to display awareness of a few sparse facts[360], stating rather ambiguously that "Lubavitch... was now [in 1947] giving him more and more to do"[361]. This seems to be the sum-total of their knowledge on this matter[362].

---

[358] Heilman and Friedman pages 32 and 40. To present this fact as a reflection of Ramash's general detachment or even disinterest in his father-in-law and his activities is misleading in the extreme. Initially, in fact, Ramash and his wife did reside in 770, in the very room which would become Ramash's office for the rest of his life. Due to pragmatic considerations, however, that arrangement was temporary. The three-story house at 770 Eastern Parkway already accommodated two households, as well as offices, a cheder, a synagogue and a library, leaving precious little space to house yet another couple. That small room in which the couple lived upon their arrival in the USA would soon become the hub of several new organizations founded by Rabbi Yosef Yitzchak and run by Ramash. [Before Ramash's arrival, Rabbi Yosef Yitzchak had himself used that room to receive people in private audiences – 'yechidut', on occasion he recited chasidic discourses there, and on one occasion he used that room to hold a farbrengen. See Beit Chayeinu (above note 357), pages 136-138].

[359] Heilman and Friedman page 136.

[360] Here again they mention Ramash's choice of residence in New York, but this time they make sure to mention that it was "just a couple of blocks from what would become the world headquarters of Chabad Lubavitch". At this stage in their narrative it seems that it suits their agenda better to underscore Ramash's 'increasing' association with the Lubavitch court. Certain facts must, therefore, be re-presented with a different twist, while previously 'forgotten' events such as the publication of HaYom Yom are conveniently remembered (see Heilman and Friedman page 142).

[361] Heilman and Friedman page 141.

[362] Thus the authors even suggest that when Ramash travelled to Paris to meet his mother in 1947 "perhaps he actually took the time to reacquaint himself with the Paris he had fled in the midst of the war and consider whether he could again resume the life he had left there". Quite aside from any other considerations, the suggestion that Ramash was considering moving back to France even as he was

Executive Chairman – Threefold

Let us now explore the facts as testified by the documents:

On the 16th of Sivan 5701 (11th June 1941), just twelve days prior to the arrival of his daughter Chaya Mushka (Moussia) and son-in-law, Rabbi Menachem Mendel Schneerson, from war-torn Europe, Rabbi Yosef Yitzchak founded 'Machane Israel'. The function of this organization was to strengthen and sustain the study of Torah and Jewish practice through the example and influence of its members who would actively inspire and encourage others to repentance, Torah study and good deeds. 'Merkos L'Inyonei Chinuch' was founded that same summer, its function being to educate Jewish children in the traditional spirit of Torah true Judaism through all available means including the establishment of schools, extracurricular study groups and youth groups[363]. A few months later 'Kehot Publication Society' was established, as a branch of 'Merkos L'Inyonei Chinuch' for the publication of Hassidic works as well as educational material for adults and children in English and a variety of other languages[364].

Ramash was appointed executive chairman of all three organizations and throughout the next decade he penned hundreds of letters in those capacities.

---

working to secure American immigration papers for his ailing mother whom he had not seen for twenty years, borders on the absurd.

[363] In a letter penned in 1943, less than two years after the arrival of Ramash in New York, Rabbi Yosef Yitzchak describes the activities of "Merkos L'Inyonei Chinuch" which had by that time "published about 6000 copies of 'Talks and Tales' in Yiddish and English, a calendar for children and more, all of which were well received... 'Merkos L'Inyonei Chinuch'... has already established many schools for girls with much success... organizes Shabbos gatherings for boys and girls... speaking to them about the Torah portion of the week and telling stories about great leaders of the Jewish people concerning matters of Jewish faith...". In the same letter he describes the function of 'Machne Israel', "to strengthen the [Jewish] religion in regards to the observance of the Sabbath, Family Purity... study of *Mishnayot* by-heart and more..." (Rayatz, *Igrot Kodesh* vol. 7, page 156). For full documentation of the work of these organizations until 1950 see Rabbi Shalom Dovber Levin, *Toldot Chabad BeArtzot HaBrit* (above note 207), chapters 57-64.

[364] For a more detailed discussion of these three organizations, see *Igrot Kodesh* vol. 1, pages 15-20.

In a letter dated the 15th of Av 5702 (29th July 1942) Rabbi Yosef
Yitzchak instructed the officials of the Chevrah Kadisha, led by Rashag,
to appoint Ramash as head of the committee[365]. Ramash also shared the
vice-chairmanship of Agudas Chasidei Chabad (the president was
Rabbi Yosef Yitzchak), the umbrella organization of Chabad-
Lubavitch[366].

[From an early age Rabbi Yosef Yitzchak had been trained to con-
front new challenges to traditional Judaism and Chasidism specifically
according to the needs of the time. As political and intellectual ferment
spread across Russia at the turn of the century, his father had founded
the Yeshivah *Tomchei Temimim* and appointed him as its executive director[367]. With the rise of communism Rabbi Yosef Yitzchak had set up
an underground network of activists, who had spread throughout Russia, managing to keep the embers of Judaism alive through decades of
desperate struggle[368]. With his arrival in New York he realized that the
freedoms of American society and the social pressures of the American
dream had combined to create a new reality that needed to be confronted. The new organizations were specifically established in order to
deal with the challenges posed by Western society. As executive chairman it was Ramash's job to ensure that indeed America would be "no
different"[369], that Jews would not be enticed into the comforts of assim-
ilation but rather would remain proud practitioners of their Jewish heritage. It was perhaps precisely due to his 'worldly' background that

---

[365] Rayatz, *Igrot Kodesh* vol. 6, page 386:

"אל ידידי הבוררים של חברה קדישא אשר על יד אגודת חסידי חב"ד בארצה"ב וקאנאדא . . בזה הנני
למלאות את ידם . . לבחור בועד מועצה של החברה קדישא במספר חברים שימצאו לנכון, ולראש ועד
המועצה את חתני הרב רמ"מ שליט"א שניאורסאהן'".

[366] Ramash's name appears in this capacity on the stationary of the organization.

[367] Regarding the circumstances surrounding the establishment of *Tomchei Temimim*,
see Rabbi Moshe Rosenblum, *Divrei Yemei HaTemimim* chapter 1 (published in *Kerem
Chabad*, ed., Y Mondshine, Vol. 3, Kfar Chabad 1987, page 11ff).

[368] For a full survey of these activities see R. Shalom Dovber Levin, *Toldot Chabad
BeRussia HaSovietit* (above note 183).

[369] When Rayatz came to the United States and confronted the prevalent ignorance
and religious apathy, with many people claiming that it would be impossible to
insist on traditional standards in the *'goldene medinah'*, he responded with the
unequivocal statement that *'America is nisht anderesh'* (America is no different).

Ramash was picked for this daunting task. Under his guidance, all three of these organizations flourished, on both a local level and a national level, creating the template for the international expansion of similar activities which would unfold over the next fifty years.]

Scholarly Correspondence

In addition to his work directing these three organizations, which may be categorized as communal activity, Ramash was also heavily involved in scholarly pursuits. In the second issue of the journal *Kovetz Lubavitch*[370], a section entitled *Teshuvot uBiurim* ('answers and explanations') was launched, in which Ramash penned answers to questions presented primarily by rabbinic figures in all fields of Torah scholarship with breadth, depth, clarity and unusual erudition[371].

Additionally Ramash wrote hundreds of letters during this period, many of which were devoted to scholarly correspondence. Even those letters that dealt with administrative issues usually featured some scholarly content or lesson in Divine service according to Chasidic teachings. Several volumes of these letters have been published[372] thereby providing valuable testimony to Ramash's erudition as well as to his activities following his arrival in the United States. His correspondence with leading chasidim and rabbis from the United States, Europe and Israel attests to the fact that his status as a well-known and much respected figure only grew with time.

As early as Febuary 1939 when Ramash was still living in France, we find the revered chasid, Rabbi Yerachmiel Binyominson[373], then in

---

[370] This journal first appeared in the winter of 1944. On its front page it is described:

"קובץ ליובאוויטש': נוסד מטעם המזכירות של כ"ק אדמו"ר שליט"א מליובאוויטש, יוצא מזמן לזמן, על ידי חבר מערכת.

[371] Introduction to *Igrot Kodesh* vol. 2, pages 5-6. Many of the letters published in *Kovetz Lubavitch* are reprinted in this volume of *Igrot Kodesh* and are cited in the footnotes to the introduction. A collection of the Rebbe's *Teshuvot uBiurim* columns were printed by Kehot Publication Society (Brooklyn, 1974).

[372] *Igrot Kodesh*, vols. 1-4 and volume 21.

[373] Born in 1885, Binyominson studied in *Tomchei Temimim* in Lubavitch and was a renowned Torah scholar. At the time he served as a Rabbi in England, and it seems

London, turning to him with queries regarding the possible reconciliation of different rabbinic views on the subject of the Kabbalistic doctrine of "*tzimtzum*"[374]. Beginning in 1942 there is already evidence of a very steady correspondence with Rabbi Menachem Zev (Volf) Greenglass[375], a prominent Chabad rabbi and a teacher in the *Tomchei Temimim* yeshivah of Montreal[376] where there resided a group of illustrious chasidim[377], both regarding communal affairs and scholarly matters. A very warm correspondence covering diverse aspects of Halachah, Kabbalah, Agadah and Chasidic thought with Rabbi Eliezer Ephrayim Yolles[378], the non-ChaBaD Rabbi of Philadelphia, began to develop in the same year. In addition to similar correspondence with many chasidim of note and influence such as Rabbi Shlomo Yosef Zevin (chief editor of the Encyclopedia Talmudit and a world renowned scholar[379]), Rabbi Dovber Rivkin[380], Rabbi Avrohom Elyah Ax-

---

that he had been in contact there with the famed Rabbi Eliyahu Eliezer Dessler (who later served as *mashgiach* in the Ponivezh yeshivah in Israel and authored *Michtav Me-Eliyahu*) and it was his enquiry regarding the doctrine of "tzimtzum" that Binyominson forwarded to Ramash.

[374] *Igrot Kodesh* vol. 1, pages 19 and 23.

[375] See *Igrot Kodesh* vol. 1, pages 38, 41 and 49 for some examples.

[376] Examples of letters addressed to the students and faculty of this yeshivah can be found in *Igrot Kodesh* vol. 1, pages 42, 81 and 186.

[377] For examples of letters addressed to the community see *Igrot Kodesh* vol. 1, pages 75 and 108.

[378] For examples see *Igrot Kodesh* vol. 1, pages 65, 198, 292, 304 and 312.

[379] For particularly scholarly examples of Ramash's correspondence with Zevin see *Igrot Kodesh* vol. 2, pages 241 and 260.

[380] This is the same Rivkin mentioned earlier in connection to the passing of the Rebbe Rashab. In a letter dated Thursday of *Parshat Ekev* 5703 (1943) he writes in response to Ramash: "My beloved friend (*yedid nafshi*)... the gaon . . . Ramash... I read, once, twice, a third and a fourth time, that which your honor transcribed concerning Divine Providence, and I saw that you wrought wonders . . . with great knowledge, depth and breadth..." (*Igrot Kodesh* vol. 1, page 168). At the time, Rabbi Rivkin was serving as a Rosh Yeshivah in *Torah Vodaas*, a prominent non-Chabad yeshivah in Brooklyn. For other examples of Ramash's correspondence with him, see ibid., vol. 2, pages 82 and 85.

elrod[381], Rabbi Yitzchok Dubov[382] and Rabbi Moshe Gourary,[383] Ramash responded to enquiries about diverse aspects of Torah scholarship to a host of interlocutors from both the ranks of the rabbinate and the laity. It is surprising that all this was lost on the authors of *The Rebbe*, as a cursory glance through the multiple volumes of his published correspondence would have easily furnished them with the relevant material[384].

Ramash's Relationship with Rabbi Yosef Yitzchak

Rabbi Yosef Yitzchak referred many of the scholarly questions that had been enquired of him to Ramash, such as that of Rabbi Yisroel Noach Belinski[385] mentioned above. In a letter to Rabbi Belinski in 1948, Rabbi Yosef Yitzchak writes, "I have handed these to my son-in-law, *ha-rav ha-gaon ha-rav ha-chasid*, Rabbi Menachem Mendel *shlit"a* ... He has shown me his detailed response which addresses all aspects of your enquiry. I trust that his written response will be studied with the

---

[381] Axelrod had learned in *Tomchei Temimim* in Lubavitch and at the time served as Rabbi in Baltimore where he had been visited by Rayatz in 1928. For the earliest examples of Ramash's letters to him, see *Igrot Kodesh* vol. 1, pages 44, 62 and 277.

[382] Dubov was a respected Chabad Rabbi in Manchester, and a lecturer in the non-Chabad Yeshivah there. He too had studied in *Tomchei Temimim* during the lifetime of Rashab. For examples of Ramash's scholarly letters to him, see *Igrot Kodesh* vol. 2, pages 55, 275 and 348.

[383] Rabbi Gourary was a student of *Tomchei Temimim* and at the time a leading figure in the Chabad community in Israel. He was also known as an outstanding scholar of Chasidic thought. For examples of Ramash's correspondence with him concerning communal matters see *Igrot Kodesh* vol. 2, pages 112 and 307. See also ibid., vol. 3, pages 15 and 231.

[384] For a quick reference list of some of Ramash's scholarly letters between the years 1944 and 1948, see the preface to *Igrot Kodesh* vol. 2, page 5 and the footnotes thereon. Additionally, the publisher's introductions to the first four volumes of *Igrot Kodesh* clearly demonstrate the breadth of Ramash's scholarly (and communal) work spanning the 1940s.

[385] Rabbi Belinski was a senior Chasid, a respected graduate of the Yeshivah *Tomchei Temimim* in Lubavitch. He held a position on the faculty of *Tomchei Temimim* in Samarkand, Uzbekistan, and later in Brunoy, France. See also the reference above note 197.

attentiveness it deserves"[386]. In 1946 Rabbi Yosef Yitzchak writes: "In answer to your letter... regarding the publication of a scholarly periodical by the students of the Yeshivah *Torat Emet*...[387] send all the material to my son-in-law, the gaon and chasid, Rabbi Menachem Mendel Schneerson and follow his directives"[388]. In a letter penned in the spring of 1945 Ramash writes to Rabbi Yerucham Leiner, a prestigious scion of the Radziner Chasidic dynasty: "Due to the many demanding commitments that require the attention of my father-in-law, the Rebbe, he gave your honor's letter to me to look into and reply to... I would be very pleased if you would let me know your opinion on what I write below"[389]. Again this letter marks the beginning of a warm correspondence.

In a letter penned in 1945 and addressed to Rabbi Shlomo Yosef Zevin, Rabbi Yosef Yitzchak describes at some length an English book entitled "The Bible Unauthorized". His respect for the scholarly opinion of Ramash is evident therein: "When my son-in-law, Rabbi Menachem Mendel Schneerson, arrived here [in the United States], I requested that he review the volume and tell me what he thought of it..."[390].

A closer examination of Ramash's correspondence at this time reveals the deep reverence Ramash held for his father-in-law and the finality with which he regarded his opinion. It is telling that in his letters, Ramash, in virtually all cases, deals with concerns directly relating to his father-in-law, no matter how apparently insignificant, at the very beginning of his letters; only afterward does he move on to discuss other matters of importance.

Additionally Ramash would often consult Rabbi Yosef Yitzchak regarding queries that he had been approached with, whether they concerned matters of Chasidic thought, communal affairs and even as-

---

[386] Rayatz, *Igrot Kodesh* vol. 14, page 405. For Ramash's treatment of Rabbi Belinski's queries, see his *Igrot Kodesh* vol. 2, page 392, letter dated Ellul 5708.

[387] This was the Chabad Yeshivah in Jerusalem.

[388] Rayatz, *Igrot Kodesh* vol. 9, page 107.

[389] *Igrot Kodesh* vol. 2, page 36.

[390] Rayatz, *Igrot Kodesh* vol. 9, page 5.

pects of Jewish law. In a letter dating from 1943, for example, he writes: "I asked... my father-in-law, the Rebbe... and these are his words in answer...". What follows is a cryptic Kabbalistic explanation which Ramash continues to elucidate, citing sources that support the answer[391]. In a letter responding to a halachic query written in 1948 he cites various authorities before concluding with the remarks of "my father-in-law, the Rebbe... regarding practical application..."[392].

Ramash became increasingly known, not only for his breadth of knowledge and expertise in aspects of Jewish scholarship, nor specifically in his role as the head of the relevant organizations, but simply as a personal representative of Rabbi Yosef Yitzchak. In many letters we find people turning to Ramash as an avenue through which to gain access to his father-in-law. It may be true (as the authors state, albeit without evidence or examples of this) that "Shmaryahu Gourary was often a stand-in for him [Rabbi Yosef Yitzchak] on public occasions", and that Rashag, as well as being the executive director of the *Tomchei Temimim* network of Yeshivot, was very much the public face of Chabad and the primary fundraiser for the Yeshivah[393]. However, as we shall demonstrate, on a more personal level it was increasingly to Ramash that the chasidim were turning to as the representative of their Rebbe.

In a letter to Rabbi Yolles, for example, Ramash writes, "I fulfilled your honor's request to mention you and pass on your note of supplication [*pidyon nefesh*] to my father-in-law, the Rebbe..."[394]. Indeed Rabbi Yosef Yitzchak himself clearly acknowledged and supported Ramash in this role. The letter cited above[395] refers to an episode that is demonstrative of this phenomenon. Rabbi Yolles customarily came to receive the traditional willow branches (*aravot*) used on *Hoshana Rabbah* (the seventh day of Sukkot), from Rabbi Yosef Yitzchak. One year

---

[391] *Igrot Kodesh* vol. 1, page 196.

[392] *Igrot Kodesh* vol. 3, page 2. See also *Igrot Kodesh* vol. 3, page 149.

[393] See below for a more detailed account of Rashag's activities during this period.

[394] *Igrot Kodesh* vol. 1, page 198.

[395] footnote 201.

when he entered the Rebbe's room, Rabbi Yosef Yitzchak sent him to his son-in-law, Ramash, saying: "His hand is like my hand".

On one occasion Ramash begins a letter to Rabbi Yosef Wineberg with the following statement: "In answer to your letter requesting that I ascertain the reason why you did not receive a reply to your letters to my-father-in-law, the Rebbe..." and then continues to deal with other concerns[396]. In a letter to the aforementioned Rabbi Axelrod (dealing with communal efforts, as well as scholarly correspondence), Ramash begins: "Your two letters... have been received. I passed the information on directly to my father-in-law, the Rebbe, and I am certain that your honor has already received an answer in this regard"[397].

Scholarly Publications

In addition to his copious communal and scholarly correspondence, during this period Ramash was also heavily engaged in his work as executive chairman of the 'Kehot Publication Society'. As well as the regular transcription, annotation and publication of his father-in-law's talks and discourses, Ramash personally edited and annotated many other volumes and oversaw the production and publication of numerous works in a variety of languages. Examples of works that Ramash personally compiled, edited, annotated and prepared for publication include: *Torat HaChasidut, Limud HaChasidut* (1945), *Torat Shalom* (1945), *She'eilot UTeshuvot* and *Chidushei Tzemach Tzedek* (1946), *Kitzurei HaTzemach Tzedek LeTanya* (1948) and *Torat Shmuel. She'eilot uTeshuvot* and *Chidushei Tzemach Tzedek* are multi-volume Halachic works while the rest are works of Chasidic thought. Virtually all of these are original works by the previous Rebbes of Chabad which Ramash prepared for print, editing them and adding annotations and comments. (*Torat*

---

[396] *Igrot Kodesh* vol. 1, page 137. Weneberg had been a student at *Tomchei Temimim* in Warsaw and Otwock, Poland. He became a well-known representative and fundraiser on behalf of various Chabad institutions. Later he authored a popular commentary on the Tanya based on his weekly radio-broadcast lessons. Interestingly, a scholarly query posed by Ramash in this letter, was answered by his father-in-law in a public talk, delivered ten days later. See Rayatz, *Sefer HaSichot 5703* (Kehot Publication Society: Brooklyn, 1965) page 139.

[397] *Igrot Kodesh* Vol. 1, page 277.

Shalom is a collection of public talks of the fifth Rebbe, Rabbi Shalom Dovber, compiled by Ramash at the request of his father-in-law).

Additionally Ramash authored a Passover Hagadah, *Hagadah Shel Pesach im Likuttei Ta'amim uMinhagim*. Amongst its other features, its encyclopedic scope (in an age when scholars could not rely on computer search-engines to find far-flung sources) made it a unique contribution to the literature on the *haggadah*[398]. He also authored a biography of the fourth Rebbe of Chabad, Rabbi Shmuel Schneerson, the Maharash (1834-1882), and a slim volume entitled *Hayom Yom* in which he compiled pearls of wisdom, Chasidic stories and sayings from the talks of his father-in-law[399]. Another work concerning the history of Chabad, edited and annotated by Ramash is *Admur HaTzemach Tzedek U'Tenuat HaHaskalah*.

Ramash was also the editor of a journal for Jewish youth entitled *Talks and Tales*. He was personally involved in the meticulous editing, formatting[400], production and distribution of this journal (both the Yiddish and English editions), and assumed responsibility for its contents[401].

---

[398] See above note 212.

[399] This booklet was compiled by the express request, and in accordance with the guidelines, of Rabbi Yosef Yitzchak, as detailed in a letter addressed to "my dear son-in-law . . . the gaon . . . Rabbi Menachem Mendel Schneerson..." (Rayatz, *Igrot Kodesh* vol. 7, page 30). After its publication, Rabbi Yosef Yitzchak wrote in a private letter: "It is packed with pearls and diamonds . . . G-d has blessed my son-in-law, the gaon, Rabbi Menachem Mendel, may he live for many good and long years" (ibid. page 231).

[400] See, for example the personal testimony of artist Michel Schwartz, published at: http://www.chabad.org/375089

[401] See, for example, *Igrot Kodesh* vol. 1, page 36ff (letter dated 23rd Iyar 5702) and vol. 21, page 91 (letter dated Ellul 5708). In the first of these two letters Ramash provides reasons for the precise choice of wording in *Talks and Tales*; in the latter he responds to a businessman who was inspired by the contents of the *Talks and Tales* to pose some rather provocative questions about the Tannaic sage, Rabbi Yochanan ben Zakkai, and the attitude of the Talmudic rabbis towards him.

The letter begins "בכל עת שבע רצון אני אם אוכל לענות בעניני תורה, הנלפע"ד" and concludes with a lengthy paragraph in which Ramash dispels his consultant's suggestions that as a businessman he should stick to commercial matters and not engage in Torah-related correspondence:

Indeed, heavily burdened as he was, Ramash was not always able to keep up with his ever-growing correspondence. In a letter to Rabbi Greenglass penned in 1946 he explains: "I have not written due to the many obligations especially in the area of publication...[402] recently I have had to edit... a booklet about Purim and Passover in French (similar to the one about Tishrei), one about Purim in English, the first volume of *Our People* in English, the final proofreading of [the Chasidic discourse] *Mayim Rabim*. In the middle of being proofread are: the appendices to Tzemach Tzedek... the booklet *Ha-Tzemach Tzedek Ve-haHaskalah*, a collection of the Rebbe [Rashab]'s talks... At the beginning of being proofread . . . *Kuntres Eitz HaChaim*, a booklet about the Rebbe Maharash... the talks of the Rebbe [Rayatz]... a book of Chasidic discourses... a book of questions and answers between a teacher and a child regarding Jewish religion and practice in English, a code of Jewish law for youth in English[403] and more. "... In addition to all of the above there is the work on behalf of 'Merkos Le'Inyonai Chinuch', 'Machneh Yisroel' and 'Kehot' besides [actual] publication..."[404].

Scholarly Talks

Ramash's reputation spread by way of his letters and publications to all places where Chabad chasidim had settled, and the high esteem

---

"הגע בעצמך: **אלפים ואלפים שנה** היתה נשמתו, שהיא היא העיקר אצל כל בנ"י, עוסקת בתורה ואחרי חיינו בעוה"ז, הגשמי, תחזור הנשמה להתעסק בתורה ולהתעמק בחכמתה שהיא אין קץ **לנצח נצחים,** אלא שבינתיים במשך איזה **עשירית שנים** זימן לו הק' ב"ה עסק של מסחר. ואיך אפשר להביט ע"ז שזהו עסקו, וענין התורה ענין נוסף. אלא שכאו"א מאתנו צריך זהירות ללמוד תורה בהתאם אל האמת, כפי שהורונו חז"ל".

[402] Indeed, the most recent letter addressed to Rabbi Greenglass prior to this date (available to us) was written about seven months earlier, a rare gap in their usually frequent exchange of letters.

[403] For an example of Ramash's type of scholarly and editorial input into this publication, see the facsimile of his handwritten notes published in *Nitzutzei Ohr* (above note 77), Hebrew section, pages 18-19.

[404] *Igrot Kodesh* vol. 2, page 90. A similar letter dates from 1949, and is addressed to Rabbi Nissan Neminov (a legendary chasid who had studied in *Tomchei Temimim* in Lubavitch, and at the time served on the faculty of *Tomchei Temimim* in Brunoy, France). In this letter, Ramash excuses himself for not having fulfilled "my promise to explain the [Rayatz's] talk in the booklet from the festival of Passover" due to his heavy workload, see *Igrot Kodesh* vol. 3, page 172.

in which the chasidim held him only deepened when they had the chance to meet him personally.

His first public appearance in America came just three days after his arrival in New York when the elder chasidim at 770 who knew him from before the War insisted that he lead a farbrengen. Ramash responded that it would have to wait until after the next weekday Torah reading (in three-day's time, on a Thursday) when he could recite the *HaGomel* (blessing of thanksgiving) for having been saved from the War and his safe arrival in Ameirca. That Thursday night Ramash held a farbrengen for the elder chasidim joined by the 770 Yeshivah students. The event started at 9:00pm and finished in the early hours of the morning. He spoke for hours on end, stopping intermittently for the singing of chasidic *nigunim*, the 'toasting' of *l'chaim*, and at one point to test the 770 students on their knowledge of his father-in-law's *Likuttei Dibburim*. The breadth and depth of his talks, which analyzed the *HaGomel* blessing according to Jewish law, Kabbalah and Chasidut astounded all in attendance[405].

Not long after his arrival he was asked to deliver the weekly Mishnah lesson after Sabbath morning prayers at 770[406] (and he would often address the Chasidim at the celebration associated with the *siyyum hamishnayot*[407]). Then in the summer of either 1942 or 1943 he was instructed by his father-in-law, Rayatz, to 'farbreng' monthly with the congregants at 770 on the Sabbath on which the forthcoming month would be blessed (*Shabbat Mevarchim HaChodesh*)[408]. He would also speak at the Kiddush on the occasion of an *Aufruf* preceding the wed-

---

[405] See *Kovetz Kaf Chet Sivan-Yovel Shanim* (Kehot Publication Society: Brooklyn, 1991), pages 20-21.

[406] *Yemei Melech*, volume 2, page 566.

[407] See, for example, *Kovetz Lubavitch* issue no. 3, page 40. See the description of the Rebbe's address on that occasion in a letter written by Rabbi Shmuel Zalmanov (dated 11th Tammuz 5704) and published in *Heichal Menachem* vol. 1 (Kehot Publication Society: Jerusalem, 1994), page 256ff:

"אולי לא תפסתי היטב את דבריו בשמיעה בעלמא . . נוסף לזה אשר ההדרן בכלל הי' מלא וגדוש בבקיאות כמעט מרוב הש"ס והי' חולף ועובר מענין לענין בשעתא חדא".

[408] *Yemei Melech* vol. 2, page 568.

ding of a community member or rabbinical student[409]. In addition, he would be invited to speak at the wedding ceremony itself. Some of these wedding discourses, as well as some of Ramash's own handwritten preparatory notes for them, have been published[410].

Ramash's personal *Reshimot* from the 1940s also contain preparatory notes for speeches to be delivered at Bar Mitzvahs, Chabad organizational events and communal Siyum celebrations concluding the study of Mishnah or Talmud[411].

During this period Ramash also began to hold Talmudic lectures on the intermediate days (*Chol Hamoed*) of Sukkot and Pesach geared specifically to yeshivah students from across the Orthodox spectrum[412]. What may have been his first such talk, delivered on *Chol Hamoed Sukkot* 1941, was prepared for print by Ramash himself. His four page analysis of the opening Mishna of the Talmudic tractate *Bava Metzia* and some of the classical commentaries thereon is followed by a twenty five page analysis of the Talmudic discussion in light of Chasidic and Kabbalistic teaching[413]. These bi-annual lectures, which also attracted non-Lubavitch Yeshivah students in the New York City area[414], continued into the early years of his leadership.

Personal Encounters

It is noteworthy that as early as 1928, following the marriage of Ramash to Chaya Moussia, Rabbi Eliyahu Chaim Althaus, a well known and respected chasid who had served as Ramash's attendant

---

[409] *Mekadesh Yisrael* (above note 220), Introduction.

[410] *Mekadesh Yisrael* chapter one.

[411] See *Reshimot* nos. 158-187.

[412] *Yemei Melech* vol. 2, pages 715-718. See also *Yemei Beresihit* pages 18-19, and footnote 25.

[413] *Hatza'at Tochen Sichah Be-hitva'adut uMesibat Bnei Torah, Choveret Rishonah, Shnayim Ochazin Be-Tallit* (Kehot Publication Society: Brooklyn, 1996).

[414] See the testimony of world-renowned Jewish music composer Ben Zion Shenker on *Living Torah*, Disc 85 Program 340. Shenker describes these Talmudic lectures, which he regularly attended during the mid-1940s together with fellow Torah Vodaas classmate, Rabbi Moshe Wolfson (today *Mashgiach* of Yeshivah Torah Vodaas).

and closely observed his conduct on the day of the wedding, wrote a letter in response to the request of his family "and the request of the chasidim [who had remained in Russia] to inform them of the details of the wedding in Warsaw", in which he described his impressions of Ramash at length:

> I was with the groom for the twenty-four hours preceding the *chupah*... I became aware with complete certainty that his great fear of G-d has not altered even a hairs-breadth, 'fear of G-d is his treasure' (Isaiah 33:6), he will certainly cause G-d's will to radiate...
>
> In the afternoon, the groom stood to pray his last *minchah* before the chupah... with intense concentration he poured out his soul in a quiet voice (*kol demamah dakah*). This was a tremendous sight, an awe-inspiring scene, for there was no one with us aside for myself and the groom ... It appeared to me that he was casting his supplications before G-d and raisng his soul towards Him... In my heart I praised and thanked G-d for what my eyes beheld... before me stands the famed Mendel son of Levik... an erudite scholar... girded with a silk belt, fasting, studying *Reishit Chochmah* the entire day...[415]

This short excerpt of his lengthy and enthusiastic letter exemplifies the deep impression made by Ramash on those who observed him up close even as a young man, and is strongly corroborated by the private letters of Rabbi Yoel Kahn, written over twenty years later.

In the second letter sent by Kahn to his father after arriving from Israel – just days after the passing of Rabbi Yosef Yitzchak – he de-

---

[415] Rabbi Althaus' eye-witness account has been published in a number of booklets. See, for example, *Teshurah Yovel HaShivim Yud Daled Kislev 5689-5759* (Kfar Chabad, 1999), pages 48-49. See also the letters of Rabbi Althaus to Rayatz (written to the latter in late 1929 when he was in the USA) in which he describes the impression that his newly-wed son-in-law (the Rebbe) made in the Chasidic court in Riga over the High-holiday period and the festival of *Sukkot*. Sections of these first-hand accounts have been published in *BeOr HaChasidut* (above note 184) and more recently in *Kovetz LeChizuk HaHitkashrut, Rosh HaShanah* (Brooklyn, 5771). See also the facsimile of one of Althaus' reports of the Rebbe's talks delivered on the festival of Shemini Atzeret and Simchat Torah 1929 in Figure 25 at the end of this book.

scribes Ramash as a *"penimi* to the extreme" (in Chabad vernacular the title *penimi* refers to an individual who acts upon pure inner conviction, shying away from recognition and fanfare[416]). Kahn was clearly impressed by the tremendous depth of feeling and self-control exhibited by Ramash, writing that "he appears to be a cold person, sitting in a composed manner and speaking quietly, and suddenly he bursts into tears, before continuing to speak quietly in the same controlled tone". A few months later he writes, again in a private letter to his father: "In my opinion, the chasidim in the Holy Land simply do not recognize the extent of his greatness, he is a man of another sort entirely, the Rebbe [Rayatz] said about him: 'he has complete insight, level-headed insight, resilient insight, he is another sort entirely'. He also said many other such things about him... his obedient submissiveness to the Rebbe is indescribable, always at the [Rebbe's] table Rashag would speak, ask questions, he [Ramash] sat like a servant before his master. Even now, when in the Rebbe's room he stands with astonishing humility..."[417].

Rashag Revisited

Notwithstanding the above, Rashag had ample reason to believe that, in the event of Rabbi Yosef Yitzchak's passing, the leadership would ultimately fall to him. He was a more than passable scholar with a fluent knowledge of hundreds of Chasidic discourses. And not only was he the executive director of the *Tomchei Temimim* network of Yeshivot[418], but he himself taught Chasidic thought in the Yeshivah in

---

[416] The conduct of a *'pnimi'* is not affected by circumstances external to himself. The *pnimi* knows what needs to be done and does not waste a moment, applying himself wholly to its pursuit and fulfillment without fanfare. He deliberately avoids external attention as much as possible, aware, as he is, that any unnecessary publicity may distract him from the obligations placed upon the self. See above note 8.

[417] *Yoman miMichtavim* page 2.

[418] To which position he had been appointed by his father-in-law. See Rayatz, *Igrot Kodesh* vol. 7, pages 152, 254, and pages 282-287. For a detailed description of Rashag's work on behalf of the Yeshivot see *Toldot Chabad BeArtzot HaBrit* (above note 207) chapters 36-56.

770[419]. He had dabbled in various business enterprises[420] and was in many ways a man of ambition who enjoyed the prestige and authority that came with his position as his father-in-law's public representative.[421] The astute man that he was, Rashag must have known that his brother-in-law was far more erudite than he, and could not but respect his brother-in-law's depth and piety. But Ramash was also extremely reticent and it seemed unlikely that he would accept a public position as Rebbe, unless he was faced with no alternative. As the older and more visible son-in-law, Rashag, who dressed in the traditional rabbinic style, and who was well connected and respected by many of the wealthy donors who supported the various Chabad institutions[422], had ample reason to believe that though he was not the more qualified, he was the more likely candidate.

Part 2 – The Succession

A Coup d'Etat?

The authors attempt to portray the period directly following the burial of Rabbi Yosef Yitzchak as a time of escalating political ferment and open rivalry between Rashag and Ramash. "By the beginning of the shiva" they write, "cracks in the family unity began to appear... according to Barry Gourary, each of the son-in-laws 'sat shiva' in separate rooms..."[423].

But as neither of the sons-in-law actually sat *shivah* (for only the wife and daughters of Rayatz were obligated by Jewish law to sit *shivah*), this can hardly be seen as a sign "of what would become a contest over the future of ChaBad Lubavitch". Whilst it is true that each "led independent services", this was presumably in fulfilment of the Chabad custom that each mourner (or, as in this case, son-in-law who had

---

[419] See *Yoman miMichtavim* page 7 (end), page 15 (letter dated 20th of Adar Rishon 5711).

[420] See above note 149. [See also Rayatz, *Igrot Kodesh* vol. 15, page 35, end].

[421] See Rayatz, *Igrot Kodesh* vol. 7, pages 96 and 361.

[422] See Rayatz, *Igrot Kodesh* vol. 7, pages 288-290 and 376.

[423] Heilman and Friedman pages 37-38.

undertaken to recite Kaddish) should lead the congregation in prayer if possible.

The allegation that during the seven-day period of mourning "each man was implicitly in competition with the other" is based on pure speculation. The documented facts however suggest that nothing could have been further from the minds of the two dedicated sons-in-law, who shared the collective burden of grief on behalf of all the chasidim. In the letter from that period that "both of them signed"[424] there is no mention of any "need for solidarity" in the political sense. All evidence goes to show that both men were sincere in their grief and genuine in their resolve to do whatever was necessary to strengthen the spirit of the chasidim, so as to ensure that their father-in-law's spiritual legacy would not die with his physical passing.

Ramash did not make any attempt to gain "control of the organization[425] ... with the help of Chaim Hodakov"[426]. Nor did he seek to es-

---

[424] The authors (page 38) write: "To be sure, in the immediate aftermath both of them signed a letter telling everyone that Lubavitch would go on, and that there was a need for solidarity. However . . ." In endnote 26 they refer to an interview with Zalman Schachter as the 'source' for this letter. See, however, Figure 26 at the end of this book for a facsimile of the original.

The letter published both in Hebrew and English reads: "In this hour of bereavement and grief, a tremendous responsibility falls upon our shoulders and yours: to safeguard, with G-d's help, the gigantic spiritual heritage which our late Rebbe has left us all... Let us solemnly rededicate ourselves to carry on . . . in the spirit of self sacrifice exemplified by our late teacher and leader of saintly memory...".

[425] The authors suggest that Ramash was motivated to assume leadership of the movement, because "he saw that in 1950's post war America, for a nearly forty-nine-year-old new immigrant there was no real career outside Lubavitch...". (Heilman and Friedman page 43. See also page 96). However, as we have already demonstrated at some length, by the 1950s Ramash was committed to a career in the movement that had already occupied him on a more than full-time basis for nearly a decade.

Nevertheless, to indulge the authors' argument for just a moment, let us say this: Tens of thousands of Jewish refugees and Holocaust survivors went on to build very fruitful careers in new countries after the war. Many of them were not young. Most of them had no previous knowledge of the language of the new country they found themselves in. There is therefore no reason to assume that Ramash, a man who clearly possessed exceptional intellectual and leadership capabilities, would

tablish himself as a rival to Rashag – indeed, he was by nature uncomfortable with any publicity – neither did he need too. As we have already demonstrated, Ramash had been appointed to run Merkos L'Inyonei Chinuch and other prominent organizations almost a decade before and was already widely recognized as a scholar of outstanding knowledge and a man of deep piety.

As his father-in-law had become more infirm and less accessible, Ramash had increasingly become the link between the chasidim and their Rebbe and it was to him that they looked for clarification of Chasidic concepts in general, and Rayatz's teachings, responses and directives in particular[427]. In the last year of his father-in-law's life, the dimension of Ramash's correspondence had grown to the extent that it already became impossible for him to write to everyone individually. Beginning in 1949 he began to write 'general personal letters' מכתבים) כלליים-פרטיים). Frequently he would compose a general letter dealing with issues that were relevant to a broad segment of his recipients, to which he would add the name of the addressee, and a couple of lines dealing with issues of a more specific nature, as necessary.[428]

In sum, by the time the question of succession came up, Ramash was already a well-known figure, especially to the Chasidic leadership and the Yeshivah students who frequented his father-in-law's court. To those who knew him on a more personal level, he was especially respected as an individual of unique depth and piety. Although extremely reserved, he was conscientious and wholly dedicated to the furtherance of his father-in-law's concerns. Bearing all the above in mind, there was presumably no need for him to "build on the groundswell of support from young followers" or make efforts to gain

---

have had less potential, especially when one considers the fact that he had a quick grasp for languages (speaking at least five fluently before reaching American shores) and was apparently acquainted with the English language while yet in France (see Rayatz, *Igrot Kodesh* vol. 15, page 353).

[426] Heilman and Friedman page 42.

[427] As well as the examples cited above, see *Igrot Kodesh* vol. 3, pages 44, 51, 144 and 197.

[428] See the preface to *Igrot Kodesh* vol. 3, page 5.

"new respect from... old time Hasidim"[429] nor is there any evidence to support such assertions.

The authors rightly point out that "a Rebbe was not simply a political or institutional leader", but "also... an intermediary between his followers and the Almighty, capable of bestowing blessings as well as transmitting the will of G-d... Like a father, he also guided his Hasidim in the most personal decisions of their lives"[430]. This was not a mere figurehead position that could be filled by default. The connection that chasidim had with their Rebbe was intensely spiritual and a replacement would have to measure up to extraordinary criteria. For this reason, when the question of succession did eventually arise, few seriously considered Rashag as a viable candidate for the unique position that his father-in-law had held. Though Rashag was well respected, sufficiently skilled, charismatic and learned enough to fill the roles of institutional leadership, he did not possess the transcendental qualities that chasidim saw in Ramash. Nevertheless, as a consequence of Ramash's reticence and Rashag's more public image, it is fair to assume that had Rashag seriously entertained the possibility of there ever being a successor to his father-in-law, he may have seen himself as the more likely candidate.

Rather than transcribing the documented facts in full and in chronological order, the authors' narrative represents a confusing mix of random statements that freely mingles fact and conjecture. Wider context is usually ignored, key details are omitted and no heed is paid to chronology. The effect is rather bemusing in that Ramash comes off as vaguely opportunistic; an ill-informed reader could not be blamed for supposing that Ramash was not well-known, nor particularly learned or experienced, but was nevertheless shrewd and very charismatic[431].

---

[429] Heilman and Friedman page 42.

[430] Heilman and Friedman pages 32-33.

[431] In this vein, the author's allege (page 57) that the chasidim were "charmed" by Ramash's aura of "mystification", claiming that "forty-nine-year old Menachem Mendel . . . turned out to **all the Hasidism's amazement** (emphasis added) to be a scholar in ChaBaD wisdom and Jewish sources" although "it was not clear to the Hasidim where he had acquired his deep knowledge".

By playing his cards right he managed to win the day against the odds[432]. Below we present a summary of the events leading to the ap-

---

In partial concession, however, they then describe a few aspects of his Torah scholarship throughout his life. Beginning with his studies and correspondence with his father, they also note that "he had surely always studied alone, during his years in Berlin and Paris", and conclude that "in the years since coming to New York in 1941 he had spent much time in the library at his father-in-law's court delving into the esoterica that was in it, and he had published a calendar that served as a kind of manual for ChaBaD daily practices and customs".

These passages seem to contradict the implication of the author's earlier statement that "there were reports – many of them **emerging later, after his star had risen** (emphasis added) in the Lubavitch leadership – that he had been involved with ChaBaD and other Torah scholarship throughout his years outside the court".

At any rate, they fail to discuss the nature and degree of Ramash's Torah scholarship and the vast library of scholarship that Ramash himself had published, nor do they they mention his vast correspondence by virtue of which Ramash's erudition had become common knowledge. **No one** was 'amazed' that Ramash **was** "a scholar in ChaBaD wisdom and Jewish sources".

If there was **one thing** that had long been obvious to the chasidim, it was that this was an individual who was first and foremost steeped in the study of Torah. In the words of Rabbi Shmuel Zalmanov a chasid and confidant of Rayatz, "he spends nights like days in diligent study". (See facsimile of original letter, quoted at length below, in *Yemei Bereishit* page 173).

[432] Several years before the passing of Rayatz the Rebbe travelled to Paris to meet his mother who had managed to make her way out of the Soviet Union. He would ultimately spend three months in Paris tending to his ailing mother, meeting and addressing many refugees and laying the groundwork for the establishment of Chabad educational institutions in France. At one particular gathering the Rebbe engaged in a unique presentation. Heilman and Friedman describe it as follows:

"Demonstrating an ability to remember the people's names and using the occasion to offer little sayings that connected those names with the unique characteristics of each person, an exercise that totally charmed those in the room. It was a virtuoso performance, **and he knew it**" (emphasis added).

In response to the question as to why the Rebbe would offer such a "performance", Heilman and Friedman characteristically suggest:

"No doubt news of his charm and abilities would be spread by Hasidim and others in attendance, who soon would likewise make their way to America and would help pave the way for his conquest of Lubavitch" (Heilman and Friedman page 141 and endnote 45).

We find once again that there is no basis whatsoever for this type of conjecture. First of all, the Rebbe was addressing an audience of survivors and refugees and it is

pointment of Ramash as the Lubavitcher Rebbe in the order that they
actually transpired.

Early Developments

With the passing of Rabbi Yosef Yitzchak the mood of the chasidim
was somber to put it mildly. In the first days and weeks most were
simply in shock, the loss being too great to come to terms with and few
had the presence of mind to look ahead with any kind of clarity[433].
Nevertheless, from the very beginning, we find signs that the chasidim
were beginning to look to Ramash for guidance.

Rabbi Yitzchak Dubov[434] had been in New York for his son's wedding when Rabbi Yosef Yitzchak passed away. In a letter written a few
years later he recalled: "I saw with my own eyes the attachment of the
young men and the Yeshivah students to [Ramash, who by the time of
writing was already] the Rebbe... they practically made me their emissary to speak to the Rebbe regarding his nomination..."[435]. Perhaps he

---

more plausible to suggest that he was using this opportunity to personally give each
one of them some meaningful words in order to boost their morale rather than using it as a forum to campaign for any future contest; secondly, there was absolutely
nothing novel about the Rebbe's "performance" in Paris nor was there any need for
the news to travel back to New York. The chasidim living in New York were already well versed in the Rebbe's Hebrew-name analysis (often devoted to the
names of people participating in his *farbrengens*) to which they had been exposed
from his earliest days on American soil (see, for example, *Kovetz Kaf Chet Sivan–
Yovel Shanim* (above note 405), pages 20-21 and the introduction to *Mekadesh Yisrael*
(above note 220)). Indeed name analysis would continue to be a frequent feature in
his homilies (and occasionally in personal encounters) throughout the following
five decades. The importance of this hermeneutic to the Rebbe is perhaps illustrated
by the fact that the first scholarly essay he ever published was on the Biblical, Talmudic and Kabbalistic sources for Hebrew name analysis. (See *Kovetz Lubavitch* Iyar
5704, reprinted in *Teshuvot uBiurim*, Kehot Publication Society: Brooklyn, 1974, page
1ff and in *Igrot Kodesh* vol. 1, pages 286-291). Name analysis was also a distinctive
feature in the writings of the Rebbe's father and teacher, Rabbi Levi Yitzchak
Schneerson (see also *Sichot Kodesh 5735* vol. 2, page 469).

[433] See *Shemuot veSippurim* vol. 3, pages 135-146. *Yoman miMichtavim* page 1.

[434] See above note 382.

[435] Rabbi Dubov's letter was published in the *Kfar Chabad* magazine, issue number
176.

was spurred to act by the knowledge that living away from the main Chasidic community he would soon have to return home to face the new daunting reality in relative isolation. Be that as it may, on Tuesday the 13th of Shevat 5710 (31st January 1950), no less than three days after the previous Rebbe's passing, Rabbi Dubov approached Ramash urging him to accept upon himself the mantle of leadership. Ramash protested adamantly exclaiming, "The Rebbe lives!" He was alluding to the well known Chasidic principle articulated by the founder of the Chabad movement that "the life of a tzaddik is not a life of flesh, but rather spiritual life – faith, fear and love [of G-d]… therefore… after his passing… anyone who is close to him may receive from his spirit…"[436]. It was this principle that Ramash would live by and reiterate time and time again in the coming months. When Rabbi Dubov persisted – pointing out that, although the previous Chabad Rebbes had also continued to live on spiritually after their passing, yet that had not stood in the way of the appointment of their successors – Ramash questioned the very assumption that he was fit for leadership by exclaiming, "What do you suppose? That Mendel Schneerson is a Rebbe?!"[437]

On his return to England Rabbi Dubov, together with two leaders of the Chasidic community in London, Rabbis Avrohom Sender Nemtzov and Bentzion Shemtov[438], led the signing of a communal 'letter of hitkashrut (attachment)', 'binding' themselves as chasidim to Ramash as their Rebbe. In a letter dated the 25th of Adar 5710 (14th March 1950), Ramash dismissed the 'letter of *hitkashrut*' with a cryptic reminder of his earlier refusal to consider the issue of succession: "I received your letter of the 2nd of Adar [19th February]. Surely you remember what we spoke of when you were here… ". To Nemtzov,

---

[436] Tanya, *Igeret HaKodesh*, 'Explanation' to Epistle 27.

[437] See *Yemei Bereishit* page 84.

See also *Igrot Kodesh* vol. 3, page 260: "I was shocked… that you demand of me things that were not given to me, and are not within me…". See also ibid. page 308.

[438] Rabbi Shemtov was a legendary Chasid; he had studied in *Tomchei Temimim* in Lubavitch and was famous for his self-sacrifice on behalf of Judaism in the face of Soviet oppression. See Rayatz, *Igrot Kodesh* vol. 2, page 68, where Rabbi Yosef Yitzchak describes his efforts and imprisonment at the hands of the soviet government.

Ramash wrote: "I received your letter of the 2nd of Adar. Surely Rabbi Yitzchak Dubov has conveyed what I told him in this regard when he was here..."[439].

One month following Rabbi Yosef Yitzchak's passing the senior chasidim in Israel gathered in order "to deliberate matters regarding the progression of the community of the chasidim of Chabad"[440]. The outcome of these deliberations was summed up in a letter written on the 28th of Adar (17th March):

> On the thirtieth day since the passing of our Rebbe... we gathered together, a whole group from amongst those who are the most attached to him... it is specifically the irreplaceability of our great Rebbe that obligates us... to continue the thread of his life... and most importantly... to continue the golden chain... to seat the one [a veiled reference to Ramash, as will become clear presently] upon his holy seat...

Attached to this letter was another addressed to "the organizational committee of the chasidim in the United States", this one more explicit:

> Ramash, may he live for long and good years, is from the offspring of the dynasty, a direct descendant, therefore it is fitting to urge him that he should succeed the Rebbe... We request that you answer us in this regard[441].

Both letters were signed by three of the most prominent and erudite elders of the Chabad community in Jerusalem: Rabbis Shlomo

---

[439] Facsimiles of both letters, written in the Rebbe's own handwriting, have been published in *Yemei Bereishit* page 104.

[440] Letter on the stationary of Colel Chabad, Jerusalem, dated the 4th of Adar 5710. A facsimile of this letter has been published in *Yemei Bereishit* page 115.

[441] Sections of both these letters are printed in the introduction to *Igrot Kodesh* vol. 3, pages 21-22 and *Yemei Bereishit* page 116. The authors refer to this letter in endnote 38.

Yosef Zevin[442], Nachum Shmaryahu Sosonkin[443] and Avrohom Chein[444].

In a letter written at approximately the same time, the non-Chabad Rabbi Yolles, who had been close to Rabbi Yosef Yitzchak and knew Ramash personally, expressed his surprise that Ramash had not yet been appointed Rebbe:

> Why do you delay attaching yourselves to that holy and pure *tzaddik*? Although I understood from the pure and trustworthy words of the holy Rabbi, Ramash, may he live for many good years, that he does not want to lead the holy community, it is nevertheless incumbent upon you, the chasidim of Chabad to overcome even the will of a *tzaddik*, with 'an arousal from below' (*itaruta di-letata*), for the sake of G-d's glory. I am not a Rebbe, but I am the son and the disciple of a Rebbe... and I have thank-G-d a sense for the spirit of a Rebbe...[445].

Secret Hopes

In the second of the above-mentioned letters from the Chabad Rabbis in Jerusalem we are given a clue as to why the senior chasidim in the United States had not been as quick as their overseas counterparts to officially proclaim their desire to see Ramash succeed his father-in-law. "If you see fit" they write, "to publish the enclosed letter,

---

[442] The Rebbe had met and made a favourable impression on Rabbi Zevin when the two were still in Russia (in the mid 1920s). See Rabbi Nachum Zevin's preface to *Ishim veShitot* (Jerusalem 5767) page 23. (See also *Hitva'aduyot* 5744 vol. 2, Lahak Hanochos: Brooklyn, 1984, page 766).

[443] Sosonkin was a prestigious chasid serving as Rabbi for the Chabad community in Jerusalem. See his autobiography published in N.Z. Gotlieb (ed.), *Zichronotai* (Jerusalem, 1988).

[444] R. Avrohom Yehudah was a son of the famed Chasid, Rabbi Dovid Zvi Chein, known as "the *Radatz*", who had been Rabbi of Chernigov, Ukraine. See *Lubavitch veChayaleha* page 282. R. Avrohom served as the Rabbi of *Beit Medrash HaRambam* in Jerusalem and was the author of *BeMalchut HaYahadut* (Mossad Harav Kook: Jerusalem, 1959-1964). The first volume of this work is prefaced with a biographical sketch of his life and an appreciation by Rabbi S.Y. Zevin.

[445] For the source and Hebrew text of this letter, see above note 201.

and it will not cause any unpleasantness or the like, do so, and if you see that it is still too early for various reasons, do as you understand"[446]. It therefore seems that the leading chasidim in New York were reluctant to reveal their true intentions at too early a stage for fear of offending Rashag[447].

In terms of their private hopes, a letter from Rabbi Yisroel Jacobson[448] to Rabbi Chaim Shaul Brook[449] dated the 2nd of Iyar (19th April 1950) speaks for itself:

Today we[450] went to the gravesite of the late Rebbe with a request for mercy, that G-d should help us to go in the right and true way, in accepting the leadership of the one who is fit for it, according to the true intention of our late Rebbe... his honored son-in-law, Ramash, may he live and be well, conducts all the affairs, he answers those who ask advice and send him letters, he is given notes of supplication [*pidyonot*][451]. He is a man of transcendent stature; on many occasions did I

---

[446] This segment of the letter is published in the editor's introduction to *Igrot Kodesh* vol. 3.

[447] See *Yoman miMichtavim* page 5, letter dated 11th of Av 5710.

[448] Rabbi Jacobson was the founder of 'Agudas Chassidei Chabad of America' and one of the senior chasidim in America at the time. He had studied in *Tomchei Temimim* in Lubavitch, and played a key role in the efforts to rescue Rabbi Yosef Yitzchak from war-torn Europe. See Rachel Altein (ed.), *Out of the Inferno* (Kehot Publication Society: Brooklyn, 2002).

It is noteworthy, that the authors themselves admit that Jacobson and others like him did not support Rashag "because they were more impressed by Menachem Mendel", and due to their personal knowledge of Rashag's ambitions. "While Jacobson was willing to cede control to Menachem Mendel," they conclude, "he was not ready to do so to Shmaryahu Gourary" (Heilman and Friedman pages 53-54).

[449] Rabbi Brook was a student of *Tomchei Temimim* in Lubavitch. He served on the faculty of the Chabad Yeshivah in Tel Aviv and was an influential *mashpia* (Chasidic mentor) to many.

[450] The inclusive "we" presumably refers to the inner circle of Chasidic elders who took upon themselves to ensure continuity and appoint Ramash as Rebbe.

[451] On page 46 Heilman and Friedman write that "already during the high holidays... Menachem Mendel had begun accepting *pidyones* on behalf of his father-in-law." In reality, however, this had become standard practice for the chasidim several months earlier.

hear our late Rebbe extol him with wondrous praise, and many
chasidim and Temimim heard similar things.[452]

In another telling letter, dated the 21st of Sivan (6th June 1950),
Rabbi Shmuel Zalmanov[453] writes to his uncle, a prestigious chasid living in Israel "concerning... the matter that concerns all the chasidim..."
After describing the depth of his twenty-two year personal relationship
with Rabbi Yosef Yitzchak, he continues:

> There is not even a shade of doubt that we cannot leave the
> matter as it is now; it is clear that we must continue the golden
> chain of Chabad leadership until the coming of the redeemer,
> may it be speedily in our days. It is incumbent upon us to give
> praise and thanksgiving to G-d, who left us one son-in-law of
> the Rebbe who is fit and suited to accept upon himself the
> crown of leadership, he is Ramash, may he live for good and
> long years ... he is a man of stature... in his genius and
> wondrous breadth of knowledge... and besides for this, in his
> great [personal] service [of G-d]... he spends nights like days
> in diligent [Torah] study and matters of [Divine] service.
> Though he is extremely reserved, his holiness and purity
> shines through and seeps out... Most importantly his awesome
> humility and commitment to our late Rebbe... Our holy Rebbe
> loved him very much and praised him before those who were
> close to him with wondrous praises.
>
> However at the moment he refuses to accept the leadership
> despite all the pleas and urging of the chasidim here, and
> though in many aspects he has agreed to our requests... he
> says he will not accept it upon himself publicly... The matter
> must be brought to fruition... simply for our sake and for the
> sake of our children... to attach them to the tree of life and

---

[452] A facsimile of the original letter is published in *Yemei Bereishit*, page 146. See
Figure 27 at the end of this book.

[453] Rabbi Zalmanov had served as one of the editors of the journal '*Hatomim*', edited
Kovetz Lubavitch (see above note 370) and had already authored the first volume of
Sefer Hanigunim at the behest of Rayatz in 1949 (see editor's preface to Rayatz, *Igrot
Kodesh* vol. 8, page 15ff).

educate them in light of the truth that our Rebbes have bequeathed us; and the revered and saintly Ramash... has the power and the strength to guide us... with success, physically and spiritually...[454].

These letters speak for themselves. At this early stage, however, rather than declare their hopes publicly in an official statement and risk offending Rashag, these leading figures decided to bide their time hoping that things would eventually fall into place.

Nevertheless pressure was building at a local level as well and in mid-April 1950 after the Passover festival and less than three months following the passing of Rabbi Yosef Yitzchak, the aforementioned Yoel Kahn wrote to his father:

For the last days of Passover many chasidim came, there have already been many secret meetings, and they decided to appoint the son-in-law of the Rebbe, Ramash, as his successor... almost everyone gives him their notes of supplication to [read at Rabbi Yosef Yitzchak's final resting place, referred to as] the *Ohel*... on the last day of Passover some honored members of *Anash* [*anshei shelomeinu*=members of the Chasidic fraternity] asked him to say a Chasidic discourse[455], obviously he refused, and afterwards at the farbrengen he spoke at length, [saying] that nothing has changed [despite the physical passing of Rabbi Yosef Yitzchak]...[456]

Throughout this time Ramash continued his work for "Machne Israel", "Merkos L'Inyonei Chinuch" and "Kehot Publication Society" as before and his deep relationship with his father-in-law remained unaffected by his physical passing. At both public farbrengens and in letters

---

[454] A facsimile of the original handwritten letter was published in *Yemei Bereishit* page 173. See Figure 28 at the end of this book.

[455] The delivery of the traditional Chasidic discourse (*ma'amar chasidut*) is seen as a trademark of the Rebbe's relationship with his chasidim; see, for example, *Ashkavta deRebbe* (above note 348), chapter 5, note 1.

[456] *Yoman miMichtavim* pages 2 and 3.

he repeatedly expounded on the deep connection between a chasid and his Rebbe and exhorted the chasidim that despite the physical passing of their Rebbe, they must study his teachings and implement his directives with ever-increasing enthusiasm.[457]

Yet the chasidim and especially the Yeshivah students were increasingly turning to Ramash himself for guidance. Though most did not formally see him as the Rebbe yet, when reading through correspondence from the time, one detects a deepening sense of awe towards Ramash and a growing awareness that he was endowed with some transcendent spiritual quality. As Kahn writes in a letter:

> I do not say that this is a 'ninth era' ([i.e. a ninth Rebbe, counting] from the Baal-Shem-Tov), and perhaps even this is impossible for us to know; however, he is certainly a saintly and transcendental individual. . .[458]

Rashag had not been invisible to the chasidim during this time; he too often spoke at public farbrengens and at the festive meals held in the previous Rebbe's apartment. On these occasions the two brothers-in-law sat on either side of Rabbi Yosef Yitzchak's empty chair, exactly as they had done during his lifetime. Rashag would tell stories, while Ramash sat in the same reverential silence that he had always assumed in his father-in-law's presence. The chasidim, however, were generally more impressed by Ramash's silence than Rashag's presentations[459].

Renewed Efforts

Ramash's repeated refusals to accept the position of Rebbe did not deter the above-mentioned Rabbi Dubov in the slightest. By now he had began to refer openly to Ramash with titles reserved for a Rebbe,

---

[457] The public talks of Ramash from this period have been published in *Torat Menachem Hitva'aduyot 5710* (Kehot Publication Society: Brooklyn, 1992).

[458] *Yoman miMichtavim* pages 4 and 5.

[459] *Yoman miMichtavim*, page 3, letter dated Thursday eve, *Parshat Tazria and Metzora* 5710. For more examples of Kahn's reactions to Rashag's public talks, see also the letter dated the eve following Shabbos, 15th of Tammuz 5710, on page 6, describing the events of the 12th of Tammuz, the anniversary of Rabbi Yosef Yitzchak's release from Soviet imprisonment.

as well as avoiding mention of his first name (another sign of awe reserved for a Rebbe). In a letter penned on the 24th of Tammuz (9th July
1950) he exhorts a colleague:

> Regarding the crowning of the Rebbe, may he live and be well,
> in truth the obligation rests upon you to try and achieve this...
> Thank G-d, I correspond with the Rebbe and he answers me
> regarding all my queries. He really feels that the previous
> Rebbe is alive, just as the previous Rebbe said and felt
> regarding his father, our holy Rebbe [Rashab]...[460] In truth, this
> is the entire service of a Rebbe to make the supernal realm
> manifest in the lower realm...
>
> In my opinion, all the chasidim outside of America must crown
> him with the title of Rebbe, and then the objective would be
> achieved automatically, despite the fact that he does not want
> it. My consideration is that the chasidim there [in the United
> States] are not able to do anything...

Based on the corroboratory documentation it is clear that the reason for their hesitation was twofold: In America the chasidim had to
contend both with Ramash's unwillingness as well as with the need to
be sensitive to Rashag's feelings.

In another letter Rabbi Dubov writes:

> Although he does not want it, we must crown him with the
> title of Rebbe. It is clear to me that he is fit for it, for I know him

---

[460] As mentioned previously (note 382), Rabbi Dubov had been a student in the
Yeshivah in Lubavitch during the lifetime of Rashab.

already from Riga[461] … For my part I have a Rebbe already, however it is neccessary that **he** should agree to it[462].

The senior chasidim in the Holy Land now decided to call a second meeting, this time a public affair to which the entire community was invited, for the express purpose of proclaiming Ramash as the new Rebbe[463]. The meeting was held sometime during the month of Menachem-Av (July-August 1950) and Rabbi Shlomo Yosef Zevin penned a 'letter of *hitkashrut*' addressing Ramash with those titles reserved for a Rebbe. "With the passing of the crown of our head" he wrote, referring to Rabbi Yosef Yitzchak, "we have become orphans without a father… and there is no Menachem [comfort] to us." By using Ramash's name, Rabbi Zevin was hinting to Ramash's refusal to take up the reins of leadership and so comfort the orphaned chasidim.[464]

"Is it possible" Rabbi Zevin wrote, "that from now on we must survive, G-d forbid, without that center of spirituality and glory by whose light we have conducted ourselves throughout the generations? Without a Rebbe to teach us knowledge?"

"A conclusive answer is unanimously in all our mouths: No! It is not possible! Thank G-d that He has left us for great salvation a scion of the Rebbe's household, he is the revered and saintly son-in-law of the Rebbe, may he live for long and good years… G-d has given him wisdom and intelligence to know, understand and comprehend all realms of the Torah… Upon him rests the obligation… to grant the public merit and stand at the head of the chasidim… for who is there that can

---

[461] Dubov lived in Riga between 1921 and 1928. See R. Raphael Nachman HaCohen, *Lubavitch veChayaleha* (Brooklyn 1983) page 239. He served as rabbi for one of the local synagogues in Riga (See the memoires of Rabbi Israel Jacobson published in *Zikaron Livnei Yisrael* (Kehot Publication Society: Brooklyn, 1996, page 107).

See also the facsimile of the Rebbe's handwritten letter to Dubov published in *Hearot HaTemimim VaAanash* (Morristown, New Jersey) issue no. 698 (13th Iyar 5753) page 12 in which the Rebbe writes:

"זוכר הנני את כת"ר מריגא ועל יסוד זכרוני הנני כותב..."

[462] Both of Dubov's letters are recorded in *Yemei Bereishit* page 199.

[463] See Introduction to *Igrot Kodesh* vol. 3, page 22.

[464] The Hebrew term for "comfort" is "*Menachem*", the first name of Ramash himself, allowing for a poetic double entendre.

compete with him as a teacher! ...This is his supernal destiny that G-d has chosen for him... We are sure that the Rebbe will certainly not withhold the good and will fulfill this request of ours - which we know with certain knowledge is also the request of all the chasidim in the Holy Land and throughout the diaspora..."[465]

Among the leading signatories to this letter were Rabbi Avrohom Chaim No'eh[466], Rabbi Nachum Shmaryahu Sosonkin, Rabbi Nissan Horowitz[467], Rabbi Avrohom Chein and Rabbi Moshe Gourary.

A similar gathering was held on the 18th of Ellul (31st August 1950) in Lod, Israel and the following day an article in the *Hamodia* newspaper ran the following headline: "The gaon Rabbi Menachem Shneerson, crowned as Rebbe of Lubavitch". The article reported that "Rabbi S.Y. Zevin opened the proceedings in which approximately a thousand Chabad Chasidim took part coming together from all corners of the land... Afterwards Rabbi Ya'akov Landau of Bnei Brak,[468] Rabbi Levi Grossman of Tel Aviv[469] and Rabbi Gershon Chein of Haifa[470] spoke ..."[471]

---

[465] *Yemei Bereishit* page 202.

[466] Rabbi Naeh was a renowned Torah scholar, author and halachic authority in Israel. For a well documented biography see, most recently, *Noda Bashearim, Lidemuto shel Amud Hahora'ah Hagaon Rabbi Avraham Chaim Naeh* (Chazak: Israel, 2010). Rabbi Naeh had also corresponded with the Rebbe, see his letter dated 24th Nissan 5711 (*Noda Bashearim* page 339):

"אודיע לכת"ר שכ"ק אדמו"ר שליט"א בקי הרבה בשו"ע אדמו"ר, והוא משיב לכל השואלים, גם אתי יש לו מו"מ...".

[467] Rabbi Horowitz was a spiritual mentor ('*mashpia*') in the Chabad community in Jerusalem.

[468] Rabbi Landau served as Rabbi of Bnei Brak. He was a close confidant of Rashab in Lubavitch and Rostov.

[469] Grossman formally served as rabbi in Kiev, Ukraine. He immigrated to Israel in 1936 and was appointed as rabbi of North Tel Aviv. He was also the author of *Shem UShe'eirit* (Tel Aviv, 1943).

[470] Chein had formerly served as rabbi of Alexandria in the Ukraine [see *Toldot Chabad BeRussia HaSovietit* (above note 183) page 242]. In Israel he was appointed head of the Beth Din in Haifa.

[471] A facsimile of the newspaper article appears in *Yemei Bereishit* page 238.

Pressure Builds

It is hard to get a clear picture of Rashag's attitude towards the growing movement to crown his younger brother-in-law as Rebbe. Knowing Ramash as well as he did, it is difficult to imagine that he really thought that he was more suitable than him to shoulder the responsibility that came with the privilege of leadership. It is more likely that it simply went against his nature to take a less visible role and yield the limelight to his ever reticent younger brother-in-law[472]. Although he had become accustomed to being the more publicly prominent of the two, it now seemed that that prominence was slowly slipping from his grasp. He began to make efforts to keep up his public image, and though he had been known specifically as a teacher of Chasidic discourses, he now began to tell stories and speak in a more casual style, reminiscent of Rabbi Yosef Yitzchak's public talks[473]. As we have seen, the leading chasidim in America understood the emotional turmoil that Rashag was going through and tried to stall for time, cushioning the inevitable blow of Ramash's rising popularity[474]. It is likely too that one of the reasons that Ramash was so vehement in his rejection of any attempts to push him into a position of official leadership

---

[472] The ever observant and analytical Kahn recognized the complexity of Rashag's feelings and realized that he could not really be opposed to his brother-in-law's leadership. Less than a month after the first anniversary of the Rebbe Rayatz's passing, Kahn wrote to his father: "Lately he [Rashag] is completely disorientated due to the fact that the Rebbe accepted the leadership. Some chasidim say that he is in opposition to the Rebbe, however I think it is incorrect to say that he is in opposition, it is simply an emotional issue not an intellectual matter..." *Yoman miMichtavim* page 15, letter dated 20th of Adar Rishon 5711.

Kahn was certain that Rashag himself understood that Ramash was the legitimate spiritual heir to Rabbi Yosef Yitzchak and that only he could really fill the role, thereby providing the spiritual fortification that would carry the Chabad ideal forward into the modern era. It was only a matter of time before he would come to accept Ramash as Rebbe. See also *Yoman miMichtavim* page 13.

[473] See *Yoman miMichtavim* pages 8-9.

[474] See also *Yoman miMichtavim* page 10.

was to protect the sensibilities of his older brother-in-law as much as he was able to, without compromising the needs of the chasidim[475].

In a letter written by Kahn to his father on the day following Simchat Torah 5711 (October 1950) he describes how – for the first time – Ramash was publicly called to the Torah using the traditional titles reserved for a Rebbe:

> Every year they would make two *minyanim* apart from that of the Rebbe (Rayatz), in which the two sons-in-law would be called up as *Chatan Bereishit*. This year they did likewise... the *gabbai* in the *Beit HaMidrash* is Rabbi Yochanan Gordon, however, being that he... read from the Torah in Rashag's Minyan, Rabbi Dovber Chaskind[476] called him (Ramash) up. **Since Rashag was not present** (emphasis added), they called on him with that title... This occurred in the presence of about fifty or sixty chasidim, it was as though not only Berel [Rabbi Chaskind] was saying it, but the entire congregation... it was like a coronation of sorts, but the Rebbe (Ramash) displayed no visible reaction... only when he made the blessing did he cry a little...[477]

It was clear to all that Ramash did not want to fully assume the position of Rebbe; he constantly maintained that Rabbi Yosef Yitzchak remained a spiritual guide to his chasidim. Ramash perceived his physical passing as a calling for the chasidim to realize a deeper level of commitment that transcended the physical relationship with a Rebbe.

Furthermore he did not see himself as a suitable candidate for the position and its ensuing title. In answer to the many requests that he accept the mantle of leadership, he would object by pointing out: "For

---

[475] See *Yoman miMichtavim* page 7, letter dated the day proceeding Yom Kippur 5711.

[476] Chaskind was a prestigious Chasid, who served Rabbi Yosef Yitzchak (by whom he had been given power of attorney, see Rayatz, *Igrot Kodesh* vol. 8, page 587) in a secretarial capacity and as a personal representative. His daughter later married Rashag's son, Shalom Dovber (Barry) Gourary.

[477] *Yoman miMichtavim* page 7.

this there must be the capability, essential powers... and revealed ability..."[478].

On the other hand he was acutely aware of the chasidim's need for reassurance and guidance, as well as his own obligation to ensure that they would indeed continue in the path that Rabbi Yosef Yitzchak and his predecessors had mapped out. It was for this reason that he attempted to tread a fine line between informal guidance and official leadership.

In anticipation of the 19th of Kislev (28th November 1950) of that year Rashag issued a letter to the Chasidic community on his own stationary, rather than on the stationary of one of the organizations under his direction (as Ramash continued to do throughout that year). The first anniversary of his father-in-law's passing was fast approaching; a day that might mark a decisive conclusion to the question of succession, and perhaps Rashag was making a final attempt to draw chasidim closer to his corner. A translation of the letter was issued in English, perhaps as an attempt to rally the wider community of American Jews who were descended from Chabad families and continued to offer their support to Chabad institutions. As Rabbi Yosef Yitzchak's public representative and the primary fundraiser for *Tomchei Temimim*, they would likely be quicker to recognize Rashag as a Rebbe than the less visible Ramash.

On the eve of 19th of Kislev Rashag held a farbrengen with the chasidim for about two and a half hours, once again drawing on various stories and anecdotes in the style of his late father-in-law. The next evening the senior chasidim congregated at Rabbi Yosef Yitzchak's table with the two brothers-in-law sitting facing each other on either side of their father-in-law's vacant seat. Rashag spoke a little while Ramash only broke his silence to say *l'chaim*. After singing the *nigunim* (Chasidic melodies) of the Alter Rebbe [Rabbi Schneur Zalman of Liadi: 1745-1812), everyone went downstairs to the synagogue, where Ramash held

---

[478] *Igrot Kodesh* vol. 1, page 485. A facsimile of the original letter is published in *Yemei Bereishit* page 143. The Rebbe's Hebrew words are:

"ומה שכותב "אנא חוסו עלינו און זייט כו'" – הרי לזה צ"ל היכולת, כחות העצמיים, כחות ההיוליים, כחות הגלויים, ושלימות לבושי מחדו"מ וכו' וכו'".

a farbrengen. Kahn described all these events and noted that during the farbrengen led by Ramash, "the synagogue was filled from one end to the other; I have never before seen such crowding as this"[479].

Appointment and Acceptance

By now it had become undeniably apparent that, despite his repeated refusal to officially accept the mantle of leadership, the vast majority of chasidim had come to see Ramash as his father-in-law's successor. The situation was such that the leading chasidim felt that the time had come to issue a public declaration of Ramash's appointment as Rebbe by the general community of Chabad chasidim. Their concern for Rashag was outweighed by the need for a guarantee of continuity and they could only hope that Rashag would soon come to terms with the inevitable. Rabbi Shmuel Levitin[480] composed a 'letter of *hitkashrut'* which the senior chasidim and leading Chabad Rabbis handed to Ramash on the 24th of Tevet 5711 (2nd January 1951), the anniversary of the passing of the first Rebbe of Chabad.

The letter read: "We the undersigned have accepted upon ourselves with truth and a complete heart the leadership of... our master, teacher, and Rebbe, Rabbi Menachem Mendel... son of Rabbi Levi Yitzchak... and to be attached and committed to him with all our hearts..."[481] It was signed by chasidim from throughout the United States. Ramash's reaction was to burst into tears, protesting that "this

---

[479] *Yoman miMichtavim* page 11.

[480] Rabbi Levitin was arguably the most prestigious and influential of the senior chasidim in the United States at the time. He was a senior member of the faculty of the central Lubavitch Yeshivah (*Tomchei Temimim*) in 770 and was extremely close to Rayatz who referred to him as "the rav" [In chapter two note 6, Heilman and Friedman note that, "It was Rabbi Levitin who had been at Rabbi Yosef Yitzchak's side when the latter's mother died in January 1942, who had even recited Kadish on his behalf at the gravesite..."]. For a brief biographical sketch on Rabbi Levitin see Rabbi Binyamin Eliyahu Gorodetzky, *Sefer Zikaron* (Jerusalem 1983), page 343ff. See also Rabbi Yisroel Alpenbein, *Chasidim HaRishonim* (Kfar Chabad, 2005), vol. 2, page 299ff. Rabbi Levitin was heavily involved in the campaign to appoint Ramash as Rebbe and worked behind the scenes to pacify Rashag to secure his support. (See *Yoman miMichtavim* page 12, letter dated 19th of Shevat 5710).

[481] *Yemei Bereishit* page 346.

[serving as Rebbe] does not have any relevance to me" and requesting that the delegation leave his room[482].

Two days later an article appeared in the Yiddish newspaper *Der Morgen Journal* reporting that the chasidim had appointed Rabbi Menachem Schneerson as the new Rebbe and that they would gather on the 10th of Shevat 5711 (17th January 1951) to formally accept his leadership[483]. When the Rebbe became aware of this public statement, he asked his secretary Rabbi Chadakov to call up the newspapers and have them publish a denial in his name. Instead, Chadakov summoned three leading chasidim, Rabbis Shmuel Levitin, Yisroel Jacobson and Shlomo Aharon Kazarnovski[484], who succeeded in convincing the Rebbe not to publish a denial of the facts. Whether he liked it or not, the chasidim had appointed and accepted him as their leader. Whether he would accept the position thrust upon him was another question altogether[485].

After the morning prayers on the tenth day day of Shevat, the first anniversary of Rabbi Yosef Yitzchak's passing, the many chasidim who had gathered from throughout the United States and Canada wrote notes of supplication which they handed to their chosen Rebbe. Rabbi Meir Ashkenazi entered Ramash's room together with several leading Chabad Rabbis and handed a 'letter of *hitkashrut*' to him on behalf of all the chasidim[486]. "Accepting the leadership" he pleaded, "will bring the ultimate redemption closer, for the redemption is dependent on 'the dissemination of the wellsprings [of Chasidism]', therefore if the Rebbe accepts the leadership and delivers a Chasidic discourse, the redemp-

---

[482] *Yemei Bereishit* page 344. A facsimile of a letter by Rabbi Shmuel Zalmanov describing these events is published on page 363 of that volume.

[483] A facsimile of the article appears in *Yemei Bereishit* page 349. Similar articles appeared in other Yiddish newspapers, facsimiles of which appear in *Yemei Bereishit* on pages 348 and 350.

[484] Rabbi Kazarnovski was a senior Chasid, who enjoyed a close relationship to Rabbi Yosef Yitzchak and his household.

[485] *Yemei Bereishit* page 351.

[486] Similar 'letters of *hitkashrut*' were sent from Chabad communities across America (*Yemei Bereishit* page 373), in Europe (*Yemei Bereishit* pages 362 and 370) and in Israel; a facsimile of the latter appears in *Yemei Bereishit* page 373.

tion will be hastened." For the first time the pleadings of the chasidim met with a positive response. "Yes," Ramash said, "but you [the chasidim] must help me"[487].

Ramash then went to the *Ohel*, the resting place of his father-in-law and Rebbe, where he spent several hours reading the many notes that had been given to him that morning. According to Kahn's report, when the communal letter was given to him, he groaned to himself, "but nevertheless began to read it, weeping copiously". Ramash arrived back at 770 with only a quarter of an hour left before sundown. After the afternoon prayer the study hall where the farbrengen was to be held later that evening began to fill up[488].

At 9:45pm the newly appointed Rebbe entered the synagogue followed by Rabbis Kazarnovsky and Yolles. Rabbi Yolles sat on his right. The Rebbe spoke for a while of the continued influence of Rabbi Yosef Yitzchak and of three loves – love of G-d, love of the Torah and love of the Jewish people – explaining that "these three loves are essentially one". Citing the American custom of making a 'flagship statement' he explained that this would be his inaugural 'statement' to be announced and publicized everywhere.[489]

After about an hour, Rabbi Avrohom Sender Nemtzov, the senior chasid from London who had been among the first to commit himself as a Chasid of the new Rebbe, stood up and pleaded: "The congregation requests that the Rebbe say a Chasidic discourse. Talks are good, but the congregation requests a Chasidic discourse... The Rebbe should say Chasidus!"[490]

Silence ensued and then the Rebbe began to speak slowly and deliberately. "In the Chasidic discourse published for the day of the [previous Rebbe's] passing, the Rebbe begins with the verse from Song of Songs (5:1), *Bati LeGani*..." The Rebbe paused for several 'long' seconds

---

[487] *Yemei Bereishit* page 376.

[488] *Yoman miMichtavim* page 11. See also *Yemei Bereishit* pages 376-377.

[489] *Torat Menachem Hitva'aduyot 5711* vol. 2 (Kehot Publication Society: New York, 1992) pages 210-211. A recording of this talk is available at: http://www.chabad.org/555604/

[490] *Yemei Bereishit* page 381.

and the tension in the air was palpable. The Rebbe then began his first Chasidic discourse with the very same words with which his father-in-law had begun his last.

Listening to the Rebbe's voice, which seems to gently throb with restrained emotion, one can sense the anticipation running through the crowd as it dawns on them that the Rebbe was now officially and publicly assuming the position of leadership. This was an extremely powerful event, with the Rebbe mentioning each of the previous Rebbes throughout his discourse, recalling in that eternal moment the ideals and achievements of his predecessors as well as underscoring the need to actualize those ideals, thereby bringing about the ultimate redemption.

After concluding the discourse the Rebbe reminded his chasidim that the fact that they now had a Rebbe did not in any way diminish the responsibility entrusted to each individual chasid. "In Chabad," he said, "the Rebbes always demanded that the chasidim act independently..."[491] He went on to explain that this gave them not only privilege but also responsibilities. At the conclusion of the farbrengen, the Rebbe called for unity "between all those connected to my father-in-law, the Rebbe". Kahn reported to his father that after the Rebbe had returned to his office all the chasidim sang and danced, "even the elders such as Rabbi Eliyahu Simpson[492] joined in the dancing"[493].

A survey of the documented facts reveals the absolute fallacy of Hielman and Friedman's assertions that the entire process leading to

---

[491] On page 50 Heilman and Friedman construe this statement as "license" for himself to act "on his own, without the legitimacy that a will may have afforded him, and secure the leadership of Lubavitch." However, it is clear from the context that his intention was to charge the chasidim with the responsibility to act, and warn them that they must not rely completely on the new Rebbe. Indeed this has always been the hallmark of Chabad. As opposed to some other chasidic groups where the emphasis is placed on the Divine service of the Rebbe, in Chabad each chasid is charged to constantly focus on his own personal service of G-d, with the role of the Rebbe as guide to his chasidim rather than officiating on their behalf.

[492] He was a senior chasid, who as a student in Lubavitch had been one of a select group of 'chozrim' who memorized, reviewed and repeated the Chasidic discourses of Rashab.

[493] Yoman miMichtavim page 12.

the succession was cleverly orchestrated by Ramash himself who "had been careful not to accept the position... until he was certain that there would be little or no resistance... He wanted it to seem to himself and the world as if it had come from the followers... as if he had not wanted to wrest his position from his older brother-in-law"[494]. In truth, the movement to crown Ramash as Rebbe was led by the most senior and prestigious chasidim of the time, in America, Europe and the Holy Land, who unanimously pinned all their hopes for the future on Ramash specifically. Not only did Ramash not encourage their efforts but on the contrary, so strong was his resistance that it took the better part of a year to convince him of his duty to give in to the wishes of the chasidim. Indeed, it was not until the chasidim had publicly announced their acceptance of him as their Rebbe that he accepted the responsibility that had already been thrust upon him despite his reluctance[495].

Part 3 – Conclusion and Epilogue

'All Beginnings Are Difficult'

Both the Rebbe and the chasidim were sensitive to the difficulty of Rashag's position. The chasidim stalled for time and cushioned the blow as much as they were able to, but ultimately they were forced to put the collective good of the community over the needs of the individual. They were confident in their hope that with the passage of time Rashag would come to see things more objectively and acknowledge Ramash as the rightful heir. In a letter dated the 24th of Shevat 5711 (31st January 1951), Kahn wrote to his father:

---

[494] Heilman and Friedman page 50.

[495] We are afforded a revealing glimpse into the Rebbe's thoughts in this regard by the following comment recorded by Herbert Weiner in his *Nine-and-a-Half Mystics* (above note 252), page 175. Weiner interviewed the Rebbe in the early 1960s. On one such occasion he asked the Rebbe how he could shoulder the enormous responsibility that comes with his position. The Rebbe replied: "To begin with, it is always pleasant to run away from responsibility. But what if running might destroy the congregation? And suppose they put the key into your pocket and walk away? What can you do then – permit the books to be stolen?"

This Shabbat... was the first time that Ramash was called to *maftir* with the title reserved for a Rebbe in the presence of Rashag... Rashag stood with his face to the wall, and the Rebbe too showed some emotion. The Rebbe recited the *haftarah* quickly. It is understandable that in the first weeks this is going to be hard, however with the passing of time things will work themselves out, both with regard to [Rashag's] acceptance of the [Rebbe's] leadership... and with regard to the Rebbe himself...[496]

A letter written by the leading chasidim to Rabbi Yosef Yitzchak's widow, Rebbetzen Nechomah Dinah, is a typical example of a source taken out of context and censored by the authors, thereby leading to false impressions and incorrect implications.

The letter was penned by the most senior chasidim of the time, chasidim who, in their words, had "been together with our holy Rebbe [Rayatz]... for thirty years" – the span of his leadership – "and the older amongst us were for many years together with the Rebbe [Rashab] ..." Such prestigious individuals cannot be cavalierly dismissed as "Lubavitcher supporters of Menachem Mendel"[497].

The authors present this letter in an attempt to bolster their assertion that "Nechama Dinah clearly favored the son-in-law who had lived in her house... [Rashag]" as the successor of her husband. The truth, however, is that this particular letter concerns a specific episode that came to a head over a month after Ramash had already been appointed as Rebbe.

In a letter dated the 26th of Adar-Sheni 5711 (3rd April 1951), Kahn puts things in context:

The Rebbetzen always spoke in praise of the Rebbe [Ramash], saying in the name of the previous Rebbe that 'if he had lived in the time of the Alter Rebbe, they would also have reckoned with him.' At first, when the chasidim began to speak with the Rebbetzen [asking] that she should pressure him to accept the

---

[496] *Yoman miMichtavim* page 13.

[497] Heilman and Friedman page 51.

leadership, she said: 'He has the head of a genius, he will succeed by default'.

Only very recently there are people who are taking advantage of her . . . she is very upset with the chasidim... Yochanan Gordon was one of the [previous] Rebbe's household, and similarly Dovber Chaskind, but now they are not able to go the Rebbetzen's house for she says that they embarrass Rashag... and that they want to take all the institutions from him. And she adds, 'What do they want from my son-in-law [the Rebbe], he is an excellent [*zaidiner*] young man, and they [the chasidim] drag him into everything...' All this is a result of... slander.[498]

As we have already noted, it was clearly very difficult for Rashag to come to terms with the new situation, one so different from the circumstances he had been used to up until then. Though he was still treated with the respect due a son-in-law of the previous Rebbe, his public prestige had quickly dissipated into relative unimportance as chasidim across the globe eagerly fixed their eyes and pinned their

---

[498] *Yoman miMichtavim* page 16. Reference is made in Heilman and Friedman page 51 to an article published in *HaPardes* (vol. 25 no. 8, page 34), which was subsequently retracted (vol. 25 no. 9, page 81). The retraction takes issue with the report that "the new Rebbe of Lubavitch was the organizing force behind the Lubavitch Yeshivas in America, and that thanks to his efforts the network of Yeshivah *Tomchei Temimim* was set up and other organizations established. Similarly it was reported mistakenly that the new Rebbe successfully orchestrated a spiritual revolution amongst hundreds of young Americans who were completely cut off from their Jewish source." The retraction goes on to remind the readership that it was Rashag who stood by his father-in-law's right hand, by whom he was appointed "as executive director of the Yeshivahs".

In the original article however there is no mention at all of Ramash being associated with *Tomchei Temimim*, which was indeed led by Rashag (no one claimed otherwise). Mention is made, however, of the Lubavitch school systems, which were under the directorship of 'Merkos L'Inyonei Chinuch', and headed by Ramash. Even by the standards set by the retraction there was, in truth, no mistake or fallacy in the original article. Indeed everything reported therein regarding the Rebbe's communal work prior to his assumption of leadership can be verified on the basis of first-hand documentation as described above. Perhaps this rather inexplicable 'retraction' was also the work of slander-mongers like those described by Kahn and an attempt to deliberately mislead the public.

hopes on his younger brother-in-law. This situation seems to have led him to cling defensively to his autonomy.

As the leading chasidim explained in their letter to the Rebbetzen: "Since Chabad's inception... it was established that the Rebbe... uniformly presided spiritually over all institutions". Quite understandably Rashag did not wish to acknowledge Ramash as the official 'president' [nasi] of the organizations that he ran. It was therefore this attempt to challenge the complete authority of their accepted Rebbe that caused the leading and most prestigious chasidim to intervene. And with the help of some opportunistic rumor-mongers, they managed to spark the displeasure of Rebbetzen Nechamah Dinah. Apparently she had been led to believe that these chasidim were using the Rebbe's titular honor as an excuse to take away all of Rashag's authority[499]. In truth they only meant that Ramash, as Rebbe, should be recognized as the official 'president' of the *Tomchei Temimim* Yeshivah network in the same way that Rabbi Yosef Yitzchak and his father had been before him. Rashag would remain the 'executive chairman' exactly as he had been in the lifetime of his father-in-law.

In fact it was in an attempt to clear the air and explain their real position that the long and very respectful aforementioned letter was composed. "Traditionally," they explained, "the running of various institutions was handed over from the Rebbe to those who were close to him; however they were no more than representatives... to direct [the institutions] on a practical level. But... the spiritual leader... of each institution was always the Rebbe...". With this clarification they intended no disrespect to Rashag, they explained, for "so it was with the Alter Rebbe... and so it was by the Rebbe, the Tzemach Tzedek – even though a son of the Alter Rebbe still lived, the uncle Rabbi Chaim Avrohom... who was much older than the Tzemach Tzedek. Also alive at that time was the son of the Mitteler Rebbe (Rabbi Dovber Schneerson: 1773-1827), Rabbi Nochum, nevertheless... they too completely and willingly agreed to submit themselves to him as chasidim do to a

---

[499] It is widely known that by this point Rebbetzen Nechamah Dinah was almost completely deaf. It would be entirely understandable if this communication handicap contributed to the confusion.

Rebbe...". The letter continues to explain that the senior chasidim had concluded that the only way for Lubavitch to survive was to appoint Ramash as Rebbe: "We do not need to recount his great genius and extraordinary merits, you know them far better than we, and you also heard this from the previous Rebbe much more than we merited to hear... We do not want, G-d forbid, to take away from Rashag anything that the [previous] Rebbe gave to him; on the contrary, we wish to help him in every possible way... But the power and presidency that the previous Rebbe had over all Chabad institutions, that we cannot give him... It belongs now to his successor, the Rebbe, Ramash..."[500].

An Agreeable Resolution

As has been mentioned, deep down Rashag was fundamentally aware of the fact that Ramash was more suited to serve as Rebbe than he, and despite his initial opposition, with the passage of time he himself would also become a chasid of the 'new Rebbe'.

---

[500] Heilman and Friedman (page 51) write: "Angered by this letter, Nechama Dina... responded in a letter of her own by calling them 'chutzpahnikes' (arrogant). In the letter, she 'refused entry into her house to those who had mocked' Gourary and claimed to consider herself the 'only Lubavitcher Rebbetzen', or rebbe's wife".

In endnote 71, they refer to Avrum M. Ehrlich's *"Leadership in the HaBaD Movement [A Critical Evaluation of HaBad leadership, History, and Succession,* Jason Aronson: New Jersey, 2000], 399", as the source for the particulars of this letter. Apart from the line about "chutzpahnikes" (which I could not find), they paraphrase Ehrlich faithfully enough, except that Ehrlich makes no mention of any such letter penned by Nechama Dinah in an angry tone. He merely quotes Chanah Gourary's testimony at the infamous seforim trial in the late 1980s: "She describes Nehama Dina as having believed and written in her will that she was the only Lubavitcher Rebbetzin..."

Rebbetzen Nechamah Dinah did in fact write a letter to the Chasidim but that letter was written prior to the one sent by the elder chasidim described above. Indeed the letter of the chasidim implies that they were writing **in response** to her letter. By confusing the chronology of this correspondence one is left with the impression that the controversy escalated, while in actuality the opposite is true.

It is true however, that Chanah (Rashag's wife and oldest daughter of Rabbi Yosef Yitzchak) remained forever embittered. According to Kahn (*Yoman miMichtavim* page 32) it was she who refused to invite the Rebbe to Barry's wedding, whereas Rashag himself "very much desired" that the Rebbe should attend. As we shall demonstrate, Rashag had by then long overcome his earlier reservations and enthusiastically accepted his brother-in-law as Rebbe.

The first evidence of reconciliation dates from the 5th of Kislev 5712 (4th December 1951). In a letter Rashag wrote in his role as executive chairman of *Tomchei Temimim*, he refers to "my revered and saintly brother-in-law... the Rebbe, Rabbi M.M. Schneerson, may he live for long and good years..."[501].

On the 11th of Kislev (10th December) of that year, Kahn wrote in a letter to his father:

> Last Thursday night... the donors who give money to the Yeshivah, together with Rashag, visited the Rebbe... since the Rebbe has now been appointed 'official' president of the Yeshivah *Tomchei Temimim*... The Rebbe told me (a few days earlier...) that he would like a few Yeshivah students to come in [together with the donors]... I and another student entered together with Rashag and the donors. Rashag related to the Rebbe very nicely (and if it were not for a few chasidim who love dispute and garb it in [a façade of] holiness... there would already be harmony). First he presented the donors to the Rebbe, saying that they are very involved on the Yeshivah's behalf... Afterwards he concluded that they had come now... to request the Rebbe's blessing..."[502].

Indeed in honor of the dinner held later that month in support of the Yeshivah, the Rebbe's words to the donors and Rashag on that occasion were published and distributed to all who participated[503].

In subsequent years there is much evidence of the very cordial relationship that existed between the two brothers-in-law as well as the deep regard and esteem that Rashag held for the new Rebbe. In a letter written in late 1952, Kahn reported:

> Rashag's relationship with the Rebbe is very good... to the extent that he reprimanded a student for being lazy and not reviewing the Chasidic discourses [of the Rebbe]...[504]

---

[501] See Figure 29 at the end of this book.

[502] *Yoman miMichtavim* page 23.

[503] *Yoman miMichtavim* page 25, letter dated the evening following *Shabbat Parshat Shemot* 5712.

By this time Rashag had also begun attending the Rebbe's far-brengens[505]. On the last day of Passover 1953 Rashag fully entered into the joyful spirit of the farbrengen and, after drinking more wine than he was accustomed to, he began to speak to his brother-in-law in the third person. Kahn recorded his words:

> To me it is clear that you [he used the respectful second-person **plural** *ir*] will lead us to Moshiach! The only heir of the Baal-Shem-Tov is **my** brother-in-law (he stressed the word **my**, as if to say that he takes personal pride in this). I give to you all the powers that I have as the older brother-in-law. I said it at the *Ohel* and I say it now in public...

In the middle the Rebbe tried to interrupt him, protesting that he should not talk like this in public. But Rashag said, "This is the truth. Everyone may hear it"[506].

In a compelling letter penned on the day following Sukkot 1972, Rashag addressed "my revered and saintly brother-in-law, the Rebbe...", writing:

> As I stand now under the impression made by the conduct and [Divine] service of my brother-in-law, the Rebbe, throughout the month of Tishrei, though I am not a man of words, I nevertheless wish to express in writing the feelings of my heart... I wish to bless my brother-in-law, the Rebbe, that G-d should energize him as he energizes thousands of Jews with his Torah teachings. May G-d give him many years filled with light, happiness and good health...
> And I wish to be blessed by my brother-in-law, the Rebbe, that I should have the merit of being together with him for many more years, together with my family, and that I should benefit from the radiance of his Torah and holy service. May G-d help

---

504 *Yoman miMichtavim* page 30.

505 *Yoman miMichtavim* previous note.

506 *Yoman miMichtavim* page 31.

that my brother-in-law, the Rebbe, should soon bring us to greet our righteous Moshiach, speedily in our days, *Amen*[507].

In addition, Rashag would constantly seek his brother-in-law's advice and blessing on a wide variety of issues, both public and personal. In one letter, dating from 1960, Rashag writes: "Today I received an invitation from the Israeli ambassador... to take part in a reception in honor of Mr David Ben-Gourion... I ask his [the Rebbe's] opinion as to whether I should go to the reception or not..."[508]

The following text is one of the many requests for personal blessings and *pidyonot* ('notes of supplication') traditionally written by a chasid to a Rebbe, this one sent by Rashag to his brother-in-law. Such notes are written in a distinctive style; usually a sum of money for charity is enclosed. This pidyon was written on the eve of Rosh Hashanah, 1977:

> ...To arouse great mercy and true kindness on behalf of myself, Shmaryahu son of Sheindel, and on behalf of my wife, Chanah daughter of Nechamah Dinah... May G-d grant me doubled success in running the Yeshivah ... and may the number of students in the Yeshivah increase and may there be success... physically and spiritually ...May G-d give me the ability to achieve everything with ease and surety, and that I should be able to fix times to study Torah with peace of mind... May G-d help that we should have pleasure [*nachas*] from our son, Sholom Dovber son of Chanah and his family... Attached is $200 as a *pidyon nefesh*[509].

Throughout the years, Rashag continued to enjoy the respect of the vast majority of his brother-in-law's chasidim; he prayed at the front of the synagogue and sat in a place of honor at the top table during the Rebbe's farbrengens which he rarely missed. Every year on Simchat Torah Rashag alone would dance together with the Rebbe in the centre of the synagogue. Until Rebbetzen Nechomah Dinah's passing in 1971,

---

[507] A copy of this letter is kept in the personal collection of this author.

[508] A copy of this letter is kept in the personal collection of this author.

[509] A copy of this *pidyon* is kept in the personal collection of this author.

her two sons-in-law would continue to celebrate festive meals together in her apartment as they had done in her husband's lifetime. On these occasions the two would engage in lively discussions, with Rashag respectfully forwarding one question after another to his brother-in-law, the Rebbe, and the Rebbe responding in kind. Many of these conversations (Rashag's questions together with the Rabbe's responses) have been published in two volumes entitled *HaMelech BiMesibo*[510].

In 1981 Rashag suffered a stroke. Rabbi Chaim Shlomo Diskin, who now resides in Kiryat-Ata Israel, was his attendant at the time. In a private communication to this author, Diskin relayed his memories from that period:

Every day Diskin would help Rashag exercise. Twice during that year Rashag went into *yechidut* with the Rebbe, a private audience as a chasid of his brother-in-law. On both occasions Rashag told his attendant that as he would be too busy with spiritual matters in order to prepare himself for *yechidut*, he would not have enough time to exercise. He also asked Diskin to come fifteen minutes early to take him to the *yechidut* so as not to keep the Rebbe waiting. After his stroke, Diskin recalls, Rashag was not always able to attend his brother-in-law's farbrengens. Yet he was always asking people to keep him posted as to what the Rebbe had said, showing a lively interest in whatever was going on 'downstairs' (Rashag's apartment was on the third floor of 770). Once, when there was a children's rally in the main synagogue in 770, he asked Diskin to find out if there was a free phone line available so that he could join the broadcast and listen in on the Rebbe's talk[511].

---

[510] *HaMelech BiMesibo* (Kehot Publication Society: Brooklyn, 1993).

[511] Although the authors grudgingly admit that "in the end, Menachem Mendel's main rival Shmaryahu Gourary himself ultimately accepted the authority of his brother-in-law (and testified on *his* behalf at the library books trial)", they qualify their acknowledgment by arguing, "What else could he do, where else could he go? His life was in the movement, to which he had given so much."

Considering however the extent of Rashag's obvious enthusiasm and respect for his brother-in-law's piety, erudition and leadership, even in private letters, it is difficult to explain away such a deep commitment as mere acceptance of the inevitable. The available documentation and testimony attests to the fact that Rashag, perhaps

When Rashag passed away in 1989, the Rebbe accorded him great honour[512] and also prayed in his apartment on several occasions during the first month of mourning [513]. He also instructed that a special edition of the Tanya be printed in his memory. On the first anniversary of his passing (6th Adar 5750/3rd March 1990) the Rebbe gave a public address devoted to Rashag's legacy, which he later personally edited for publication. In this address the Rebbe said that Rashag's Yahrtzeit should be designated as a day of special significance and commemoration for all.

> The main work of the one who's *Yahrtzeit* is today (throughout most of his life)... the direction of the *Tomchei Temimim* yeshivah (with the power of my father-in-law, the Rebbe, who was appointed (by his father, the founder of the Yeshivah) as executive director of the Yeshivah) and through his efforts and service many students were educated... as we can see with our physical eyes – students who are deeply involved in the study of Torah, Talmud and Chasidut, and in the spreading of Torah and Judaism, and *hafatzat ha-ma'ayanot chutzah* (the 'dissemination of the wellsprings to the outside')... which will bring about the redemption..."[514].

---

more than many others, knew and appreciated his brother-in-law's greatness and actually considered himself privileged to be his brother-in-law.

The authors also write (page 54): "After Shmaryahu Gourary accepted Menachem Mendel's sovereignty, he never again really tried to exhibit the qualities of a rebbe, never published talks that were meant to display his erudition, scholarly acumen, or even his knowledge of Hasidic traditions...".

However, while this is not intended to detract from Rashag's credentials, it is noteworthy, that there is no evidence that Rashag **ever** wrote or published any scholarly material at all.

[512] See, for example, the Rebbe's remarks published in *Sefer HaSichot 5789* vol. 1, page 266 and page 279.

[513] *Beit Chayeinu* (above note 357), page 175.

[514] *Sefer HaSichot 5750* vol. 1, pages 320-325. On that occasion, the Rebbe expounded upon Rashag's name שמריהו בן מנחם מענדל. In this 'exegesis' the Rebbe emphasised how Rashag and his work were intrinsically connected to the messianic redemption (ibid. page 323).

Illustrations

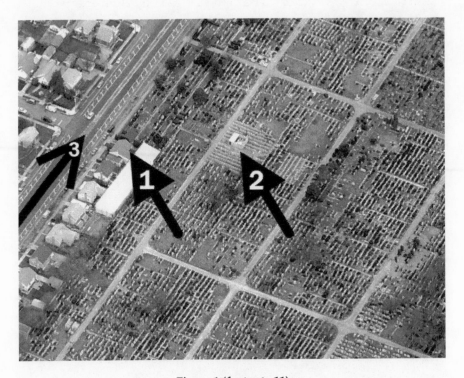

Figure 1 (footnote 11)

1 - Location of Aron Kodesh within 'chapel' (on the Easternmost wall)
2 - Location of headstones of Ramash and Rayatz
3 - Direction of prayer within 'chapel' (toward the East; not toward headstones)

Figure 2 (footnote 15)

Figure 3 (footnote 16)

ABONNEMENTS TÉLÉPHONIQUES.   — 174 —

43. Abonnements de saison (1).

a. A ligne provisoire. — Concédés aux personnes qui, à l'occasion d'un séjour limité, désirent utiliser le téléphone pour une période maximum de 3 mois.

Durée maximum : 3 mois ; pas de durée minimum (les redevances étant dues par périodes mensuelles indivisibles).

L'abonnement peut partir d'une date quelconque.

b. A ligne permanente. — Concédés aux personnes ayant une résidence fixe, mais ne pouvant utiliser leur poste que pendant une partie de l'année.

Durée indéterminée, la période d'utilisation annuelle étant au minimum de 3 mois, consécutifs ou non.

Les périodes d'utilisation partent d'une date quelconque. (Voir n° V, page 180.)

44. Abonnements temporaires (2).

Concédés aux organismes ou personnes qui le demandent à l'occasion de manifestations diverses : expositions, foires, marchés, congrès, réunions sportives, etc. (Voir n° V, page 180, § 3°.)

C. — FACULTÉS CONFÉRÉES PAR TOUS LES ABONNEMENTS.

A. — A TITRE NORMAL.

45. Droits de l'abonné.

L'abonné au téléphone peut :

1° Contre payement des taxes réglementaires :

Correspondre avec les abonnés et les postes publics du réseau d'attache et des autres réseaux ;

Transmettre des messages (N° 18), des demandes de communication avec avis d'appel (N° 15) ou préavis (N° 14) ;

Transmettre et recevoir des télégrammes (Voir service télégraphique N° 38, p. 125) ;

2° Gratuitement :

Recevoir des communications, recevoir des télégrammes rédigés en langage clair français et ne dépassant pas 50 mots.

46. Annuaire.

Inscription gratuite pour tout titulaire d'une ligne principale d'abonnement. Elle n'est pas obligatoire, et comporte exclusivement :

1° Le numéro d'appel de l'abonné ;

2° Son nom (suivi de son prénom si cela est indispensable) ou la raison sociale, ou la dénomination commerciale ;

3° Sa profession ;

4° Son adresse.

Les abonnés du réseau de Paris peuvent obtenir sur leur demande :

1° Une inscription gratuite dans la liste par rues ;

2° S'ils exercent une profession, une inscription gratuite dans la liste professionnelle.

Fourniture aux abonnés. — Gratuite, pour tout titulaire d'un abonnement principal (3). Dans la région de Paris, les abonnés du réseau de Paris reçoivent les deux volumes de l'annuaire de Paris ; les autres abonnés de la région de Paris reçoivent seulement le premier volume. Les abonnés des départements autres que la Seine, Seine-et-Oise et Seine-et-Marne, reçoivent la partie de leur département.

Distribution. — A domicile gratuitement aux abonnés de province et moyennant une taxe de 2 francs aux abonnés de la région de Paris.

(1) Ne donne pas droit à la fourniture gratuite de l'Annuaire.

(2) Ne donnent droit ni à l'inscription gratuite à l'Annuaire, ni à la fourniture de cet annuaire.

Pas de durée minimum. Il n'est pas signé d'engagement pour les abonnements d'une durée inférieure à 5 jours.

(3) Sauf pour les abonnements de saison, les abonnements concédés à l'occasion de manifestations diverses et les lignes spécialisées à l'arrivée.

Guide officiel des PTT 1938

Figure 4 (footnote 16)

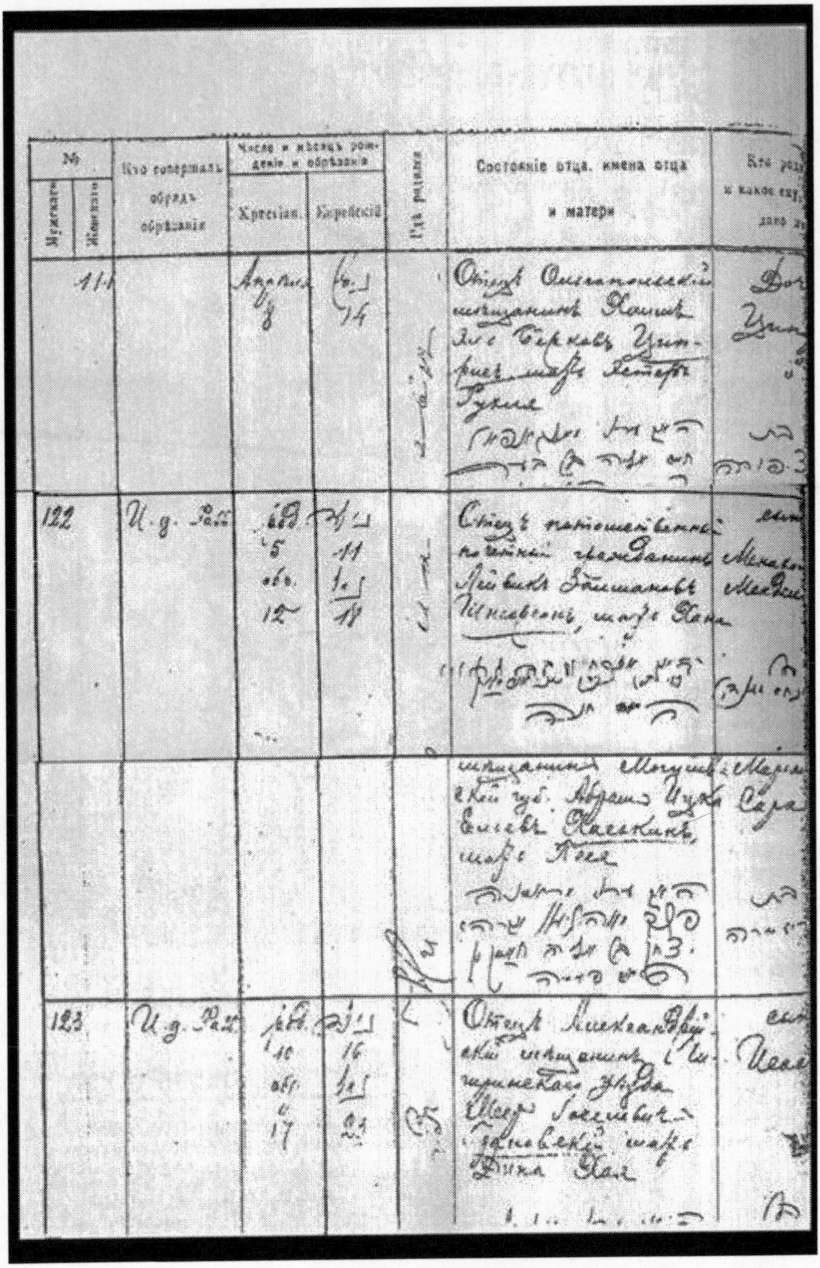

Figure 5 (footnote 50)

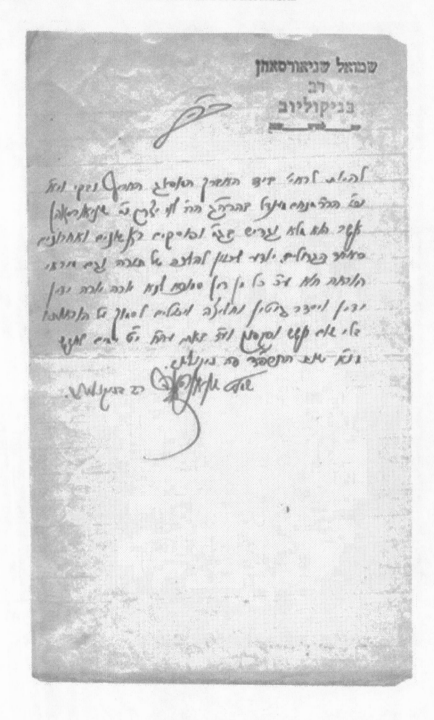

Figure 6 (footnote 64)

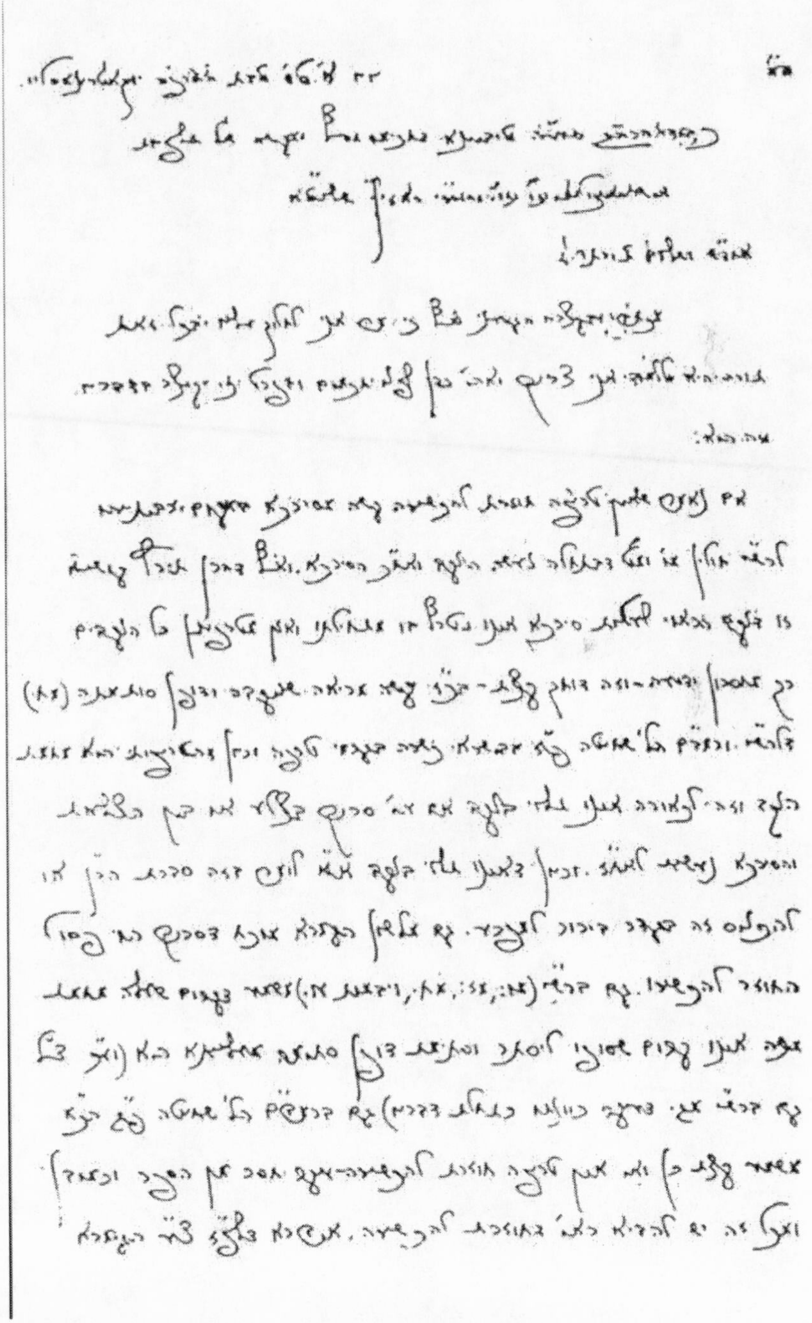

Figure 7a (footnote 73)

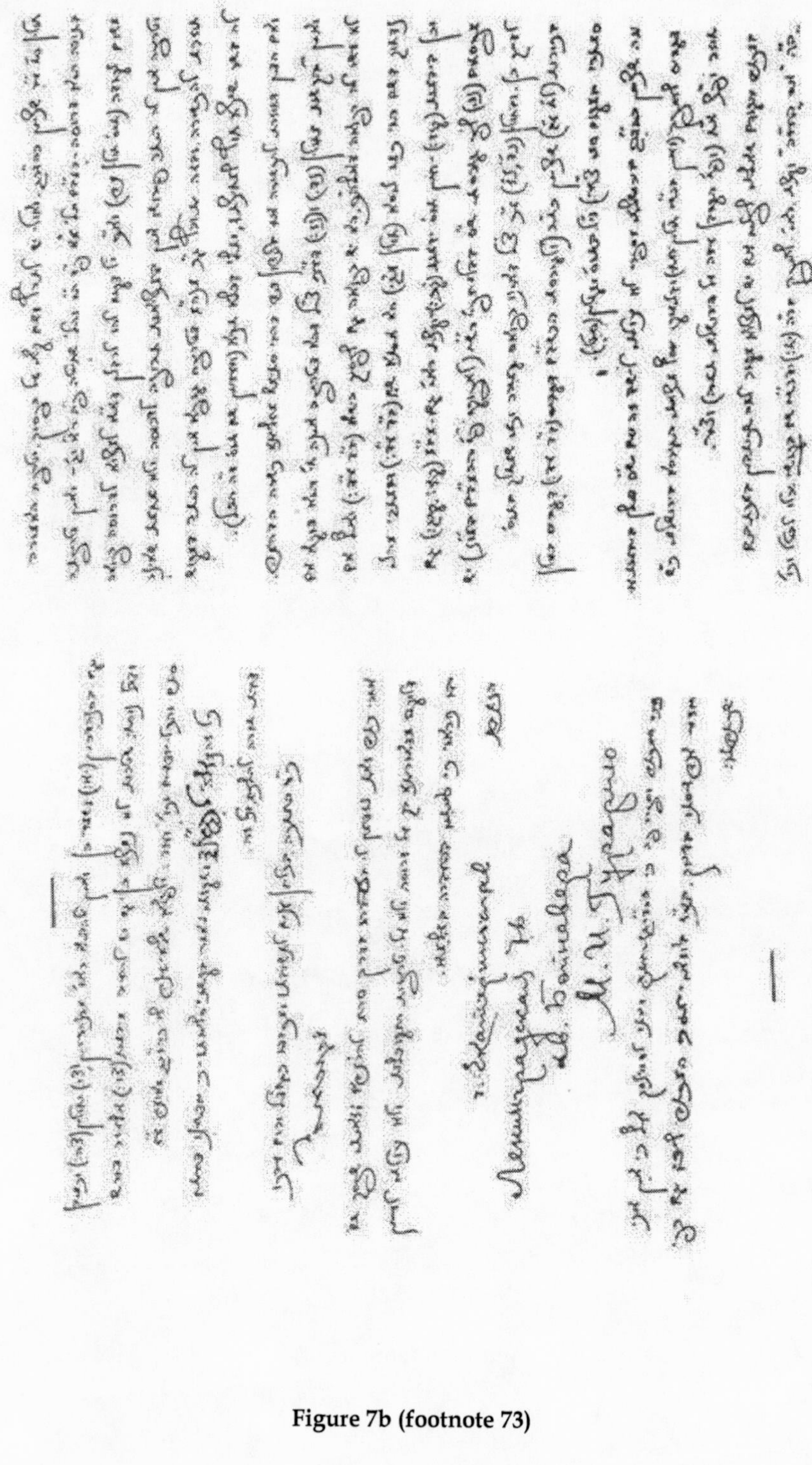

Figure 7b (footnote 73)

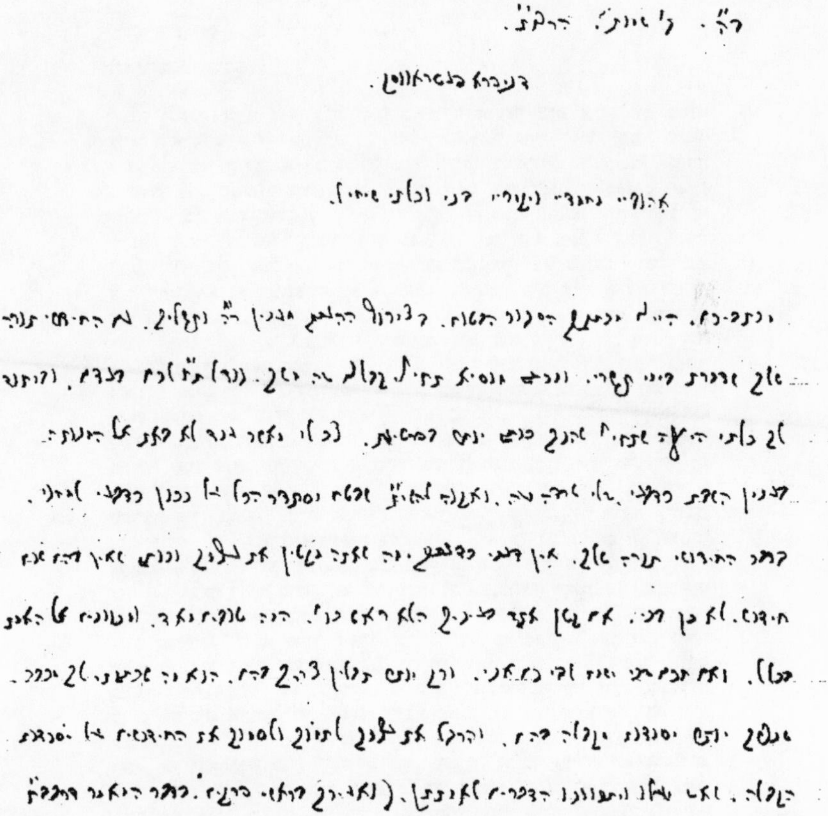

Figure 8 (page 32)

ב"ה, ערב יום הכפורים התרצ"ט.

דניפראפעטראווסק.

ובאשר היום הוא ערב יו"ם כפורים (מספר ב"פ אור, ועם מספר
ער"ב הוא מספר פור"ת עדמ"ש בן פורת יוסף, שזה שייך לספרי' ורבי'. ובכלל
לכל הברכות והצלחות). הנחשב כיום הכפורים כמארז"ל כל האוכל ושותה
בתשיעי כו', ששיעור האכילה ושתי' ב' ימים הוא לנגד יסוד ומל' שאין
להפרידן, כי נקראים כפות תמרים שתמר סליק דכר ונוקבא יחד. ולנגד זה
שיעור איסור אכילה ביוהכ"פ הוא כמתר, כי אז הוא עליית התמר, בזמן
נעילה כד תחמי שמשא בריש דיקלא, והכותבת אז היא כותבת הגסה, ואא
ע"ד התחומרתא דחינונינתא שמצא רב הונא בסוטה דמ"ט ע"א, שהיא שמינה
ויש בה ריח טוב. רב הונא שמו הוא מלשון הון יקר ונעים שקאי על דעת
עליון המחבר חכ' ובינה שהם יקר ונעים. הזן הוא עשירות שעשירות הוא
מצד דעת עליון והוא הנמשך ע"י תקיעת שופר שברי"ה. כי ע"י שופר נמשך
עשירות וכמארז"ל כל שנה כו' היא מתעשרת בתופה שהפירוש הוא אחר
תקיעת שופר, וכמ"ש והשבע לעשיר איננו מניח לו לישון, השבע לעשר הוא
השבעה הכלים הנמשכים ע"י השופר, אינו מניח לישון להעבד הכתוב מקודם
מתוקה שנת העובד. והוא מה שהשופר מעורר מן השנה והתרדמה. הנה אז
מתחיל בנין המל' שנעשית בחי' תמ"ר היפך מר"ת נפש מרתא בת בייתוס
שנעשה מי"ז בתמוז עד ת"ב, וכמא' אמרו לפני מלכיות כו' ובמה בשופר.
הנה בר"ה ע"י התקיעות נעשית תמר, אבל לא דחינונינתא עדיין, ואימתי
נעשית חינונינתא הוא ביוהכ"פ בגמר נעילה שאוי יש ג"כ תק"ש, שהוא
גדול מן שופר דר"ה כידוע. אז נעשית חינונינתא מלשון וחנון ע"י התחנונים
שביוהכ"פ. שמגיע זה ברום המעלות בתיקון השלישי די"ג ת"ד. (והוא בחי'
ביום השלישי יקימנו ונחי' לפניו, שביום השלישי קאי על יוהכ"פ). הפני
משערות. והוא הארחא שתחת החוטם ששמש גמשך לחפה דא"א שיאמר סלחתי
כמ"ש בזהר הקדש באד"ר. והוא ביוהכ"פ שאז הוא סלחתי וכמ שאומרים
בריש יוהכ"פ, ויאמר ה' סלחתי כדבריך, אז נעשית התמורתא, חינונינתא
שמינה מפנימיות החכ' ויש בה ריח טוב מפנימיות בינה, ומצא אותה רב
הונא השייך לתק"ש כנ"ל, וקאי גם על התק"ש שבנגמר נעילת יום הכפורים,
ונתנה לרבה ברי' ורבה נתנה לרבא בן בנו כדאיתא התם, לרמז שמזה נמשך
בנים ובני בנים, כי כל ענין מה שתמר סליק דכר ונוקבא הוא בכדי שיהיו
בנים ובני בנים וכמ"ש לא ימושו מפיך ומפי זרעך ומפי זרע זרעך שאז אמר
ה' מעתה ועד עולם.

ובכן הנני מברך ברכות הורים אותך בני יחי' לאויט"א ישימך אלקים
כאפרים וכמנשה ואותך כלתי תחי' לאויט"א ישימך אלקים כשרה רבקה רחל
לאה. ואתכם יחד יברכך ה' וישמרך ה' יאר ה' פניו אליך ויחנך ישא ה' פניו
אליך וישם לך שלום, ושם את שמי על בני ישראל ואני אברכם. בשנה
תכב   לקוטי   **אגרות קודש**   לוי יצחק

הטובה הזאת הבאה עלינו לטובה יפקדכם ה' בבן זכר זרעא חייא וקיימא
ויחדש השי"ת 'על כולנו שנה טובה ומתוקה שנת חיים ושלום וכל טוב בגוף
ונפש בגשמיות ורוחניות, שנת גאולה וישועה ע"י משיח צדקינו, וימלא השי"ח
את כל משאלות לבבנו לטוב. האמתי הגלוי אלינו לחיים טובים ארוכים
ולשלום. יתקבלו תפלותינו ובקשתינו בתוך כל תפלות ובקשות אחינו בני
ישראל לרחמים ולרצון לפני אדון, והי' אך טוב חסד ושלום והשקט חיים
טובים ארוכים לשלום כחפץ אביך וחותנך המצפה לרחמי שמים.

לוי יצחק ש"ם

Figure 9 (footnote 96)

כסלו רפ"ט.

עתה חביבי מחמדי שמע לדברי, בהנוגע לכללותך בשטומ"צ אי"ה
למד"ט. והוא בערך שבוע או יותר קודם הנשואין, תלמוד טושו"ע יורה דעה
סי' קצ"ג וד"ל. הקריאה לתורה קודם הנשואין יהיו מסתמא בש"ק פ' ויצא

רז   לקוטי   אגרות קודש   לוי יצחק

אי"ה. הנה אחר עלייתך לתורה יברכוך במי שברך כו' ויאמרו בעבור שאביו
ואמו (בשמותם ושמות אבותיהם) נדב'מ צדקה בעדו וצוו לברכו כר אמן. (ובטח
תודיע מקודם באיזו יום יהי' הקריאה לתורה במדי שגם אנחנו נשמח בפה
אי"ה). ובמוצש"ק תודיע בדיפעש מעלייתך לתורה, וגם במכתב מכל בפרטיות.

ביום החופה תטבול א"ע בדיוק במקוה (ישראל ה', שהמ' סאה רומזים
על ד' יודי"ן דשם ע"ב, שההשרש הוא המזל נצר חסד, ושייך זה מאד לחתן,
ודוק) ומיד אחר חצות היום תלמוד פרק "כ"ה" בתניא בכוונה עצומה (לא
בעיון, רק בכוונה כו') ותומ"י אחר זה תתפלל מנחה עם על חטא בכוונה
גכונה ועצומה. וכל המרבה לבמת אז בתענית זה שנחשב כיוהכ"פ (שגם
אז הי' ענין נשואין, שבנות ישראל יוצאות וחולות כו', במדריגה יותר
גבוה מן ט"ו באב) הר"ז משובח. תחת החופה תלבש קיטל חדש (מובן
לך שמאד חפצתי גם האבנט מבגד הצ"צ ז"ל זיע"א, שאצלי, אבל מר,
ומח' טובה הקב"ה מצרפה למעשה) על הבגד, סורטוק של משי (שמסתמא
תפרת לך, כאשר בקשתיך). ותיכף אחר החופה אם הפצך תוכל ללבוש
בגד אחר. בעמדך תחת החופה כל העת תחשוב ביראת־שמים (כן אמר
לי להנגשאין שלי אדמו"ר ז"ל גבנ"מ זיע"א) ושיהיו לך בנים יראי־שמים
דור ישרים יבורך מב"ג תחי' אשר ברכך ה'. מיד אחר החופה בהקדם
היותר אפשרי, תודיעני בדיפעש שהיי הנשואין למד"ט בשטומ"צ, ואחרי
הנשואין תתפלל כל התפלות, (וכן ברכות השחר) באבנט, גם תתחיל להניח
תפילין דר"ת ג"כ כל ימיך אי"ה.

נא מחמד נפשי עשה ככה, וייטב לך כל הימים, כחפץ אוהבך אהבת
נצח ובלי מצרים. חפץ באשרך והצלחתך תכה"י.

Figure 10 (footnote 100)

Figure 11 (footnote 124)

במה שכתבו שמוציאים לאור הוצאה מיוחדת מחיבורם כתב: (1) ונכון במאד מאד

במה שכתבו שיודעים אנו כמה הדוקים הם קשרי הידידיות בין וכו', עיגל חלק זה שבקטע וכתב: הרבה יותר

מאשר יודעים (2)

ולבסוף כתב:

כוונתם רצוי' וכו', אבל אין הנ"ל נהוג בבית הרב כלל ומכמה דורות – ואתם הסליחה (3)

Figure 12 (footnote 136)

[ב׳ אד״ר פ״ט׳]

...שהנך מתענה בכל יום ויום עד עת המנחה, אדרבא הנני שובע רצון מזה שהודיעה אותי, ומחזיק טובה הנני לה בעד זה, ואיני מבין אותך כלל, מהו השיטה הזאת, מאין לקחת ומי למדך כאלה. כמדומה שלע״ע רחוק הנך מגבורת שמשון, ולמה אתה עושה כאלה, אין זו דרך התורה, ולא דרך התשובה כלל וכלל, נצרך לשמור את הבריאות בכל תוקף ועוז, והנני מצוה לך במפגיע שבל תעשה כזאת בשר״א, לא רק עד המנחה, אלא גם עד אחר תפלת שחרית, תאכל בכל יום ויום פת שחרית קודם התפלה (רק תקרא ק״ש מקודם, ואם באפשר עם תפילין[2] מה טוב.) והשתדל ביותר לשמור את בריאותך, וכל המרבה הר״ז משובח.

...לע״ע הנני מסיים, ואבקשך עוד הפעם על כל האמור לעיל, ונא ונא אהובי, לכתוב לפרקים קרובים ביותר, ומכל בפרט, ויהי׳ ה׳ עמך, תעלה ותצלח מעלה מעֵלַה בגו״ר כחפץ אביך אוהבך מעומקא דליבא כה״י.

לי״ש

באלו הימים מסתמא אשלח לך עוד ענין א׳ אי״ה

Figure 13 (footnotes 153 and 156)

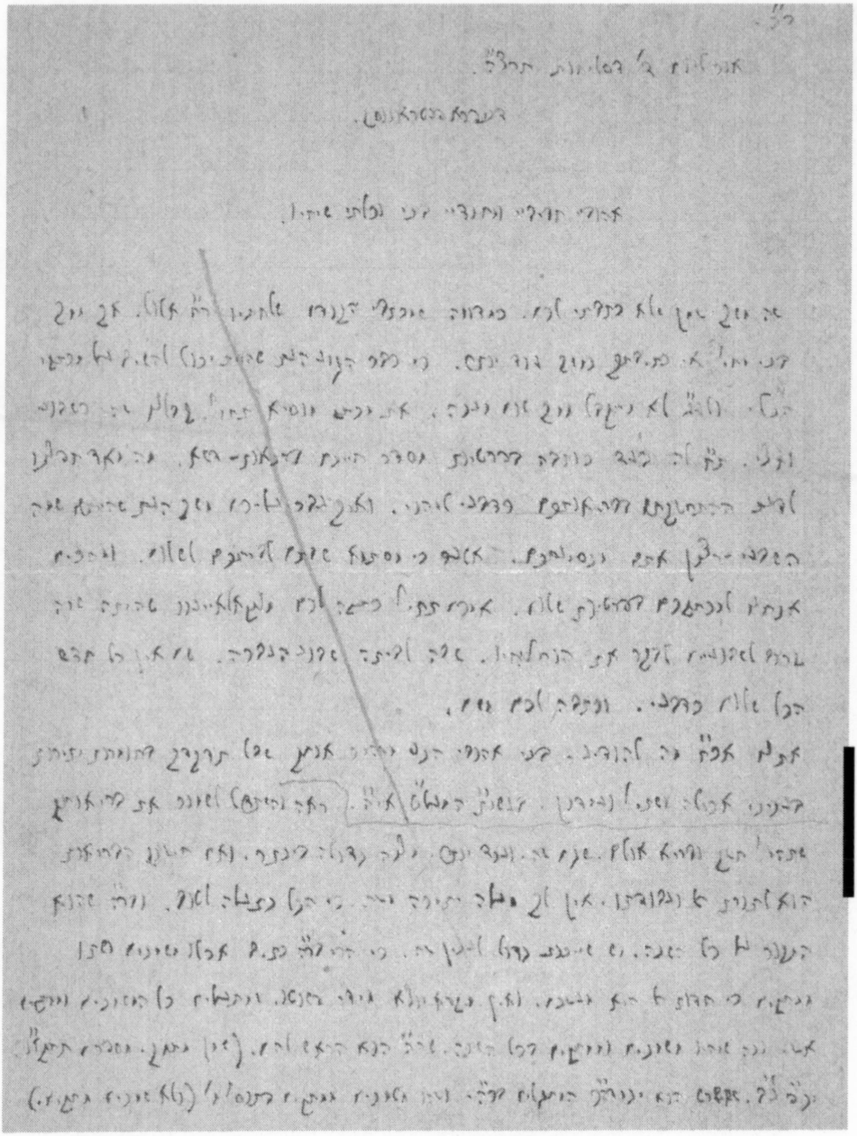

Figure 14 (footnote 159)

‎. . . בני אהובי הנני מזהיר אותך שבל תדקדק בחומרות יתירות בעניני אכילה ושתי' ועידן בעשי"ת
‎הבעל"ט אי"ה, ראה והשתדל לשמור את בריאותך שתהי' חזק ובריא אולם, שגם זה, ועוד יותר,
‎מצוה גדולה ביותר. ואם חיזוק הבריאות הוא לתורת ה' ועבודתו, אין לך מעלה יתירה מזה, כי הכל
‎נתעלה לטוב . . .

Please note: When the Rebbe submitted his father's letters for publication he
struck out some private passages including those that make reference to his
own supererogatory or ascetic conduct to indicate that they should be omitted
from the printed text.

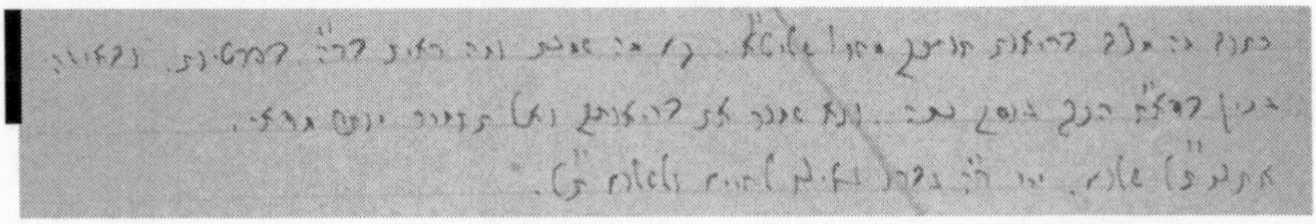

Figure 15 (footnote 159)

כתוב מה מצב בריאות חותנך מחו' שליט"א, גם מה שמעת ומה ראית בר"ה בפרטיות, ובאיזה ענין בדא"ח הנך עוסק עתה. ונא שמור את בריאותך ואל תחמיר יותר מדאי.

Please note: When the Rebbe submitted his father's letters for publication he struck out some private passages including those that make reference to his own supererogatory or ascetic conduct to indicate that they should be omitted from the printed text.

•

 י"ט טבת, צ"ט.

הנך כותב שהתחלת להניח תפילין דשמושא רבא, לוא יהא כן, אם כי לכאורה הלואי הספקנו מבלי להסיח דעת מתתפילין דרש"י ור"ת. ויהי' ה' בעזרך להרגיש המוחין שבתתפילין הללו ג"כ, ויהיו לכם חיים ארוכים טובים ונעימים. כי ע"י תפילין נמשך חיים כמארז"ל במנחות דמ"ד מפסוק ה' עליהם יחיו ע"ש. ובפסוק כתיב ג"פ חיים, יחיו חיי רוחי, והחייני, הוא לנגד הג' תפילין דר"ת דרש"י ודשמושא רבא הנרמזים בפסוק שמר תם וראה ישר כי אחרית לאיש שלום. והם לנגד כתר חכמה בינה, היינו חיים ארוכים טובים ונעימים. והם מכוונים ג"כ לנגד הג' דברים חיי מזוני בני התלוים במזלא. (כי מזוני ובני הם ג"כ בחי' חיים, וכמארז"ל שעני חשוב כו' וכן מי שאין לו בנים). ובני בעיקר שייכים לתפילין דשמושא רבא, שהם בכתר ומשם נמשך בני. כידוע באי"ה הנאמר בשרה איה שרה אשתך. ושמושא מורה על זה, שהוא ג"כ מלשון שהשמש דש בדרד"יל. וזהו לאיש שלום ששמו הי' שלום ומגיע זה ביסוד הנקרא שלום. והוא אי"ש שלרים מספר השמות עסמ"ב, קס"א קמ"ג

לקומי   אגרות קודש   לוי יצחק   תכג

קנ"א. שביסוד הנקרא בן פור"ת (ע"ה) יוסף, ומזה נמשך אשה כי תזרי"ע וילדה זכר. ובחי' דבני נכלל ג"כ חיי ומזוני, והוא מה שג"פ חיים הוא מספר צדי"ק יסוד עולם. והיינו מה שבתתפילין בכלל צריך להניחם במקום שמוחו של תינוק רופ"ס, אם כי תינוק עצמו א"צ להניח תפילין. הוא כי ע"י תפילין נמשך שיש בני, תינוק, ודוק במִלָת   רופ"ס ותמצא עד היכן הדברים מגיעים. ובכן יהי רצון וחפץ מלפני השי"ת שאיה מקום כבודו שתזכרו ותפקדו במהרה בבני חיי ומזוני רויחי, ותחיו יחד חיי ענג.

לוי יצחק ש"ס

Figure 16 (footnote 162)

Figure 17 (footnote 220)
passport photograph
(issued 1 October, 1927)

Figure 18 (footnote 220) end 1928

Figure 19 (footnote 220)
February 28, 1935

Figure 20 (footnote 220)
June 14, 1942

Figure 21 (footnote 220)
March 17, 1949

Figure 22 (footnote 220)
February 6, 1951

Satmar, M'lochim, Lubavitch

While it was reported that Satmar officials condemned the hanging (nothing was said about the attack on the Israeli flag), their claim that they had nothing to do with the demonstration was given scant credence. In the meantime, more mischievous sparks were scattered. In Williamsburg the Yiddish weekly newspaper, the *Algemeiner Journal*, sympathetic to Lubavitcher causes, became forbidden reading. Newsdealers carried it at their own risk. Harassing phone calls were made to subscribers, distributors, and advertisers. These pranks took a more dangerous turn when the *Algemeiner's* offices in Borough Park were ransacked and later burned to the ground. A candy store in Williamsburg that carried the newspaper was also razed by fire.

The Satmar Hasidim received most of the blame and the negative publicity associated with the Purim happening. The Lubavitcher Rebbe apparently did not know of Cohen at the time and placed the blame squarely on Satmar. At a Shabbes farbrengen ten days after the events he observed that he had waited ten days for a sign of repentance before speaking out.[8] Responding to the Satmar claim that only children were involved, he cited pictures of the attack on the mitzvah tank in the press showing many older men with long white beards standing by, laughing and smiling.

Conflicts

In midsummer of 1976 differences between Satmar and Lubavitch were sharpened by their responses to events in the Middle East. On June 27 an Air France jet flying from Tel Aviv to Paris with a manifest of approximately 250 passengers and crew was seized by 7 pro-Palestinian guerrillas. After refueling the plane in Libya they forced the crew to fly to the Entebbe airport in Uganda. Claiming to be members of the Popular Front for the Liberation of Palestine, the kidnappers threatened to blow up the plane and kill all of their hostages unless 53 terrorists were freed from prisons in Israel, France, West Germany, Kenya, and Switzerland. The Israelis, 2,300 miles distant, launched a rescue mission on July 3. Under cover of darkness they landed three cargo planes at Entebbe. To confuse the terrorists and delay their initial response one of their number drove up in a Mercedes Benz dressed as Idi Amin, Uganda's head of government. In a lightning assault on the terminal Israeli troops killed all 7 hijackers and saved 103 passengers and crew members (143 passengers had been released earlier through negotiation).[9]

The daring raid was hailed throughout the world as a brilliant rescue and a blow against terrorism. The elated Lubavitcher Rebbe called the event a miracle; the Satmar Rebbe, however, scorned it as a misguided risk.

Figure 23a (footnote 236)

HASIDIC PEOPLE

Relationships deteriorated even further after the raid on Entebbe. Again the Rebbe said it was a miracle. God performed miracles through the Israeli soldier. To the Satmar this was totally unacceptable. He would do anything to destroy what he considered to be the cancer of our generation. (AF)

The community then waited for the next incident to occur. One's relationship to the Israeli government became the measure used to determine even the sacred obligation of charity.

The Satmar Hasidim give enormous *tzedakah* [charity], but they refuse to give money to any institution which is supported by the Israeli government. Forty-Seventh Street Photo gives but not to supporters of the government. I asked Goldstein for support for our yeshivah in Israel and he said, "I have one question: Do you accept money from the Israeli government?"
I said, "I have to admit that we do."
And he said: "Then I'm sorry but I can't give you anything." (IA)

Tempers rose the year following Entebbe when the Lubavitcher Hasidim sent their "Mitzvah tanks" into Williamsburg, the heart of Orthodoxy. The Satmar Hasidim considered it an intolerable intrusion. As the trucks turned down Rodney Street, where the Satmar besmedresh is located, they were greeted by flying stones, the police escort notwithstanding.

The Lubavitcher Hasidim could not understand the hostile reaction. A custom had been inaugurated under the previous Lubavitcher Rebbe of visiting places of worship in Williamsburg on the seventh day of Passover to deliver short talks on Lubavitcher philosophy. They remained determined to fulfill their previous Rebbe's program and continue their activities in Williamsburg.

For the past forty years on the seventh day of Passover we've gone to shuln in Williamsburg, Borough Park, and Crown Heights not to antagonize but to increase happiness on the holidays. We always obtain permission in advance from the president or rabbi of each shul. We didn't go to Satmar but to other shuln where we had permission. (AR)

There were warnings of violence if Lubavitchers continued this practice. The present Lubavitcher Rebbe, however, indicated that he could not stop something that his predecessor (his revered father-in-law) had initiated. This drew a sharp reaction from the leadership of Satmar.

They are not telling the people what they are doing. They came in with troops, with sound trucks, marching here and there in the street. What did they want to dispense here? Hasidism? We have our own Hasidic life. We don't need the Lubavitcher Rebbe to teach us his philosophy. We didn't go to Eastern Parkway to preach there. They look for trouble. Lubavitch had a custom that every Passover they came marching in the hundreds in the street. I called them and I told them, "Don't come to Williamsburg. Why do you

· 58 ·

Figure 23b (footnote 236)

אחי התמימים בלמדם ואת עבורתם הנאמנה נגל
כבודם עוד יותר חרבה מאד, ולאות רגשי לבבי
נרשתי שלשה רו"כ, מכיר אנכי כי ראוויים הם הילרים
התמימים להתגרב עליום מאות ואלפים, אלא שעורני
ילד, ומובמחני שאכותי יחי' ישלימו ואת אשר
החסרתי ימלאו כרותם הנריבה וכיד ר' המובה
עליהם.

בכבוד נמור, באהבה ובאחוה
נשה כ"ר נתן נוראאי'.

חידה.

נח בן שם, אחר המבול, ואברהם בן חם
ראו, כי נפלאה הארץ ללשון עם ועם.

פתרון החידה בגליון כ"א.

"עין תחת עין מבון".

שמות הפותרים:

ארשא: משה אליעזר ווינאארסקי. באברוויסק:
בנימין איזראאילעוויטש. גלובאקאיוו: אבא
שרגוביג. ישעי' באגין. מרירכי ווערטמאן. נתן מוסין.
שמעת בניםין שולמאן. שלג. סיכל ראמנחין. דוקאר:
אברהם הורעוויג. יצחק ייאסקמאניטש. מררכי
נאנטמאן. רובראוונא: שניאור זלמן מעוונזער.
שמואל מאנראם. האמעל: אברהם בוכמאן.
אברהם אבא נארעליס. ווינמכסק: ירמי' נאלצערסין.
ולאבין: בנציון סמאלמנער. נעוויל: נעצל
אוערגיקאוו. רוד סאמינסקי. סענגא צבי אחראניס.
מאריק: מיכאל מריששר. מאלאאט: אלי'
מיינצער. פלעשצעניף: מנחם נחום ליבערמאן.
פרילוק: יצחק כהנאוו. יצחק סלאווין.
צעצערסק: חיים אליעזר ריבקין. קרעמענצוג:
אברהם רוד יאנאווסקי. קאתאנצאוו: אהרן מתחי'
אירעלציג. אברהם יונה בלזומין, דובער לוסקין.
יהושע ליעוויג.

נרבת אחים.

ארעסא: אסאווסקי אברהם ותלמידיו 1 רו"כ.
בוקסטין, משה, יצחק, כאו"א 10 ק"ם.
דאלינסקי: מיכל בארסוס 12 ק"ם.
הלוכאוו: גינובערג ליסא 5 ק"ם, נאוועלסקי
שמעון 26 ק"ם, מעהליער אברהם 24 ק"ם. ליבערמאן
יוסף 9 ק"ם.
ווע ליז: בהרד שמואל 5 ק"ם, הורחי ליב 5

ק"ם, באנאדאראווסקי שמואל, תאווקין, חיים שמואל,
שלמה, כהנגר משת, מאליקאווסקי צבי, נתום,
פאטאסינסקי ש. זלמן, צירלאו פנחם כאו"א 10 ק"ם.
הורחי שניאור זלמן 25 ק"ם.
זעמבין: גילעוויטש אלטר 20 ק"ם.
חרסון: ארנאנסקי מרדכי יורא 5 ק"ם,
מיימעלמאן ישראל 7 ק"ם, קורזאן אברהם 10 ק"ם.
חאטומסק: אייזיק אסמראאו 5 ק"ם.
חאלאמאנימש: ביעליענמא שלמה, נעמין
יוסף מרדכי. נאלרין שמואל משה שמונרין נתום
שלמת, רובין פנחם, כאו"א 10 ק"ם. פרירמאן ארי'
ליב 20 ק"ם.
מאראמעץ: פיינשמיין אלי' מאיר 50 ק"ם.
מארארסקי: ניעטעליעאו משה רוד 54.
יעקאמערינאסלאוו: סלוצקי משה אהרן,
שליועכסקי אברהם רוד, שניאורמאו ישראל ליב.
נראאיו שמואל גרשון כאו"א 18 ק"ם. שניאורסאן
רובער, מנחם מענרל, כאו"א 27 ק"ם. קארלינסקי
חיים 10 ק"ם. באקשם מרדכי 11 ק"ם. קאמלאן
ראובן 22 ק"ם.
לוזקי: קנעל שלום, שער לייבל כאו"א 10
ק"ם, רובאאו יצחק 36 ק"ם.
מוהליעוו: כהנאוו אלי' 1 רו"כ.
סיגבק: באמסוז 17 ק"ם, מאכליסעל יעקב 18
ק"ם, קאבאקאוו יוסף 38 ק"ם.
מאלאמערעטצעמ'נא: אייזלין רוד 32
ק"ם, סערומיונסקי בצלאל 9 ק"ם.
נעוויל: זאמצטוווסקי שלמה אלי' 9 ק"ם,
נוחעוויץ שמואל 10 ק"ם, פאניוואוסקי אייזיק 20
ק"ם.
סמאראמעליע: נעאוסיחין בנימין, ראוין
בונש, באירימסקי רניאל, לעשוק יוסף, צבי, סומין
שלמה כאו"א 5 ק"ם, אוותרבוד גרלי', אוועו חיים,
קראליק יודא כאו"א 3 ק"ם.
צעצערסק: ריבקין זאב וואלף.
קאנאמאם: בראהינסקי פרייזא 50 ק"ם.
קלימאוויץ: מראלרקן שלמה, קאראבעלניק
ליב בן ציון כאו"א 5 ק"ם.
רודניא: פורעאוויו ירחמיאל 5 ק"ם, ראבינאוויץ
זלמן, ראםסון חיים כאו"א 10.
חאסלאוויטש: ריםבערג ברוך יעקב, זעלמאן
יעקב. חאזאנאוו יעקב. צערניאק משה אברהם.
קאזארנאווסקי יעקב מ'ל, קאראקאווסקע ישכר רובער.
האמיענאס ליב יודא, צערנין יצחק ליב כאו"א 44 ק.

Редакторъ: М. Розенблюмъ, Любавичъ.

Контора I. Шнеерсона, Любавичи, Mor. Губ.

и Типографiя I. Лурье, Гороховая, 48.

Figure 24 (footnote 256)

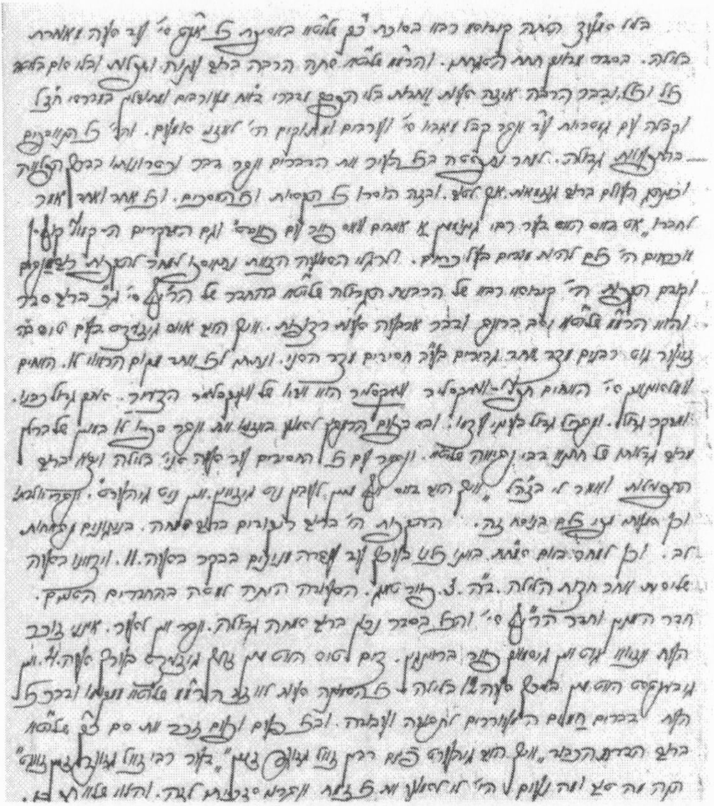

Figure 25 (footnote 415)

בליל שמע"צ היתה קידושא רבא בסוכת כ"ק שליט"א באסיפת כל אנ"ש שי', עד שעה מאוחרת בלילה, בסדר מדויק תחת השגחתו. והרמ"מ שליט"א [=כ"ק אדמו"ר זי"ע] שתה הרבה ברוב ענוה ושפלות ובלי שום בליטה כלל וכלל, ודבר הרבה איזה שעות אחדות בלי הפסק מדברי דא"ח מעורבון ומתובלין במדרשי חז"ל וקבלה עם גימטריות, ע"ד אשר קבל מאביו שי', וערבים ומתוקים הי' לאזני לשמעם, והיו כל הנאספים בהתפעלות גדולה. למחר נתפשטה בכל העיר הדברים אשר דיבר וכשרונותיו בדרך הפלאה, וכמנהג העולם ברוב גוזמאות, אך לטוב, ובזה הוסרו כל הקושיות וכל המסכים, וכל אחד ואחד אמר לחברו "אָט דאָס האָט דער רבי גינומען אַ איידים וואָס פאָר עם פּאָסט" [=הנה, הרבי לקח חתן הראוי לו]. וגם המבקרים ה-קאָן קוּפּ-ן [הכ"ף קוּ"ף?] מוכרחים היו כולם להיות מודים בעל כרחם. ולרגלי השמועה הזאת נתאספו למחר להקפות רוב אנשים, וקודם הקפות הי' קידושא רבא של הרבנית הגדולה [מרת שטערנא שרה] שליט"א בהחדר של הרב יחזקאל פייגין שי', ג"כ ברוב סדר. והוא הרמ"מ שליט"א ישב בראש, ודיבר ארבע שעות רצופות. איך האָב אויסגיזעצט דעם טיש ב"ה זייער גוט [=סידרתי את היושבים בשולחן ב"ה טוב מאוד], רבנים מצד אחד, גבירים בע"ב מצד השני, ונתתי לכל אחד מקום הראוי לו. האחים וואלשאניק שי' האחים חפץ שי', ווענקסליר – ווענקסליר הוא אביו של וואנקסליר הצעיר – שותק גדול כבנו, ומבקר גדול, ומשכיל גדול בעיני עצמו. ובא בפעם הראשון לשמוע באזניו את אשר ספרו לו במנין של ברלין, מרוב גדלותו של חתנא דבי נשיאה שליט"א [=כ"ק אדמו"ר זי"ע], ונשאר עם כל החסידים עד שעה שני' בלילה. ויצא ברוב התפעלות ואמר לי בה"ל: "איך האָב דאָס אויף מיין לעבין ניט גיזעהן און ניט גיהערט' [=בחיי לא ראיתי ולא שמעתי כזאת], אשרי יולדתו וכן שמעתי מפי כולם בנוסח זה. ההקפות הי' ברוב ריקודים ברוב שמחה, בניגונים משמחות לב וכן למחר ביום שמח"ת באנו כולנו בערך עד עשרה מנינים בבוקר בשעה 11, ויצאנו בשעה שלישית אחר חצות לילה. דאָס הייסט 3 פאַר– טאַג [=לפנות בוקר]. הסעודה היתה למטה בהחדרים השונים, חדר המנין, וחדר הרי"ף שי', והכל בסדר נכון ברוב שמחה גדולה, אשר אין לשער. אינני זוכר כעת אַזוי גוט פאַרברייננען [=שהתוועדו כ"כ טוב]. צום טיש האָט מען זיך גיזעצט [=לשולחן התיישבו] בערך שעה 4, און גיעבענטשט האָט מען [=ובירכו] בערך שעה 12 בלילה. כל השמונה שעות לא זז הרמ"מ [=כ"ק אדמו"ר זי"ע] ממקומו ודבר כל העת דברים חמים המעוררים לתשובה ועבודה, ובכל פעם ופעם זכר את שם כ"ק שליט"א ברוב הדרת הכבוד, "איך האָב גיהערט פון דעם רבי'ן זאָל גיזונט זיין" [=שמעתי מהרבי שליט"א], "דער רבי זאָל גיזונט זיין זאָגט" [=הרבי שליט"א אומר]. הנה מה טוב ומה נעים הי' לי לשמוע את כל זאת, אשרינו שזכיתי לזה...

N. DINAH SCHNEERSOHN
OF LUBAWITZ
770 EASTERN PARKWAY
BROOKLYN 13, N. Y.
Slocum 8-2010

נחמה דינה שניאורסאהן
ליובאוויטש
—•—
ב"ה, ח"י שבט תש"י
ברוקלין

כבוד ידידינו, ידידי ומקושרי כבוד קדושת
אדוננו מורנו ורבינו הרה"ק גאון ישראל
הפארחו והדרו חסידא ופרישא וצוקללה"ת
נבג"מ זי"ע זכ"מ,
ולכל אחינו בית ישראל מיקרי שם הוד קרשו
וזכרו הטוב,
די בכל אתר ואתר,
ה' עליהם יחיו,

בשבת קודש פרשת בא, יו"ד שבט, כרבע שעה לפני שמונה בבוקר, נצחו
אראלים ונשבה ארון הקודש.

אדוננו מורנו ורבינו עלה השמימה, ואנחנו נשארנו עזובים גלמודים
ונדכאים. כספינה מוטלכה בלב ים וקברניטה אין עמה.

מי יתנה גודל האבדה בתלקם ממנו אישי ובעלי ואבינו רבינו מנחיגנו
ומדריכנו, וכל"ם, מי ינוד לנו ומי ינחמנו.

וכגודל האחריות המוטלת עלינו ועליכם, הננו בזה להחעורר ולעורר
את כל אחד ואחת אשר זכו להשחחף בעבודתו הקדושה והרחבה של נשיאנו ורבינו
נבג"מ זי"ע, הכ"מ, כי בגזר השי"ח נמסיך את כל העבודה הקדושה אשר האנחלה
תחת פיסדרא וסנהיגה כבוד קדושת אדוננו מורנו ורבינו נבג"מ, כי זאת אריך
הפצו ורצונו וסגמהו בחיים ובחי החיים.

בשעה איומה זו כל אחד ואחת אשר לבו קרוע ומורחת לשמע האבדה הגדולה
של כל בית ישראל, בטח יכירו גודל החוב המוטל עליהם לעמור הכון על
משמרחם ולהמשיך עבודחם, לא יפול דבר וחצי דבר מכל אשר עשו ופעלו פראש,
וית קדשו במותר לחוסיף אומץ ביתר שאת וביתר עז, כגודל דרישת חשעה, ואיש
אל רעהו יאמר חוק.

אנא אחים ורעים, נשמור נא המורשה הקדושה שהנחילנו נשיאנו, נחלה
בלי מצרים, המוסרות הקדושים והמהורים להרבצת החורה והפצת מעינוחי
חוצה, לחיזוק החינוך הכשר, להפיח לעורה ולמח"י בגשם ובדוח לאחינו
הפליטים, ולהמשיך כל עסקנומשצריבורית בצרכי הציבור ותיחיד, באהבה
ישראל אהבת החורה ואהבת השם ובספירות נפש בפועל. נחסיר ללכת בדרך
... לפנינו מורנו ורבינו נבג"מ זי"ע, הכ"ם, לא נסור ימין ושמאל, כי
רק בזה ובכה נגרום קורח רוח לנשמחו הקדושה והמהורה הנושאה רינה ותפילה,
יחד עם נשמות אבוחינו רבוחינו הקדושים, זכוחו וזכוחם יגן עלינו ועל כל
אשר לנו, להטסיע שפעת חיים ברכה והצלחה בכל המעניינים בגשמיוח וברוחניוח
לכל אחד ואחת מאחנו עם ב"ב יחיו, ולהצליח בעבודתנו הקדושה, עד כי
ישלח לנו השי"ח אח משיח צרקנו ויגאלנו גאולה שלימה וחקיצו זדננו
שוכני עפר, והוא ב"ק אדוננו מורנו ורבינו הקמ"ק וצוקללה"ת נבג"מ זי"ע,
הכ"ם, בתוכם, בב"א.

מקרב ולב נשבר ונדכא

הרבנית נחמה דינה שניאורסאהן

הרב שמרי' גורארי', מדב"ג   הרב מנחם שניאורסאהן, מדב"ג

Figure 26a (footnote 424)

N. DINAH SCHNEERSOHN
OF LUBAWITZ
770 EASTERN PARKWAY
BROOKLYN 13, N. Y.
SLocum 6-2515

נחמה דינה שניאורסאהן
ליובאוויטש

By the Grace of G-d
18th of Shevat 5710

To our dear friends and all those who
    cherish the memory of our beloved and revered
        teacher and leader, the Lubavitcher Rebbe
            of saintly memory - זצוקללה"ה נבג"מ זי"ע הכ"מ.

On the holy day of Shabbos, the tenth day of Shevat, 7.45 in the
morning, our great and saintly Rebbe returned his soul to its Maker.
My unforgettable spouse, our dearly beloved and revered father, teacher,
and leader, is no longer with us. May the Almighty comfort all those
who, together with us, mourn our irreplaceable loss.

In this hour of bereavement and grief, a tremendous responsibility
falls upon our shoulders and yours: to safeguard, with G-d's help, the
gigantic spiritual heritage which our late Rebbe left us all: the world
renowned institutions for the spreading of the Torah and the light of
true Judaism, the institutions for the betterment of Jewish education
everywhere, the institutions for rendering material and spiritual aid
to our uprooted brethren.

Everyone who was privileged to participate in this holy work
should consider it his or her sacred duty to remain on his or her post
and continue all activities as before, but with greater zeal and deter-
mination.

Let us solemnly rededicate ourselves to carry on all those rami-
fied activities for the good of one and all, with true love: love for
our brethren, love for our Torah, and love for G-d, in the spirit of
self-sacrifice exemplified by our late teacher and leader of saintly
memory. Such was his central wish and aim in his lifetime; such, and
even more so, surely is his desire in Eternal Life.

In this way will we gratify his saintly soul, and we may hope
with certainty to receive G-d's blessings for success in our work, until our righteous Redeemer will come, and "the dead shall rise with
song," and our dear and revered Rebbe of saintly memory among them,
speedily in our time, Amen.

Nechama Dina Schneersohn

Nechamah Dinah Schneersohn

Shemaryah Gourary
Rabbi Shemaryah Gourary
Son-in-law

M. Schneerson
Rabbi Mendel Schneerson
Son-in-law

Figure 26b (footnote 424)

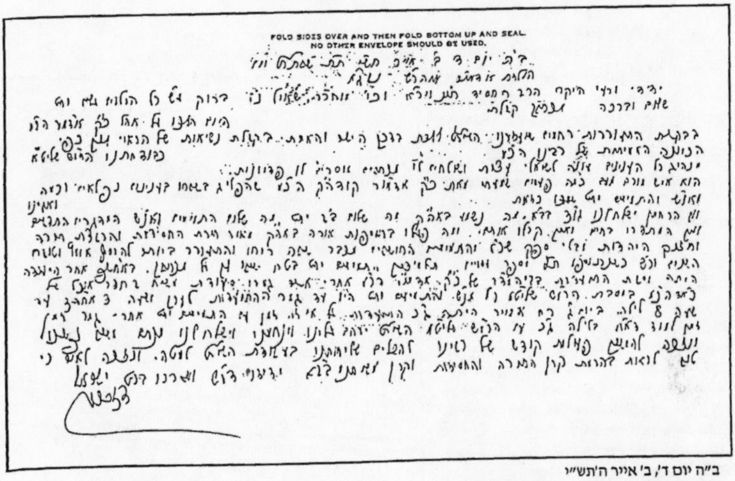

ב"ה יום ד', ב' אייר ה'תש"י

ת"ת שבת"ת יום הולדת אדמו"ר מוהר"ש נבג"מ

ידידי ורעי היקר הרב החסיד הנו"נ ואי"א וכו'

מוהר"ר שאול נ"י ברוק, עש"ק כל חנלוים עליו יחיו

שלום וברכה

מכתבך קבלתי . . היום הלכו על אהל כ"ק אדמו"ר הכ"מ בבקשת התעוררות רחמים, שיעזרנו השי"ת ללכת בדרך הישר והאמת, בקבלת נשיאות של הראוי לכך כפי הכוונה האמיתית של רבינו הכ"מ.

...כבוד חתנו הרמ"ש שליט"א מנהיג כל הענינים, עונה לשואלי עצות, ושולחים לו מכתבים, מוסרים לו פדיונות . . הוא איש מורם מעם, כמה פעמים שמעתי מאת כ"ק אדמו"ר קודה"ק הכ"מ שהפליג בשבחו בעניינים נפלאים, וכמה מאנ"ש והתמימים יחיו שמעו כזאת.

...ואבינו אב הרחמן ישלח לנו גו"צ בב"א.

...מה נשמע באה"ק, מה שלום ג"ב יחיו, מה שלום התמימים ואנ"ש המתגרים החדשים, ואיך הסתדרו בחיים ואיך קבלו אותם.

ומה פעלו בתוספות אורח באה"ק מאור תורת החסידות והרבצת תורה וחיזוק היהדות ובלי ספק שכ"א מהתמימים החשובים, מכבר שבה רוחו והתעורר ביותר לחוסיף אומץ, וטובים השנים וכ"ש כשנתוספו ת"ל מספר מסויים. תלמידיך התמימים יחיו בטח ישיבו לך על מכתבך.

באחש"פ אחר הסעודה היתה מסבת התועדות בביתמד"ר של כ"ק אדמו"ר הכ"מ — אחרי אשר גמרו סעודת משיח בחדר אוכל של כא"ד הכ"מ — במסבת הרמ"ש שליט"א. כל אנ"ש והתמימים יחיו היו עד גמר ההתועדות, לערך משעה 3 אחה"צ עד שעה 8 לילה.

ביום ג' ר"ח אייר היתה ג"כ התועדות על איזה זמן עם התמימים יחיו — אחרי גמר זמן למוד דא"ח בלילה — ג"כ עם הרמ"ש שליט"א.

השי"ת ירחם עלינו וינחמנו, וישלח לנו מנחם משיב נפשנו, ונזכה להמשיך פעולות קודש של רבינו, להשלים שליחותנו בעבודת השי"ת למטה. ונזכה לאור כי טוב לראות בהרמת קרן התורה והחסידות וקרן משיחנו בב"א.

ידידו דו"ש ומברכו בכ"ט

ישראל דזייקאבסאן

Figure 27 (footnote 452)

במכתבו של הרה״ח ר׳ שמואל זלמנוב מיום כ״א סיון תש״י לדודו הרה״ח ר׳ שמואל זלמנוב
שי״ב מזקני החסידים באה״ק הנעתק בזה מסופר על הנעשה ב״בית־חיינו״ בתקופה זו.

ב״ה ג׳ כ״א סיון ה׳תשי״י, ברוקלין נ.י.

שלום וכטיים לדודי היקר והנעלה הוריח אי״א חו״ן בעל
מדות תרומיות וכו׳ כש״ת מוהר״ש שי׳ זלמנוב, ע״ש כב״ב
היקרים שי׳.

אחדהש״ט.

...בדבר בקשתו לכתוב לו מחמעשה בבית חיים שליט״א ועי״ד
הענין המענין את כל אנ״ש שי׳.

...אתנו אלה פה שזכינו לעמוד מקרוב ומסביב למשכן ה׳, —
אני זכיתי לחיות בסמוך לרבינו הק׳ יב שנים, י״ב שנים
בירואם ובימתי חעשר שנים האחרונות בפה — ולראות פנ׳
חק׳ וחמאורות של חוד כ״ק אדמו״ר הרה״ק זנוקללה״ה
נבג״מ זייע, הכ״ימ, ולשמוע מאמרי דא״ח ושיחות חק׳
והוראותיו הכלליים והפרטים עד יומו האחרון בעלמא דין,
אשר באמת חי׳ לנו לא רק לרב מורה אלא פשוט לאב רחמן,
ואשר תמונת פנו חק׳ כמלאך ד׳ צבאות עמדה חי לנגד עינינו
ובאזנינו עוד מצלצלות דבריו חק׳ שהשמיע לנו ברבים
וביחידות — חנה קשת מאד עלינו לחעלות על חדעת שיהי׳
שוך ענין של תמצרח או חלפין, אמת חדבר, אשר בענין רב
אמרו רז״ל ועשה לך רב, יועשמ״ה בדרך קבעיו, אבל יאב״א אי
אפשר לעשות אם לחחליף, אל חדמו שזח דברי מלחמה או דברי
חגומה, יודע אני בעצמי וכן חרבה חרבח מחאכרכים דפה,
שחתתקשרות שהי׳ לנו לאבינו רבינו חיתה חתקשרות עצמית
ופנימית מעין התקשרות בן לאב וחוא אבינו רבינו האאויל לנו
התקשרות עצמית מאב ורב לבן ותלמיד, ויש לי חרבה מח
לספר בזה ואכ״מ.

אמנם אשמים אנחנו כי חטאנו, ומפני חטאינו גיטלח מאתנו
בגלוי עטרת תפארת ראשינו והוסרח מקור חיינו ומשוש לבנו,
אבל חי׳ ליפול ביאוש ועצבות, אין אף צל פפק שא״א לעווב
חדבר כמו עתה וברור חדבר אשר צריכים לחמשיך את
חשתשילתא דדחבא של נשיאות חבי׳ד עד ביאת הגואל בב״א.
עלינו ליתן שבח ותודי׳ לחשי״ת, אשר חשאיר לנו אחד
מחדב״ק חראוי וסוככר לקבל עליו כתר חנשיאות ח״ח

הרמ״ש שליט״א, אשר לבד שנוצץ ויחוסו עולם בית, אל וכד ונין לכ״ק אדמו״ר חצי״צ ני״ע, חנה חוא איש חמעלה ומשכמו ולמעלח גבוח וכו׳, חן
בנאוותו ובקיאותו חנפלאה בגגלה ובנסתר וכל רז לא אניס לי׳ בכל ספרי חבי״ד חגדפסים וחכתי״ר ולבד זאת גדל עבודתו בסיעופים ומשיט לילות
כימים בשקידה בלימוד עניני עבודה ואם כי נחבא חוא אל חכלים אבל קדושתו וטחרתו מבצבץ ויוצא מתחת חמליל חטתרי ותעלם וחעיקר גדל
עוצם ביטולו וחתנמסרותו לחוד כ״ק אדמו״ר הרה״ק חכים, אשר לא מש מעל אהלו חק׳ במשך טי״ד שנים האתרונות ורבינו חק׳ חגב אותו מאד
מאד ושיבח אותו לפני חמקורבים בשבחים נפלאים.

אמנם לע״ע חרמ״ש שליט״א מסרב בקבלת חנשיאות, למרות כל חבקשות וחחפצרות מאי״ש שי׳ דפת, ואם כי בחרבה ענינים נעתר לבקשתנו וחוא
עונח על שאלות אנ״ש בעניני גשמיים וגם רוחניים וגם מקבל פ״נ לקרוא על האהל ציון כ״ק אדמו״ר חכים, ועוד נאר עבניים, אבל בגללי אומר
שאינו מקבל עליו מפני שאין לו הוראות ובתינה כח וכו׳, ובאמת החסרון מצד אנ״ש שי׳, כי לא חי׳ אתעדלל״ת חוקה ואמתית...חי׳ באוטן אחר,
וחדבר מוכרח חוא, לא רק בשביל חכלל וחם חביד בעולם, אלא חעיקר בשביל חפרט, פשוט בשבילנו ומח גם בשביל בנינו ודור חבא לקשרם
באילנא דחיי/א ולחדריכם באור האמת שחנחילנו כ״ק רבותינו חק/ ורב כוחו ועווו של כ״ק הרמ״ש שליט״א לנחל אותנו במעגלי צדק בדרך רבותינו
חק׳ בחצלחה בגו״ר בעוחי״ר.

...וחנני בי״א חדוי״ש ומברכו בכטי״ס
שמואל

ב"ח

Tel. STerling 3-1143

הרב שמרי' גוראר׳

RABBI S. GOURARY

Bedford Avenue cor. Dean Street

Brooklyn 16, New York

Chairman of Executive Committee
UNITED LUBAVITCHER YESHIVOTH
of the U.S.A. and Canada

יו"ר ועד הפועל
מרכז הישיבות
„תומכי תמימים" ליובאוויטש
דאת"פ וקנדה

ב"ה יום ה' כסלו תשי"ב .

כבוד ידיד׳ הנכבד ומאד נעלה
חרה"ח אי"א חו"נ וכו' מוה"ר

שלום וברכה.

מקדם אני שמכתב׳ זה ימצא את ידידישיח׳ בבריאות הנכונה , ובזה הנני
מתכבד להזמין אח כרום"ע שיח׳ באוחן איש׳ להחגיגה השנתית של מרכזנו חרוחנ׳
מרכז הישיבות חק׳ תומכ׳ חמימים ליובאוויטש העתיד להחקיים איה"ש ביום א' פ'
ואר׳ , כ"ב טבח , ח'תשי"ב , בשעה 6 בערב בעולם המרכז׳ של סלון אסטאר בני׳ יארק .

מתאחדים אנו לחוג חגיגה זו ברוב פאר והדר ולשתף בו את כל היהדות
החרדית , החרדים לקיום החורה וללכל קרש׳ תיהרות חמסורחית חטוהרה וחצרופה
ואדיר חפצ׳ שגם ידיד׳ שיח׳ יקח חלק בחגיגה זו , שהם יה׳ כינוס למען החזקת
והרבצת הורה .

לוטה פה חנני שולח לו מכתב ב"ק גיסי שליט"א , ארמו"ר חרמ"ש גניאורסאהן
שליט"א , נשיא של הישיבות חק׳ תומכ׳ חמימים ליובאוויטש , ומשולשח לפיע׳ בבכנת משתה זו , וגם לבוא בחמונים להחגיגה , ביום א' לפרשה וארא אל
האבוח , כ"ב טבח ח'תשי"ב , המבקש בבקשה כפולה

אך למורח להגיד לו מטרה של החגיגה , במשחה זו יקחו בל אחד ואחר
מאחבנ"י בניאם ובנוחחם ויעוררו איש את רעהו בזה חאבה וחיבה לבוא בשורה ראשנה
בפעולות ממשיות למען החזקת מרכזנו חרוחנ׳ , שהוא כחיום מרכז הרבצת חורה לאומ׳
של חצבור העבר׳ במדינה זו , בקענערע , ובארץ ישראל שמס ואירואפא , ח"ל אלפ׳
נער׳ וילד׳ ישראל מהחנכים ברוח ישראל סבא במוסדות אלו .

ולמסרות הצלחחו חרוחנ׳ הנה מצבו חגשמ׳ אנוש הוא במאד מאד ועזרה ממשיח
ויה׳ נא מםובבו לשלוח ל׳ ציזה שוקימם מכיריו שאשׁר לפנות עליהם בבקשח׳ שיח׳
נחוצה לנו בהקדם האפשר , א׳ לזאה בקשחי נא ונא לבוא בחמונ׳ על חחגיגה ממשיח
מטובם לבוא לחגיגה זו , וגם חם ישחחסו ויקחו חלק בהחזקת מוסדנו הקרוש , מרכז
הישיבות חק׳ תומכ׳ חמימים ליובאוויטש

מקוה אני שכרום"ע שיח׳ בטח ימלא בקשוי זה וגם ימלא את הרעזערוו"יש]
קארט שהננ׳ שולחא בזה , ומה גם ישחדל בכל עוז וזרע לעורר לעורר את אנש׳ קהלחו שיקחו
חלק בהחזקת מוסדינו חק׳ , ויח׳ו משוחפים בחגיגה זו שבהצלחחה חל׳ מעמד חגשמ׳
של הישיבות חק׳ תומכ׳ חמימים

ובזכוה גודל המצוה של החזקת חורה זלומדי' ישׁׁפיע, חש"ח לו רוב טוב
גשמי ורוחנ׳ , ויזכה לראוח בחרמה קרן חחורה וקרן ישראל ע"י משיח צדקנו ב"ב
אמן .

בהודה מראש ובברכת חחורה

חרב שמרי' גוראר׳ חרב"ג

Figure 29 (footnote 501)